PIONEERS in JEWISH MEDICAL ETHICS

PIONEERS in JEWISH MEDICAL ETHICS

EDITED BY
FRED ROSNER

JASON ARONSON INC.
Northvale, New Jersey
Jerusalem

This book was set in 11 pt. Galliard by Alabama Book Composition of Deatsville, Alabama.

10 9 8 7 6 5 4 3 2 1

Library of Congress Cataloging-in-Publication Data

Pioneers in Jewish medical ethics / [edited] by Fred Rosner.
p. cm.
Includes bibliographical references and index.
ISBN 0-7657-9968-5 (alk. paper)
1. Medicine—Religious aspects—Judaism. 2. Medical ethics.
3. Medical laws and legislation (Jewish law) 4. Ethics, Jewish.
5. Jewish scholars—Biography. 6. Rabbis—Biography. I. Rosner, Fred.
BM538.H43P56 1997
296.3'642'0922—dc21 97-12965
r97

Manufactured in the United States of America. Jason Aronson Inc. offers books and cassettes. For information and catalog write to Jason Aronson Inc., 230 Livingston Street, Northvale, New Jersey 07647.

Contents

Preface

Jewish medical ethics has come of age. The modern era of this field began with the landmark monograph titled *Jewish Medical Ethics* (Philosophical Library, 1959) by Lord Immanuel Jakobovits, Chief Rabbi of Ireland, later to become Chief Rabbi of the British Commonwealth of Nations, knighted by Queen Elizabeth II and subsequently appointed to Britain's House of Lords, the first Jew in four hundred years to be honored and the first Rabbi ever to be honored. This pioneering work has since been followed by a number of other books, including Rabbi David Feldman's *Marital Relations, Birth Control and Abortion in Jewish Law* (Schocken, 1968, 1975); Dr. Fred Rosner's *Modern Medicine and Jewish Law* (Bloch, 1972); Rabbi J. David Bleich's four-volume *Contemporary Halakhic Problems* (Ktav, 1977, 1983, 1989, 1995); Rosner and Bleich's *Jewish Bioethics* (Hebrew Publishing Co., 1979); Bleich's *Judaism and Healing* (Ktav, 1981); Feldman and Rosner's *Compendium on Modern Medical Ethics* (Federation of Jewish Philanthropies of New York, 1984); Rabbi Levi Meier's *Jewish Values in Bioethics* (Human Sciences, 1986); Rabbi Faitel Levin's *Halacha, Medical Science and Technology* (Moznaim, 1987); Feldman's *Health and Medicine in the Jewish Tradition* (Crossroad, 1986); Rosner's *Modern Medicine and Jewish Ethics* (Ktav, 1986, 2nd ed. 1991); Rosner's *Medicine and Jewish Law* (Jason Aronson, Vol 1., 1990; Vol. 2, 1993); and several other books.

Hebrew books on Jewish medical ethics include Dr. Avraham Steinberg's six-volume *Encyclopedia of Jewish Medical Ethics* (Jerusalem, 1988–1996); Dr. Abraham Abraham's five-volume *Nishmat Abraham* (Jerusalem, 1983–1994); Rabbi Moshe Hershler's five-volume *Halachah Urefuah* (Jerusalem, 1980–1988); and Rabbi Yitzchak Ralbag's four-volume *Harefuah Le'or Hahalachah* (Jerusalem, 1980–1985).

This proliferation of books is supplemented by innumerable articles on Jewish bioethical topics in various journal and other publications. The Falk Schlesinger Institute for Medical Halachic Research of the Shaare Zedek Medical Center in Jerusalem publishes Hebrew and English versions of a journal titled *Assia*, devoted entirely to Jewish medical ethics.

Numerous international conferences on medicine, ethics, and Jewish law over the past decade have been sponsored by the Association of Orthodox Jewish Scientists in New York (biannually); the Institute for Jewish Medical Ethics of the Hebrew Academy of San Francisco (jointly sponsored annually by the Stanford University School of Medicine); the Lubavitch Youth Organization (jointly sponsored annually by the State University of New York Health Sciences Center at Brooklyn); the Jewish communities in Copenhagen (January 2–9, 1996) and Sweden (December 15–16, 1996); and Georgetown University Medical Center (cosponsored by Aish Hatorah) in Washington, D.C. (April 21–23, 1996).

Ongoing lectures, symposia, scholar-in-residence programs, and other educational activities in Jewish medical ethics throughout the world are too many to enumerate. This field of study and research has continued to blossom since Rabbi Jakobovits's pioneering doctoral thesis first published in 1959. Rabbi Lord Dr. Jakobovits is recognized as the father of modern Jewish medical ethics.

This book attempts to put Jewish medical ethics into historical perspective. The Foreword by Dr. Shimon Glick and the introductory chapter by Rabbi Lord Dr. Immanuel Jakobovits are followed by Dr. Samuel S. Kottek's discussion of the practice of medicine in the Bible and Talmud and its influence on the modern dilemmas and rabbinic decisions in medical practice. Dr. Edward Reichman uses the case of ***mumia*** to illustrate the impact of medieval medicine on medical *halachah*. The next five chapters compose the core of this book. Rabbi Moshe Feinstein's enormous influence on medical *halachah* is presented in two sections: one by his son-in-law, Rabbi

Dr. Moshe D. Tendler, and the other by myself, one of his disciples. Dr. Avraham Steinberg, who was very close to the late Rabbi Shlomo Zalman Auerbach, discusses in detail his personal attributes and his significant contributions to medical *halachah*. Dr. Yoel Jakobovits presents the singular contributions to Jewish medical ethics of his illustrious father, Lord Immanuel Jakobovits, who he correctly characterizes as the undisputed father of Jewish medical ethics. Finally, Dr. Steinberg discusses the renowned Rabbi Eliezer Yehudah Waldenberg, one of the living giants of medical *halachah*.

Rabbi Dr. Nisson E. Shulman then provides brief biographical notes and extracts from the works of seven of the most prominent contemporary specialists in Jewish medical ethics. Several are rabbis, several are physicians, and several are both. The book concludes with a chapter on trends and prospects, by Rabbi Lord Dr. Jakobovits, in which he speculates about future developments in this field.

I am greatly indebted to the contributors to this volume, all of whom I respect as colleagues, friends, and mentors from whom I have learned much over the years. I am also grateful to the rabbis whom I have consulted on many matters of medical *halachah*, and who have rendered me invaluable help and assistance over several decades (in alphabetical order): Rabbi Dr. J. David Bleich, Rabbi Dr. David Feldman, Rabbi Tzvi Flaum, Rabbi Lord Dr. Immanuel Jakobovits, Rabbi Dr. Moshe D. Tendler, and Rabbi David Weinberger.

Fred Rosner, M.D.
New York City

Foreword

Shimon Glick, M.D.

The list of individuals described in this volume, *Pioneers in Jewish Medical Ethics*, might lead one to believe that we are dealing with a twentieth-century phenomenon, since all of those designated as pioneers have done their work in the twentieth century. Indeed, the rubric "Jewish Medical ethics" was first coined by Rabbi Lord Dr. Jakobovits in the middle of the twentieth century. Yet, as Samuel Kottek reminds us, the Jewish people have been studying, writing about, and practicing Jewish medical ethics for thousands of years. The Jewish tradition, which dates back to Sinai, is perhaps the longest unbroken tradition in bioethics that is still followed by its adherents. Former Israeli Supreme Court justice and talmudic scholar Menachem Elon estimates that there are over 300,000 halachic responsa extending over centuries, a veritable treasure of casuistic literature unmatched by any other ethical or legal system.

Throughout the millennia, Judaism and medicine have marched hand-in-hand as allies, not as rivals. The mainstream of Jewish tradition has placed an enormous value on human life and health, has given human beings an obligation to preserve life and health, and has pursued a dual track of encouraging recognized medical therapy together with faith in the Almighty. Judaism has also, for the most part, rejected all varieties of dualism and rivalries between the body and the spirit, maintaining rather that spiritual progress can be enhanced by a healthy body. Our ancients already had insights, as well, into preventive medicine and behavioral medicine.

In an era when the Israeli government has been shaken over the question "Who is a Jew" and "pluralism" is a popular catchword, this book makes no apologies for selecting what may be fairly called representatives of Torah-true Judaism, the only kind that existed until the schisms brought about by the French Revolution and the Enlightenment. This Torah-true, or Orthodox, Judaism posits a revealed normative faith that seeks to discover divinely ordained guidelines for human behavior at every moment of human life, and in every sphere of human endeavor.

These guidelines are not, as some think, easily derived by reading a popular magazine article on Judaism or by a home-study university course on the Talmud. The guidelines derive from traditional source texts, clearly defined methodology, recognized scholars, and rigorous application of reason and logic, in accord with fundamental principles of charity, justice, and mercy, which shape these standards. The pioneers described in this volume are those who, by their scholarship, erudition, intellectual honesty, and, often, saintliness, have been recognized by their faith community as the experts.

It is no accident that the overwhelming majority of Jewish bioethical literature has emanated from Orthodox sources, and not from the competing trends in Jewish society. Jewish bioethics is casuistic in nature; it is based not on abstract philosophy but on actual cases posed to experts by individuals loyal to their faith and committed to act according to its tenets. The overwhelming majority of these individuals—health professionals and lay persons alike—are found in the Orthodox community.

It is a remarkable phenomenon, a blessing from Heaven, to have witnessed the growth of this religiously observant health-professional community over the past few decades. When I began medical school in 1951, the number of observant physicians in the United States could be counted on the fingers of one's hands. There was a widely held belief that science and religion were contradictory. There was one legendary observant physician on the Upper East Side of Manhattan who was, as a result, widely known as "Shabbes Friedman." By the time I emigrated to Israel, only a quarter of a century later, the physicians' section of the Association of Orthodox Jewish Scientists in the United States numbered in the hundreds and was growing from year to year. Similar growth was taking place in Israel and elsewhere. Conferences on Jewish medical ethics, with hundreds of physicians and health professionals in attendance, have become commonplace. Rabbi Lord Dr. Jakobovits not only created the name "Jewish Medical ethics," but he also has been instrumental in its expansion, popularization, and accreditation as a field of scholarly endeavor.

Many outsiders often suggest that having a divinely mandated system of ethics makes life easy, that no conflicts exist and that there are simple solutions, while the rest of society has ethical conflicts and dilemmas. Those familiar with the field of Jewish medical ethics, however, know that the path to the "right" decision is not easy, and that decisions are often far from unanimous. There frequently exist intense debates, even between the greatest authorities. For example, brain death, abortion for fetal defects, and artificial insemination are but a few of the areas in which major differences of opinion exist. With respect to these debates, we say: both opposing views have Divine authority. Generally, with the passage of time, a consensus develops in the religiously observant community.

Not always have the Torah views on bioethics been popular at the time they were expressed. Some of the most gentle, saintly, and modest scholars, exquisitely sensitive to human feelings and suffering, invariably stood firm when principles were involved. When Rav Moshe Feinstein, of blessed memory, stated in the 1960s that heart transplantation was a double murder, this position was regarded in many circles as evidence of a primitive, antiscientific stance that characterized the Orthodox world. But in retrospect, as has been clearly demonstrated by the scholarly work of Renée Fox[1] on transplantation, Rav Feinstein's admonitions were absolutely on target for the level of medicine at that time. As George Annas[2] recently stated: "The field of human transplantation is, to a large extent, one of technical success and ethical failure."

Some of the halachic discussions and insights, which date far back in time and place, are incredibly relevant and insightful to modern-

1. Fox. R.C., Swazey, J.P. *The Courage to Fail; A Social View of Organ Transplantation and Dialysis*, second ed. Chicago: University of Chicago Press, 1988.

2. Annas, G. "Book Review." *Ann. Int. Med.* 1994; 120–252.

day issues. For example, only in recent decades have clinical researchers begun to appreciate the pernicious effect of even seemingly trivial bias. Studies that lack double-blinding, random allocation of patients, and controls are rejected as subject to bias. The Sages of the Talmud anticipated these problems in their discussions of the potential bias of judges. We are told how judges disqualified themselves from judging cases in which any of the disputants so much as removed a piece of lint from the judge's coat. Even more remarkable is the disqualification of the High Priest from sitting on the tribunal that decides whether a given lunar year will have a month added to it to bring the lunar and solar calendars into alignment. The reason for this disqualification is the fear that the High Priest, who must carry out the Temple service barefoot on Yom Kippur, might be desirous of a warmer temperature in Tishrei, which might bias his decision. Such punctiliousness in avoiding bias seems exaggerated, perhaps, but modern medicine's experience with clinical trials has demonstrated that such precautions are not superfluous in those situations in which unbiased objective decisions are essential.

A similar insight on conflict of interest is the ruling by Rav Chaim Palache of Izmir[3] a century ago. He ruled that prayer for the death of a suffering terminal patient is permitted, but only by those not personally involved in the care of the patient. He expressed the fear that those who are burdened by the care of the patient may not be able to be objective enough. In today's era of managed care, and with the "right to die" being transformed into the "duty to die," we can appreciate the timeliness and relevance of the insight of this Turkish Jewish decisor who lived in a culture vastly different than ours. Our Torah is timeless and universally applicable.

This volume deals with a variety of subjects that seem rather remote from "ethics." These include laws about the Sabbath, *kohanim*, *chometz*, *mikvah*, redemption of the first-born, and *kashrut*, among others. These areas are normally categorized as ritualistic rather than ethical. Yet, in many ways, this integration of ritual and ethics is unique to halachic Judaism. No area of human

---

3. Palache, H. *Response Hikekei Lev*, Vol. 1, Responsum 50, Salonika, 1840; reprinted by Book Export Enterprises, Ltd., 1978.

endeavor, whether in the interpersonal realm or the ritual realm, is exempt. Ideally, meticulous attention to details of observance should characterize all areas of endeavor for the Jewish, God-fearing health professional.

The laws of the Torah are often regarded by outsiders as restrictive. On the other hand, the religious Jew's philosophy is that true freedom is acquired only by accepting the Torah life. This life, which liberates one from enslavement by one's instincts and animal drives, also often provides secondary benefits. The creative solutions that are developed to solve problems posed by the *halachah* may contribute beyond their immediate circle. For example, many of the technological solutions for Sabbath observance have been put to use beneficially in other areas of societal endeavor. Another example is the program developed to prevent the tragedy of Tay-Sachs disease while also avoiding either abortion or the tragic breakup of already-developed relationships between young men and women. Dor Yesharim's program of confidential testing of young men and women who are seeking mates without stigmatizing carriers is an innovative example of such a solution, created to solve a halachic problem.

I have had the good fortune of knowing personally almost all of the individuals described in this volume. It is, indeed, a rare privilege and opportunity to have learned from and conversed with them face-to-face. In my academic life I have had many opportunities, as well, to work with great scientists and secular scholars, among them several Nobelists. I can say with all honesty that the combination of qualities I found in the two recently deceased great sages of Israel, Rav Moshe Feinstein and Rav Shlomo Zalman Auerbach, of blessed memory, remains unmatched by any other individuals I have encountered in the secular world. In the words of our Sages, "If you are told that there is wisdom among the nations, believe it; if you are told that there is Torah among the nations, do not believe it." These two sages were intellectual giants who had at their fingertips an amazing storehouse of knowledge and who had the ability to integrate the knowledge and apply it to almost any current issue. These qualities above were not enough to give them Torah greatness; in addition, they were indeed saintly, compassionate, modest, and God-fearing beyond human comprehension. The words of the prophet Malachi, "They shall seek the law at his mouth for he is the angel of the Lord of Hosts," is interpreted by the Talmud to teach us that "only if the teacher resembles an angel of the Lord should you seek to learn Torah from him." These words were applicable to these two remarkable rabbis. They were never elected to any office, nor selected by any official process as *Gedolei Hador* (the generation's great men), but they were the undisputed possessors of this title, and deservedly so. Blessed is the generation that has such luminaries gracing it.

And, we have described in this volume other individuals, each unique in his own light, each contributing to our understanding of what it means to deal with the sensitive life-and-death issues of medical ethics in an ethical, Jewish way. We have a saying, "The Jewish people are not left widowed." The Almighty somehow always provides the Jewish people with new scholars and leaders of stature in each generation. We are fortunate in having bred a new generation of physicians and scientists who are true *talmidei chachamim*, Torah scholars, in the time-honored Jewish tradition of combining both medicine and Torah. They, too, are described in this volume. It is worth pointing out, as well, that pioneers described here by no means exhaust the list of individuals who have contributed, and are contributing, to this field in a major way.

Finally, what is the relevance of Jewish medical ethics beyond our specific faith community? Is there a message beyond this relatively small population? The answer, I believe, is a resounding "yes." Over the past three decades, the field of bioethics, which originated largely in religious settings, was taken over by philosophers and other secular scholars, who have developed a scholarly, widely recognized and respected field. Yet, over the past few years, being heard increasingly are voices of dissatisfaction with the widely accepted Western secular principles,[4] which often offer little guidance when two principles contradict each other. Furthermore, the ethical pluralism and relativism lead to a consensus around the lowest common denominator,[5] a watered-down code of ethics that

4. Clouser, K.D., Kopelman, L.M., eds. "Philosophical Critique of Bioethics." *J. Med. Phil.* 1990; 15:121–236.

5. Engelhardt, T.J.R. *The Foundations of Bioethics*, second ed. New York: Oxford University Press, 1996.

allows almost any action if it does not interfere with another person. Increasing numbers of thinking people are unhappy, as well, with the growing evidence of a slippery slope that has, in the past quarter-century, granted widespread approval for abortion and homosexuality and may be on the way to permitting euthanasia. There is increasing thirst for a more substantial ethic based on eternally valid principles. Here, Jewish bioethics—Torah Judaism—has not only a message for the Jewish world, but a universal message that has stood the test of time throughout the millennia. These ideas are represented by the pioneers described in this volume.

An Introduction to Jewish Medical Ethics

Lord Immanuel Jakobovits

If there are two spheres in which Jews have particularly distinguished themselves over the ages, almost as a national vocation, they are ethics and medicine.

The principal commitment of the Patriarchs of the Jewish people, the Ten Commandments, and the predominant message of the Hebrew Prophets attest to the supremacy of ethics as the overriding theme of Jewish history and the Jewish purpose.

Likewise, the pursuit of medicine has been by far the most favored professional vocation among Jews from ancient and medieval times to the present day. Two facts from different periods provide the ringing affirmation of this striking fact. It is estimated that over one-half of all the best-known Jewish thinkers and writers in the Middle Ages were physicians by occupation: Men like Maimonides, Yehudah Halevi, the Ibn Ezras and Ibn Tibbons, and many other scholars of the first rank were practicing doctors, several of them responsible for notable medical writings mentioned in every history of medicine.

This proclivity for a medical career, often for medical pioneering, has not abated in contemporary times. Over twenty percent of all Nobel prizes in medicine have been awarded to Jews—a proportion forty times as high as would be warranted by the numerical strength of the Jewish people.

It is, therefore, hardly surprising that the combination of these two fields in Jewish medical ethics is providing such a rewarding theme of modern scholarship and contemporary interest.

While the term "Jewish medical ethics" is only of fairly recent usage, having first served as the title for my doctoral thesis presented to the University of London in 1955 and subsequently used as the title of my book *Jewish Medical Ethics* in 1959, the subject is now well established. It is recognized as an academic discipline at several universities, notably in Israel and the United States. The subject also commands a growing library of specialized books and magazines, most of them in Hebrew or English, but some also in French, Italian, German, and other languages.

The progress of the subject is demonstrated by the fact that while the twelve-volume *Jewish Encyclopedia* published in 1901 makes no reference to any subject embraced by Jewish medical ethics, the sixteen-volume *Encyclopedia Judaica* published seventy years later does already feature some ten entries, and soon thereafter a supplement includes an entry on Jewish medical ethics itself.

The slow process in the evolution of the subject from complete obscurity to the present growth is certainly not due to any sparsity of sources. Jewish legal texts, notably the profusion of rabbinic responsa, are replete with discussions, enquiries, and judgments on the subject. These prolific sources now make up the bulk of the rich source-material accumulated over the ages. But, written as they are for the most part in the highly technical parlance of rabbinic Hebrew, they are in fact available only in trained experts—except through secondary sources now becoming ever more popular as textbooks or articles on Jewish medical ethics.

What are, then, some special characteristics in the orientation and rulings of Jewish medical ethics as enshrined in these sources?

Jewish ethics is, of course, not "situational," relative, or arbitrary. It claims authenticity by falling back on earlier precedents and thus qualifies for being included in the corpus of Jewish law. The verdicts ultimately enjoy the imprimatur of Jewish tradition and rabbinic endorsement.

In the halachic process, an opinion becomes normative on emerging as a majority view among qualified rabbinical scholars debating the subject in hand and eventually tending toward a consensus or at least a clear predominance over and among conflicting opinions.

The basic approach in Jewish medical ethics, as in Jewish law generally, is "consumer-oriented." Rules, or rulings, are not given in abstract, generalized terms by philosophers, or committees of enquiry, or groups of professionals and legislators, or even a consensus of public opinion. Instead, they evolve from an accumulation of (usually published) judgments secured from leading rabbinical scholars of world repute in response to questions submitted by doctors and patients alike—by those who seek to abide by specifically Jewish principles, particularly in dealing with often highly sensitive moral questions involving life-and-death decisions.

In the Torah, the basic law on abortion, for instance, is stated in the context of a concrete case: "If men strive together and strike a pregnant woman so that she loses her offspring, and there be no accident [i.e., the mother survives], then the offender shall pay compensation for the loss of her fruit" (Exodus 21:22). In other words, the destruction of an unborn child, while a heinous offense, is not deemed as a capital crime (otherwise, no compensation would be payable).

This "case law" then establishes the important principle that abortion does not constitute murder—a principle later enshrined in the Mishnah, Talmud, and all Jewish law codes. The fetus, though usually inviolable, is of distinctly inferior value compared to that of the mother, so that in any mortal conflict between them (say, in the case of a breech birth that cannot be completed with absolute safety for the mother except by embryotomy, or the destruction of the child), "The mother's life has priority over the life of the unborn child" (Mishnah).

Later authorities then deal with further complications of borderline cases, such as danger threatening not the mother, as in the first instance, but the life or health of the yet-unborn child—for instance, as indicated by an amniocentesis during pregnancy establishing that the child will definitely suffer from Tay-Sachs or some other genetic and eventually fatal disease. Among the rulings on this dilemma in several quite recent responsa, rabbinical experts are still divided, with some permitting an abortion even up to the seventh month of pregnancy and others strongly opposing this.

Much of medical ethics in general deals with modern dilemmas arising at or before birth, or else before or at death. Under these simple headings can be subsumed such vast areas as contraception, sterilization, artificial insemination, in vitro fertilization, experimentation on embryos, genetic engineering, and counseling, as well as—at the opposite end of life—euthanasia, determining the moment of death, autopsies and dissection, the utilization of tissue removed from the dead, and attitudes to hospices and terminal care, plus a host of other related problems.

Often enough, Jewish medical ethics comes to conclusions clearly at variance with general medical ethics. For instance, in the realm of doctor–patient relationships, truth-telling is a case in point. The modern trend, particularly in the United States, is to divulge a potentially fatal diagnosis to the patient, if only to avoid the possible threat of litigation for failure to communicate the full truth. Similarly, the commitment to the truth demands that the patient gives "informed consent" to treatments deemed necessary, even for the preservation of life.

Obviously, such a practice is bound to serve the doctors' interests. By informing the patient that he suffers from a terminal condition, the doctor cannot go wrong: If the patient in due course dies, the doctor is proved right in his diagnosis; if not, the doctor is even greater for having performed a "miracle" against all expectation.

Jewish ethics deems the physical and psychological or mental welfare of the patient to be the paramount concern. Hence, if there is any fear that the information may cause some serious setback to the patient, adding the anguish of the fear of finality to the suffering from the illness he endures, reassurance to the patient must be the first consideration, even if this means withholding the full truth from the patient. Similarly, a life-saving operation deemed imperative by a competent doctor must in principle be performed even against the wishes of the patient, since he has no more right to dispose of his own life than to dispose of anybody else's.

These are just a few examples to show some distinct attitudes adopted in Jewish medical ethics. Naturally, since no two cases are absolutely identical, each case must be carefully adjudicated by moral experts in the light of all the circumstances, as established by competent medical experts.

The concept of consent in medicine is, in any case, of only fairly recent origin, introduced within the past hundred years or so mainly in order to safeguard doctors against malpractice or compensation claims. The idea of "informed" consent is particularly questionable. Is it really suggested that a physician can impart to his patient the knowledge and experience he himself took perhaps ten years to acquire?

The principle of consent, let alone "informed" consent, is therefore alien to Jewish law and thought. The onus is on the physician to make the decision on the required treatment and to do his best to prevail on his patient to submit to it to promote his life and health.

With the relentless march of medicine and its encroachment on many of the most sacred areas of life, health, and human reproduction, the search for and application of reliable guidelines becomes ever more urgent if human existence is not to be reduced to purely mechanical conditions and procedures, in which man's uniqueness in the image of his Creator is replaced by chemical formulas, labeled test tubes, utilitarian values, and physical measurements.

No religious system commands a more rational attitude to healing and a more reverent approach to man's mortal frame, in death as in life, than Judaism. Few contributions by the Jewish people could be more significant and win wider acclaim than those that are enshrined in Jewish medical ethics.

Here are just some of the key areas that already engage the urgent attention of leading rabbinical experts and that will increasingly call for new rabbinic judgments and verdicts, as ever more moral dilemmas will ensue from the rapid advances of medical research and technology and their concomitant inroads into the moral sphere.

The Practice of Medicine in the Bible and Talmud

SAMUEL S. KOTTEK, M.D.

INTRODUCTION

While we still use the expression "the art of medicine," much of its meaning has been lost over the last two centuries. Medicine was first a craft based on empirical knowledge, on observation, and on trials and errors. Then, theoretical reasoning tried to organize the accumulated data in some acceptable way.

Particularly in Roman society,[1] educated laypersons claimed to possess some degree of medical knowledge and often had little faith in the expertise of professional healers who had gone through no formal licensing process whatsoever. Nevertheless, physicians of higher level were praised by Roman authorities. Seneca, for instance, differentiated between two classes of healers: those who were experts in the *techne* and those who added to this expertise wider learning and human feelings. The latter, he said, were not only his practical aids, they were also his friends.[2]

1. On the status of physicians in Roman society, see Scarborough (1969), pp. 109–121. I wish to thank Gerhard Baader for his useful remarks on this introduction.

2. Seneca, *On Benefits* VI (16) 4–5, in *Moral Essays*, Vol. III, p. 397 (trans. J.W. Basore, 1935).

Criticism and disparaging remarks have been showered on physicians since ancient times, and occasionally were merited. This criticism may have been an incentive for the emergence of an interest in medical ethics within the profession. In the first century C.E., Scribonius Largus introduced ethical principles in his work, although its content was mainly pharmacological. He even mentioned the Hippocratic Oath, which was seldom referred to in ancient times[3] and remained, generally speaking, an elitistic document.

Although the Hebrew people in biblical times and the Jews in the talmudic period were no doubt aware of what was going on in neighboring civilizations, there is little documented evidence of these interrelationships. No purely medical work has survived, even from late talmudic times, that pertains to the Byzantine period.[4] No comprehensive picture of the practice of medicine emerges, therefore, from examining the ancient writings of the Jewish people. On the other hand, a significant number of rules and edicts are formed in ancient Jewish writings that apply directly or indirectly to physicians and, more generally, to healers. The basic difference between ancient Jewish ethics and the ethics featured in the Hippocratic Oath lies in the fact that biblical and talmudic rules were forcefully implemented within the frame of the law, whereas Hippocrates' rules were, at best, implemented in some chosen medical guilds. *Halachah* (Jewish law) is binding and coercive for observant Jews, though dynamic and adaptable to the evolution of humankind from generation to generation. For those Jews who do not consider *halachah* as binding and for those who cast an eye on Jewish lore from the outside, it may prove rewarding to see how talmudic rabbinical authorities handled problems related to the practice of medicine. Did they consider it unequivocally acceptable to cure the sick? Should not suffering be considered primarily as a punishment for sins or a trial and, therefore, left to a debate

3. See F. Kudlien, *Medical Education in Classical Antiquity* (1970), p. 19. For Scribonius Largus, see L. Edelstein, "The Professional Ethics . . ." (1956), in *Ancient Medicine* (1967), pp. 337–340.

4. The Jerusalem Talmud was completed in the fifth century C.E., whereas the bulkier Babylonian Talmud was finally edited in the sixth century C.E.

between the patient and the Lord? What is the curative power involved in the well-balanced encounter between a sick person and a healthy one, including the physician? In other words, what is the intrinsic value or utility of visiting the sick? What was the social status of physicians in these remote times, according to the scarce information left to us? These are the main points we will explore.[5] These sayings and rulings of the Sages of the Talmud inspired later pioneers of Jewish Medical ethics, and they still inspirit this field to this very day.

HEALING THE SICK: LAWFUL OR DEROGATORY?

We shall not come back to the halachic basis of the right to heal. The noted Tanna[6] Rabbi Ishmael (second century C.E.) ruled that the verse in Exodus (21:19), ". . . He will cause him to be thoroughly healed," proves that physicians have a warrant to heal. Although there seems to have been no opposition to this ruling in mishnaic times, this was not the case in later generations of talmudic Sages. In the fourth century the Palestinian Amora[7] Rabbi Acha remarked: "Whoever is going to have bloodletting performed on himself should first utter the following prayer: 'May this procedure be a cure welcomed by the Lord and may He cure me,

5. These topics have been studied repeatedly in a series of works devoted to Jewish medical ethics. We shall mention here only the pioneering book of that name by Rabbi Lord Dr. Immanuel Jakobovits (1959). Its subtitle should be stressed for its broad and open approach: "A comparative and historical study of the Jewish religious attitude to medicine and its practice."

6. Tanna (pl. Tanaim): a Sage from the period of the Mishnah. This appellation covers a period ranging from approximately 20 to 200 C.E. Two major events of the history of the Jewish people happened during that period: the fall of Jerusalem in 70 C.E. and the fall of the last stronghold in Betar in 135 C.E.

7. Amora (pl. Amoraim): a Sage from the talmudic period; the title extends over some eight generations.

for He is the faithful physician and His cures are true ones; for healing is not a human management, only they took to it.' "[8] This prayer shows that Rabbi Acha considered the medical profession (here paradigmatically represented by bloodletting, a common cure for all kinds of diseases) as a questionable intervention. However, his opinion was countered by the Babylonian authority Abaye, who sharply remarked: "One should not speak this [i.e., utter such a prayer], for it was taught by the school of Rabbi Ishmael that Scriptures have clearly given a full right to cure" (*Berachot* 60a). Although the opinion of Abaye was generally accepted, this excursus shows that the right to heal was still open to discussion around the fourth century.

Another controversial talmudic text is found in tractate *Pesachim*. This is, again, a mishnaic statement[9] (*Pesachim* 4:9) relating that the Sages praised King Hezekiah (seventh century B.C.E.) for having put aside (i.e., concealed) *The Book of Medicines*. According to the commentary of R. Solomon Ben Isaac (Rashi, eleventh century), the reason for this concealment was that people used to implement the recipes of *The Book of Medicines* while forgetting to address the Lord and ask for His mercy. Maimonides (twelfth century) considers such reasoning as mere rejection of medicine and proposes two reasons for King Hezekiah's concealment of *The Book of Medicines*. Either the book contained astrological means that should not be put into practice [10] (although they may be studied), or it contained the formulas for poisons and their antidotes, and people began to use the poisons in order to harm others. One may contend that Rashi's comment enforces, at least to a certain extent, the approach

8. "They took to it," i.e., they became accustomed to go to a healer in case of disease. In Jewish jurisdiction, a custom (*minhag*) was often transformed into a binding law, either locally or generally. In this case, however Rabbi Acha opposed this custom.

9. In the standard edition of the Talmud, this text is part of the Gemara, not the Mishnah. It is, in fact, a *baraita* (i.e., an "outside" Mishnah) that eventually came to be included in the standard editions of the Mishnah.

10. Astrological practices were considered too close to idolatry, at least by Maimonides; most talmudic Sages, however, and a number of medieval authorities did not condemn astrology.

of Rabbi Acha previously mentioned. Medical treatment can be second only to prayer and obedience to the Lord. For Maimonides, a negative view of medicine can be acceptable only if its methods are heterodox or unethical. No trace of *The Book of Medicines* has been found. According to midrashic (i.e., homiletical) literature, its author was King Solomon, the paragon of wisdom (I Kings 3:12).[11] In the time of the Talmud, however, medical books no doubt existed in Judea and Babylonia, but no such book was, to our knowledge, condemned by the rabbis. We suggest, therefore, that if the Sages praised King Hezekiah for concealing *The Book of Medicines*, this should be pondered in the context of a faithful and pious king opposed to wicked rulers who preceded and followed him.

This same Hezekiah was, according to the Midrash, the "first case" of an individual who recovered from a deadly disease.[12] The prophet Isaiah came to him and told him to set his house in order, "for you will die and not live." But the king prayed to the Lord, and cried and asked for mercy, and the Lord heard his prayer and saw his tears. The king was allotted an additional fifteen years of life, and he wrote a meaningful song of thanksgiving (Isaiah 38:1–21).

Hezekiah not only concealed *The Book of Medicines* but also "broke to pieces the brazen serpent that Moses had made" (II Kings 18:4).[13] This serpent had been erected in the wilderness, when the Israelites were bitten by venomous snakes, and everyone who looked at it remained alive (Numbers 21:4–9). The Israelites burned incense to this serpent in later times; therefore Hezekiah destroyed it. Nowhere is it stated that this ritual procedure had anything to do with medicine. Nevertheless, the fact that Hezekiah's

---

11. See also I Kings 5:9–14. Medicine is not mentioned in the context of King Solomon's wisdom, but it is mentioned later in the Second-Temple-period literature, in the Midrash, in Josephus' writings, and in *The Testament of Solomon* (where it is combined with the power over demons).

12. See *Yalkut Shimoni*, Genesis 15:77. According to a parallel text in the Talmud (*Bava Metzia* 87a), it was the prophet Elisha who first recovered from a deadly disease.

13. It should be kept in mind that Hezekiah's destruction of the brazen serpent is biblical, whereas the concealment of *The Book of Medicines* is first mentioned in the Talmud.

destruction of the brazen serpent is cited by the Sages just before the incident of the concealment of *The Book of Medicines* should be kept in mind. It is known that the Phoenicians worshiped a god-healer in the shape of a serpent called Eshmun in a temple situated in Obot (north of Petra). Even earlier, the Sumerians revered a similar deity.[14]

If Job is portrayed as the "suffering righteous," King Hezekiah is pictured as the pious king who added ethical and theological frontiers to the practice of medicine.

JOB, THE "SUFFERING RIGHTEOUS"

Both Hezekiah and Job suffered from a disease called *shechin*.[15] Hezekiah's condition was considered as being an abscess, a boil (King James Bible), or a festering place (Koren Bible). The Septuagint translated it as *helkos* (ulcer). The prophet applied a "cake of figs" to the sore[16] and, as stated earlier, the king recovered from this "deadly disease." Job's *shechin* was a skin disease that spread "from the sole of his foot to his crown" (Job 2:7). We are not presently interested in the identification of this disease about which so much has been written; the point at stake is the meaning of Job's disease. Job's past is spotless; he is put to the test of his faith in the Lord. His three friends try to convince him that he must have committed some fault (even without being aware of it), but Job does not accept this conclusion and calls them physicians of naught (*rofei elil*) (Job 13:4). The Book of Job offers no solution to the often-discussed problem of the afflicted righteous. Its ultimate

14. See J. Schouten (1967), p. 100 ff and p. 39.

15. On King Hezekiah's condition, see J. Preuss (F. Rosner trans. 1978), pp. 341–342; on Job's disease, see ibid., pp. 339–341.

16. See Isaiah 38:21. Commentators (cf. David Kimchi, ad loc.) consider this "treatment" as miraculous, for figs do harm only in the case of *shechin*. While such means were indeed used in antiquity for softening abcesses, who can safely assert what this "dangerous" skin disease actually was?

lesson is the primary value of humility.[17] In the case of illness or suffering, one should first make a thorough examination of one's conduct. If one is unable to find any misdeed, one should humbly accept the trial. It should be stressed, however, that Job's "struggle for life," his adamant refusal to accept the concept of retaliation as a unique interpretation of suffering, is nowhere condemned. On the contrary, the friends who defended this view are rebuked (Job 42:7).

Job's case leads to some talmudic references to suffering (*Berachot* 5a–b). Rabba (fourth century C.E.)—others say R. Chisda (idem)[18]—declared: "Whoever is visited by afflictions (*yisurim*) should scrutinize his own doings, as it is written: 'Let us search and try our ways, and turn back to the Lord' (Lamentations 3:40). If he has searched but has found nothing, he should attribute [his sufferings] to neglecting [the study of] the Torah, as it is written: 'Blessed is the man whom You chastise, O Lord, and You will teach him from Your Torah, in order to give him rest from the days of adversity . . .' (Psalms 94:12–13). But if, again, he has found no such reason [for his suffering], then it resorts to 'afflictions of love' (*yisurim shel ahavah*), as it is written: 'For the Lord reproves[19] him whom He loves'" (Proverbs 3:12).

Several stories are told to illustrate such "afflictions of love." Rabbi Chiyya Ben Abba (early fourth century C.E.) fell ill, and Rabbi Yochanan visited him. He asked him, "Do you welcome your afflictions?" "Neither the suffering, nor its compensation," retorted R. Chiyya. Then R. Yochanan said: "Give me your hand," and he lifted him up. Some time later, R. Yochanan fell ill and Rabbi Chanina said: "Give me your hand," and he lifted him up. At this point, the unnamed editor of this talmudic text remarks: "Should not R. Yochanan have been able to lift himself up [as he did for R.

---

17. The literature on Job's case and on the value of suffering is impressive. Notable are the studies of G. Fohrer (1963, 1988).

18. Rabbi Chisda (ca. 217–309) was for some time the teacher of Rabba. R. Chisda showed a keen interest in topics related to health and hygiene. He is one the most frequently quoted scholars in both the Babylonian and the Jerusalem Talmud.

19. "Reproves" in the sense of testing or admonishing.

Chiyya]?" No, concludes the Talmud, this is not feasible, just as a prisoner is unable to free himself from prison (*Berachot* 5b).

This story is also recorded in the Midrash (Song of Songs Rabbah 2:35), with several meaningful changes. Rabbi Yochanan suffered from a disease (fever with shivering?) for three and a half years, and Rabbi Chanina visited him. He asked, "What is happening to you?" "What I have [i.e., suffering] is more than I can endure." R. Chanina retorted, "You should not speak like that; you should say [i.e., pray]: 'O Lord in Whom I trust. . . .'" When Rabbi Chanina saw how excessive the sufferings of his colleague were, he uttered a spell [or a prayer?], and R. Yochanan calmed down.[20] After some time, Rabbi Chanina fell ill, and R. Yochanan visited him. He said, "What is happening to you?" He said, "How fierce is my torment!" He retorted, "But the compensation will be great!" He said, "I do want neither the suffering nor the compensation." Then R. Yochanan asked, "Why do you not use for your own sake the formula you pronounced for me that was so efficacious?" R. Chanina said, "As long as I was outside [i.e., outside the realm of pain and suffering], I could help others[21]; now that I am inside, am I not in need of someone else who might help me out?"

Reflecting on the way disease and suffering were realized in ancient Jewish lore (at least according to literary sources), we notice that the Book of Job, while leaving the problem unsolved, calls for introspection and humility. On the other hand, the Sages of the Talmud were not prepared to suffer in silence, hoping for a better future; rather, they insisted on mutual assistance and active support, which included—but was not restricted to—medical treatment. This brings us the religious duty of visiting the sick.

---

20. R. Yochanan's soul was appeased, but it is not said that his fever went down. The psychological effect of his colleague's visit and prayer is obvious.

21. The Hebrew term *arev*, which means "to vouch for" or "to support," is meaningful in this context. A much-cited maxim reads (*Shavuot* 39a): "All Israelites vouch for one another" (*kol Israel arevim zeh bazeh*). This saying enhances the social dimension of the law and helps combat despair and despondency.

VISITING THE SICK

The following story is told in the Talmud (*Nedarim* 40a): "Once a pupil of Rabbi Akiva (first–second century C.E.) fell ill, but nobody visited him. Rabbi Akiva himself went to see him and asked that the room be cleaned, which revived the pupil. The pupil exclaimed, 'Rabbi, you made me come back to life!' Rabbi Akiva stepped out and promptly taught in his Academy: 'Whoever does not visit the sick is like one who sheds blood.'" Incidentally, Rabbi Akiva is known as the authority who pointed out the foremost importance of the biblical junction "Love your neighbor as yourself" (Leviticus 19:18).[22]

Another Sage asserted that whoever visits a sick person relieves him of one-sixtieth of the disease. Then why not send sixty persons to visit the sick and relieve him altogether? retorted other Sages. Well, he said, each one takes away one-sixtieth part of what the preceding visitor has left (*Nedarim* 39b). One-sixtieth is, of course, just a figure of speech.[23]

The information related to how and when a sick person should be visited is quite impressive and is tackled in much detail in rabbinic responsa. We shall discuss only one example, featuring a borderline case. Should one visit a sick person whom he hates (or by whom he is hated)? A first tentative answer is: No, for the sick person may think that he enjoys seeing him in that state. In any case, the sick person may not welcome that particular visit. Moreover, one rabbinic opinion advises the visitor to be cautious that the sick person not be induced to think that he must be seriously ill if this man who hates him comes to see him! In a more positive approach, it is stated elsewhere that if the visitor asks permission of the sick person to visit, then he may (or, rather, ought to) go, and that this may be a welcome occasion to make peace with him.[24]

---

22. See Jerushalmi *Nedarim* 9,4. The Lord Himself showed the way, when He appeared to Abraham after he had circumcised himself and his male household (Genesis 18:1).

23. The meaning is obviously psychological. The visitor relieves primarily the patient's anxiety; he also prays for his recovery.

24. More details on this particular case and on the topic "visiting the sick" in R.H. Bernstein (1974), Hebrew; see pp. 38–41.

Here again we are given evidence of the fact that illness places an individual in a position of self-questioning and renewed evaluation of his social relationships. On the side of the visitor, this reinforces his awareness of the value of being healthy. Caring and curing are obviously closely related.[25]

ILLNESS AND "EUTHANASIA"

The following curious statement is made in the Talmud (*Bava Metzia* 87a): "Until [the times of] Jacob there was no disease. But Jacob asked for mercy and disease was granted to him, as it is written: 'And someone said to Joseph, behold, your father is ill' [Genesis 28:1]." Joseph understood that his father was on his deathbed, and departed at once with his two sons in order to be at Jacob's side. According to a midrashic text,[26] in ancient times people used to die suddenly while sneezing, wherever they were. Then Jacob asked for mercy, saying, "Please, O Lord, do not take my soul from me until I have stipulated my will to my sons." This was granted to him and explains why anyone who sneezes should thank the Lord, who transformed a sign of death into a sign of life. The idea behind this reference to sneezing is, obviously, that the breath of life was thought to leave the body just as it had been insufflated into Adam, through the nostrils (Genesis 2:7).

"Euthanasia" means a good, happy, or noble death.[27] In the case of Jacob, "disease" means loss of strength, or weakness. It is stimulating to find here a positive approach, a eulogistic meaning toward disease and weakening.

---

25. See also F. Rosner, "Visiting the Sick," in "Jewish Medicine in the Talmudic Period," *Rise and Decline of the Roman World (W. Haase and H. Temporini, ed.),* Degruyter, Berlin and New York (1996), pp. 2890–2892.

26. See *Yalkut Shimoni*, Genesis 15:77.

27. Another reference to a "good" death is found in *Ketubot* 37b in the context of a person condemned to death. Based on the aphorism "Love your neighbor as yourself," the Sages declare, "Choose for him [i.e., the convict] a nice death" (*Beror lo mita yaffa*).

Although sudden death, i.e., death without suffering, is called in the Talmud "death from a kiss [of the Lord]" (*mitat neshikah*),[28] Jacob's death is seen as a "noble" death, his awareness of its approach enabling him to gather his family, to bless them all, and then to die in peace. This is not "active" or "passive" euthanasia, just euthanasia or good death.

THE JEWISH PHYSICIAN

The only officials called physicians (*rofeim*) in the Five Books of Moses (Pentateuch) probably were not really physicians (Genesis 50:2). These "physicians," who pertained to Joseph's household, embalmed his father Jacob, and it is well documented that embalmings were never performed by physicians in ancient Egypt. But physicians appear a number of times in the Bible. "Is there no balm in Gilead, is there no physician there?" exclaims the prophet Jeremiah (Jeremiah 8:22). In the Talmud, physicians are mentioned often. A number of talmudic authorities were also, at least to a certain degree, experts in medical matters.[29] Most impressive are the numerous references to the vast medical and astronomical knowledge and experience of Mar Samuel (second–third century), pertaining to the first generation of Amoraim.[30] In the Mishnah (*Kiddushin* 4,14), we find a disparaging aphorism: "The best of physicians is doomed to Gehenna." This opinion never prevailed, however, and later commentators painstakingly tried to apply this fate of the *worst* of physicians.[31]

The Talmud offers no details on the places and ways physicians

---

28. See *Moed Katan* 28a. Moses and his sister Miriam are on the list of those who died from a kiss of the Lord (cf. Deuteronomy 34:5).

29. A (partial) list of such experts is found in J. Preuss (trans. F. Rosner, 1978), pp. 19–22.

30. On the talmudic scholar–physician–astronomer Mar Samuel, see F. Rosner, in "Jewish Medicine in the Talmudic Period," pp. 2883–2887.

31. On this provocative aphorism, see my study (in Hebrew) in *Assia* (1976), pp. 5–12. A parallel statement appears in *Avot de-Rabbi Nathan* 36:5; it says that "the best of physicians" has no part in the World-to-

obtained their medical education. Some may have been trained in Hellenistic Alexandria, where a very active Jewish Diaspora was thriving, keeping strong ties with Judea. Medical knowledge was probably transmitted among the physician's family or in small schools. Thus, Minjome (or Benjamin) and his sons were desperate when a famous rabbi revealed the formula for their all-healing ointment.[32] And Thudos the physician, who was called by the Sages for anatomical consultation, came accompanied by "all the physicians," most probably his pupils.[33]

Physician's liability was, since talmudic times, related to the question as to whether or not they were licensed. Medical license was practically unheard of in ancient times.[34] In mishnaic times, the Tosefta (appendix to the Mishnah) states that a physician or surgeon who practices by the permission of the court and causes unintentional harm cannot be sued. However, "if he cut more than was adequate," he is considered guilty (Tosefta *Bava Kamma* 9, 11). Elsewhere it is stated that compensation for unintentional harm by a physician cannot be claimed "for the sake of society"[35] (Tosefta *Gittin* 4, 6). This means that the Sages considered physicians to be a social necessity, provided that their expertise was established by licensure. We do not know the criteria determined by rabbinical courts for the acceptability of a physician, but it may be surmised that they required adequate information from established physicians. In neither the Babylonian nor the Jerusalem Talmud is found any example of prosecution of a physician or even a surgeon

---

Come, which sounds even more offensive than the statement of the Mishnah.

32. See *Shabbat* 133b. It seems that the rabbi believed that such a panacea should not remain in private property. Minjome and his sons (therefore?) despised the Sages, while the latter considered them as unbelievers (*apikoros*), or, rather, skeptics. This is a rare example of a conflict between physicians and talmudic authorities.

33. See Tosefta *Oholot* 4:2.

34. On medical license in Hebrew sources, see J.O. Leibowitz, pp. XLVII–LIII, and I. Jakobovits, pp. 214–217.

35. "For the sake of society" (*mipne tikun ha-olam*), i.e., for the world to be in order, or in harmony.

who may have "cut more than was adequate"—which does, however, not prove that it never happened![36]

Physicians' fees were first considered in detail in the Middle Ages, since Nachmanides' medical rulings (thirteenth century).[37] Nevertheless, they were not overlooked in talmudic literature, as documented in the revealing aphorism: "A physician who cures for nothing is worth nothing," which may mean that an unpaid physician is likely to be careless (*Bava Kamma* 85a).[38] The real problem behind compensation for medical service was that healing is considered to be a religious duty. A talmudic saying reads: "Just as I, the Lord, act gratuitously, so you should [perform religious duties] without compensation" (*Chagigah* 7a). The problem was solved by the justification that a physician (as well as a teacher or a judge) may be compensated for his trouble and for the loss of time, though not for bestowing his knowledge, which is the core of his religious duty to heal.[39]

SOCIAL STATUS OF PHYSICIANS

As is still the case today, physicians were sometimes vilified but more often were praised for their obliging help. We have already mentioned the mishnaic saying, "The best of physicians is doomed to Gehenna." From among the numerous commentators who tried to interpret this saying in a positive light, I prefer the following:

36. The statements on physicians' liability are all located in the Tosefta, an appendix to the Mishnah. This means that these items were considered sideline aspects of the law; not unimportant, but concerning a small number of cases.

37. Nachmanides' rules on the practice of medicine were concentrated in his work *Sefer Torat Ha-Adam* (*Sha'ar Ha Michush, Inyan Ha-Sakana*). See the edited work by Charles D. Chavel (1964), pp. 22–45 [Hebrew].

38. On the other hand, the context allows taking into account the patient's position as well; psychologically, he might not take seriously a treatment that is free of charge.

39. See Nachmanides, *Sefer Torat Ha-Adam*, pp. 44–45.

"He who believes he is the best of physicians is doomed to the nether world."[40] The evil quality pinpointed in this interpretation is conceit and pride. The Talmud, while commenting on this statement of a mishnaic authority, adopts a similar approach. Strikingly, however, the talmudists of the third and fourth centuries refrain from any attack against physicians; they incriminate instead the surgeons who practice bloodletting (*gara*)! Ten grudges are raised against them, three of which relate to conceit (*Kiddushin* 82a). It seems that physicians in Babylonian Jewish society were above the level of such extended criticism.

Let us not conclude, however, that surgeons and bloodletters were as a rule negatively considered in talmudic times. Abba Umna was a practitioner, several times cited in the Talmud,[41] who may be credited with a paradigmatically ethical conduct. He used to perform bloodletting in two separate rooms, one for men and the other for women; he devised a special shirt for women that would lay bare only the area where the incision was to be made. He asked for no fees but placed a box outside where the patients could deposit money, in order not to shame those who could not pay. He would accept no payment from rabbinical students, and, when he recognized a poor patient, would give him some money and tell him, "Go and strengthen your soul," for a meal was formally indicated after bloodletting (*Taanit* 21b).[42]

Nevertheless, surgeons (or, rather, bloodletters) were considered of low social status. They could not be appointed as leaders of the community, in common with tanners and bricklayers (*Derech Eretz Zuta* 10); neither could they become king or a High Priest—not because they were unfit, but because their profession was despicable (*Kiddushin* 82a). In the latter statement, the bloodletter is cited

---

40. See the commentary of R. Samuel Edels, known as *Maharsha* (1555–1631), ad loc.

41. For instance, people asked Abba for advice in a gynecological case. He forwarded the case to the Sages, who in turn went to the physicians (*Niddah* 22b).

42. The ethical conduct of Abba-the-bloodletter was strikingly emphasized by a parable according to which Abba was granted a daily salute from Heaven, whereas other noted rabbis were awarded such favors only once a week or once a year (ibid.).

together with seven other professions, such as bathkeepers, tanners, barbers, and peddlers.

It should not be concluded from the aforementioned that physicians and barber–surgeons were two socially independent professional categories, as was later the case in the Middle Ages. The Mishnah and the Talmud describe many instances of surgical procedures performed by a *rofeh*, or physician. Even dental interventions are included: A slave whose master, while treating his tooth, caused it to fall out, must be freed (*Kiddushin* 24b). A *rofeh* used a leather apron, most probably while performing some surgical procedure (*Kelim* 26, 5). Moreover it should be kept in mind that talmudic literature extends over some seven centuries; there may well have been differing "states-of-the-art" according to time and place.[43]

An extratalmudic text, more or less contemporary to the beginning of the mishnaic period, is the famous *Book of Ben Sira* (second–third century B.C.E.). This work, which was not included in the Jewish biblical canon, is repeatedly quoted by talmudic Sages and remains a classical work in Jewish ethics.[44] Ben Sira refers to physicians as follows (Chapter 38):

> Honor the physician before you are in need of his [help];
> He too is part of the Lord's [plan];
> From the Lord he acquires his wisdom,
> And from the king he is granted presents. . . .

Ben Sira argues that the physician should be honored as would be a delegate of the Lord, whose skill is appreciated by even the king.

> My son, in case of disease do not tarry,
> Pray to the Lord, that He might heal [you]. . . .
> But secure also room for the physician,
> Keep him close to you, for he too is indispensable,

---

43. No evidence of such social differences can be detected if we compare the versions of the Talmud edited in Palestine and in Babylonia.

44. See the Hebrew text edited by M.Z. Segal, pp. 242–246 (my translation).

> There is a time when his hand is successful,
> For he too will pray the Lord [to this aim]. . . .

Ben Sira's conclusion, which long has been falsely interpreted,[45] refers to his introductory remark on the honor owing to the physician:

> Whoever behaves haughtily toward a physician
> Commits a sin before his Creator.

Ben Sira even admits that physicians may, to a certain degree, be proud of their acquired skill:

> The physician's knowledge will lift up his head
> And he will stand erect before the Great.

Thus intellectual pride is acceptable to Ben Sira, conditioned by the recognition that knowledge is granted by the Lord, as is the success of the physician's endeavors.

THE ETHICS OF PERFECTION: MAIMONIDES

Moses Maimonides (1138–1204) possessed all the necessary qualifications for reflecting on Jewish medical ethics, being fully knowledgeable in theology, philosophy, and medicine. On his inspiring conception of ethics in general, we offer here some brief thoughts. Promoting ethical faculties is, in fact, treating the soul and its attributes: "Just as a physician who cures the body has first to know the body he is treating in its whole and in its parts . . . , a physician of the soul who wishes to restore its faculties has to know the soul in its whole and its parts" (*Eight Chapters* 1).[46] Further, in

45. See, for instance, J. Preuss (trans. F. Rosner), p. 25, and H. Friedenwald, Vol. I, p. 7.

46. *Eight Chapters* is part of Maimonides' Commentary on the Mish-

the same work, Maimonides advocates a medium pathway in ethical conduct. If someone deviates from the middle toward one extreme, he should be treated, as in physical medicine, by transient removal to the opposite side and then progressively shift back to the middle way (ibid., Chapter 4).

In his theological work *Mishneh Torah*,[47] Maimonides singles out two "faculties" of the soul that should not be kept "in the middle" but should be driven back to the opposite extreme: anger and haughtiness. Thus, if someone feels he has a tendency toward haughtiness, "he should accustom himself to extreme disgrace, sit below everyone and clothe himself in shabby rags . . . until the haughtiness is uprooted from him."[48] In a first approach, Maimonides seems again to advocate the middle way. But then he ostensibly changes his mind and states that, for haughtiness, "it is not a good way for a person to be only humble" (which he considers to be the medium state), but "his spirit should be lowly to the extreme" (*shefal ruach*). Maimonides reminds his reader that even the biblical Moses, at the height of his career as a leader of the people, was "exceedingly meek" (Numbers 12:3).

In several of his medical works, Maimonides insists on the necessity that a physician be, or at least be directed toward being, perfect (*shalem*).[49] A perfect physician is one to which "the patient is ready to entrust in his hands both his soul and his body, and will follow all his directions."[50] This is not, however, an acceptable definition of excellence, although it may suggest that laypersons can (sometimes?) find out who is worthy of being trusted. Maimonides himself admits, in the same chapter, that the populace often says: "Go to this expert [a quack], not to the doctor." Medicine, writes

---

nah, more precisely an introduction to his commentary on *The Treatise of the Fathers* (*Avot*), an ethical work.

47. See, more precisely, *Sefer-Ha Mada, Hilkhot Deot*, 2:3. F. Rosner offered a translation of *Hilkhot Deot* (he translates "Laws of Moral Dispositions") in his *Medicine in the Mishneh Torah . . .*, pp. 73–107.

48. Ibid. p. 77.

49. See my study "Maimonides on the Perfect Physician," in *Moses Maimonides, Physician, Scientist and Philosopher*, pp. 25–32.

50. As stated by Maimonides in his *Book on Asthma*, Chapter 13 [trans. F. Rosner, p. 84].

Maimonides, cannot be learned from mere experience; it has to be based on knowledge; each patient requires renewed reflection, for "a physician does not treat a disease, he treats a diseased person."[51]

CONCLUSION

The late Yeshaiahu Leibowitz, one of the foremost philosophers of science who was also a trained physician, once startled his audience when he affirmed, "I am not sure that there exists a concept like Jewish medical ethics." An observant Jewish physician, he said, will act according to the *halachah*; his nonobservant colleague will act according to his conscience, while considering in detail the precise conditions of the case.[52]

Indeed, medical ethics, in spite of its impressive development during the last fifty years, is a discipline that aims at asking questions to which the answers are not always easy to formulate. The *halachah*, instead, though multifaceted, is highly dynamic. The rabbinic responsa, through the centuries, have given and still provide answers to medical problems, according to the state of the art. These responsa are always based on earlier jurisdiction and, ultimately, on talmudic lore.

The physician should be aware of being a representative or messenger (*shaliach*) of the Lord, whose blessing he solicits day after day. The sick person entreats the Lord to allow the treatment to be successful. The fact that physicians' liability and even licensing are mentioned in talmudic literature is remarkable. Social and psychological aspects related to visiting the sick were taken into account by talmudic and medieval authorities and retain their value in modern times.

The foremost principle of ancient Jewish medical ethics remains, no doubt, the primary duty to save life, all religious commandments

51. Ibid. [Rosner trans. 1963], p. 89.

52. At a meeting in Jerusalem (Hebrew University, Hadassah Medical School), 1976. See also *Refuah uMusar baYahadut*, n.d. [1976], pp. 18–23.

except three being suspended to this end.[53] This principle of danger to life, or *pikuach nefesh*, is best explained by the aphorism: "Whoever saves a life has saved a whole world."[54]

Most impressive in this context is the fact that, even in cases where there is no immediate danger to life but life *might* become endangered if the disease were allowed to develop, the law is waived in order to save the patient. The Sages of the Talmud went even further: The law may be violated for any sickness if either the physician or the patient himself believes that such a violation is required in order to avoid danger to life.[55] The patient is thus granted the same "rights" as the physician (or any other "expert") to judge whether his life is in danger. Obviously, in talmudic times, physicians were much less medically knowledgeable than in modern times. The Sages, on the other hand, were highly sensitive to the feelings of patients and to their rights within the framework of their encounter with their human healer.

The law was given to man in order that he may live by it, as it says (Leviticus 18:5):

> You shall therefore keep my statutes, and my judgments
> Which if a man do, he shall live in them—I am the Lord.

Selected Bibliography

Abramovitz, H.I. *Vachay Bahem: Pikuach Nefesh Ba-halakhah.* Jerusalem: 1957. (Hebr.)

Bernstein, R.H. *Yikre Dechaye: Hilkhot Bikkur Cholim*, Bnei Brak: 1974. (Hebr.)

Edelstein, L. *Ancient Medicine: Selected Papers of L. Edelstein* (O. and C.L. Temkin, eds.). Baltimore: Johns Hopkins Press 1967.

53. The laws that are not overruled by *pikuach nefesh* are those involving murder, prohibited unions, and idolatry.

54. On *pikuach nefesh*, see H.I. Abramovitz. Also see I. Jakobovits, pp. 67–72.

55. See *Yoma* 83a and in the Codes (*Shulchan Aruch, Orach Chayim* 328:5).

Fohrer, G. *Das Buch Hiob, Kommentar zum Alten Testament XVI.* Gütersloh: G. Mohn 1963.

———. "Man and Disease according to the Book of Job." *Koroth 9*, Special Issue, 1988; 43–48.

Friedenwald, H. *Jews and Medicine: Essays.* Baltimore: Johns Hopkins Press 1944. [2 vols.]

Jakobovits, I. *Jewish Medical Ethics: A Comparative and Historical Study of the Jewish Religious Attitude to Medicine and Its Practice.* New York: Philosophical Library 1959.

Kottek, S. "Maimonides on the Perfect Physician." In: *Moses Maimonides, Physician, Scientist and Philosopher.* Northvale, NJ: Jason Aronson, 1993, pp. 25–32.

——— (ed). *Refuah U-Musar Ba-Yahadut.* Jerusalem: n.d. (1976), pp. 18–23.

———. "Tov she-be-Rofeim le-Gehinnom." *Assia 15* 1976; 5–12.

Kudlien, F. "Medical Education in Classical Antiquity." In: *The History of Medical Education* (C.D. O'Malley, ed.). Univ. of California Press, Berkeley, CA: 1970. pp. 3–37.

Leibowitz, J.O. "The Problem of Medical License in Hebrew Sources." *Koroth 7* 1977; 360–363 (Hebr.) and 47–53 (Engl.).

Preuss, J. *Biblical and Talmudic Medicine* (trans. F. Rosner). New York: Sanhedrin Press, 1978.

Rosner, F. "Jewish Medicine of the Talmudic Period." In: *Aufstieg und Niedergang der Römischen Welt*, Part II, Vol. 37.3. Berlin: 1996, 2866–2894.

———. *Medicine in the Mishneh Torah of Maimonides.* New York: Ktav, 1984. (For the translation of *Hilchot Deot*, see pp. 73–107.)

Scarborough, J. *Roman Medicine.* London: Thames and Hudson 1969.

Schouten, J. *The Rod and Serpent of Asklepios, Symbol of Medicine.* Amsterdam: Elsevier Pub. Co. 1967.

Segal, M.Z. (ed.). *Sefer Ben Sira Ha-Shalem* (*The Complete Book of Ben Sira*). Jerusalem: s.n. 1972. (Hebr.)

The Impact of Medieval Medicine on Medical *Halachah*: *Mumia*

Edward Reichman, M.D.

INTRODUCTION

The medical halachic literature from the posttalmudic to the premodern period serves as a foundation of modern medical *halachah* inasmuch as *halachah* is a precedent-oriented system. A *posek*, or rabbinic decisor, in whatever generation he may live, invariably looks to the writings of his predecessors in order to see how they grappled with comparable problems. Therefore, in essence, all the medical halachic works discussed later in this volume are studies in posttalmudic medical *halachah*, as they invariably incorporate into their analyses the existing halachic literature of any particular topic from talmudic to modern times. A contemporary discussion on euthanasia, for example, will include reference to Moses Maimonides' *Mishneh Torah* (twelfth century); R. Judah the Pious' *Sefer Hasidim* (twelfth century); the *Shulchan Aruch* by R. Joseph Karo, including the glosses of R. Moses Isserles (sixteenth century); and *Shevut Ya'akov* by R. Jacob Reischer (early eighteenth century). What is unique to the body of medical *halachah*, however, is that while the halachic process has remained unchanged, the understanding and application of medicine has not.

Nowadays, a number of books are devoted exclusively to medical *halachah.* Had such books been written in previous centuries, their contents pages would read quite differently than those of today. Had such a book been authored in the tenth century, it would have included, for the first time, a chapter on the prohibition of using the medical remedies of the Talmud.[1] In the fourteenth century, such a text would have included a chapter on the use of astrology in medicine[2]; in the sixteenth century, a chapter on the use of mummies for medicinal purposes; and in the eighteenth century, a chapter on smallpox inoculation and vaccination.[3]

To be sure, a number of topics in today's medical halachic works, such as contraception, abortion, and euthanasia, may have appeared

---

1. During the period of the Gaonim, a ban was enacted on the use of talmudic remedies. This ban is found in a number of collections of Gaonic literature. See, for example, *Otzar haGaonim* on *Gemara Gittin* edited by M.B. Levin (Jerusalem, 1941), p. 78. Other sources are quoted in J. Shatzmiller, *Jews, Medicine and Medieval Society* (Berkeley, University of California Press, 1994), p. 148, n. 48. This ban was mentioned subsequently by R. Jacob Molin in *Likutei Maharil* and Rabbi Akiva Eiger in his glosses on *Shulchan Aruch.* On this topic, see also *Havot Yair* by R. Yair Bacharach (n. 20) and the commentary of R. Solomon Luria to the eighth chapter of *Gemara Hullin*, no. 12.

2. See H.J. Zimmels, *Magicians, Theologians, and Doctors* (London, Edward Goldston and Son 1952), pp. 137–139 and 163–164. The Ramban apparently used a medallion with the likeness of an astrological lion for the treatment of a kidney ailment. This is attested to by his student, R. Solomon ben Adret (Rashba) in his responsa, n. 413. On this topic see J. Shatzmiller, "In Search of the 'Book of Figures': Medicine and Astrology in Montpellier at the Turn of the Fourteenth Century," *AJS Review* 7–8 (1982–1983): 383–407; idem., "*Zurat Arye l'Klayot v'haMachloket al Limudei haHochmot b'Reishit haMe'ah ha-14,*" *Mechkrei Yerushalayim 9* (1990): 397–408; David Horwitz, *The Role of Philosophy and Kabbalah in the Works of the Rashba*, unpublished Master's thesis, Bernard Revel Graduate School (Yeshiva University, 1986), pp. 43–72 and 153–174.

Maimonides is one of the only rabbinic authorities in the medieval period to have opposed the use of astrology. See Alexander Marx, "The Correspondence Between the Rabbis of Southern France and Maimonides About Astrology," *Hebrew Union College Annual 3* (1926): 311–358.

3. On the treatment of smallpox in halachic literature, see Y.Z. Kahana, "*HaRefuah biSafrut haHalacha shel'achar chatimat haTalmud,*" *Sinai 14*

in works of previous generations. Yet the treatment of these topics would have differed relative to the medical understanding of each era.

This evolution of medicine and science poses difficulty for the modern reader of the premodern medical halachic literature. Each passage or responsum, depending on its period as well as on its author, deals with a different medical reality, a reality sometimes hidden from the modern reader, which impedes proper contextual understanding. The modern reader often unintentionally interprets modern medical theories into the texts of his predecessors, thereby yielding anachronistic and possibly erroneous interpretations.

Thus, when discussing the halachic determination of death, it is important to realize that the conceptions of cardiac and respiratory physiology have changed radically over the centuries. The circulation of the blood was first accurately described only in the sixteenth century. It was also believed that the inspired air traveled directly to the heart, until advances in respiratory physiology in the seventeenth and eighteenth centuries disproved this notion.[4]

Additionally, regarding the medical halachic issues of infertility, such as artificial insemination and in vitro fertilization, it should be noted that the understanding of reproductive anatomy and physiology has evolved over centuries. The existence of the human female egg was affirmed only in the sixteenth century, and the egg itself was not visualized until 1867.[5]

As a result, medical *halachah* in the posttalmudic period is not so much the history of individuals or pioneers as it is the history of ideas. To be sure, many extraordinary rabbinic figures during this period addressed medical topics; the figures included R. Hai Gaon; R. Moses ben Maimon; R. Moses ben Nachman; R. Solomon ibn

---

(1944): 76–77; Zimmels, op. cit., 107–110; David Margalit, *Derech Yisrael beRefuah* (Jerusalem Academy of Medicine, 1970), 376–379.

Abraham Nansich wrote an entire treatise on smallpox, *Aleh Trufah* (London, 1785), in which he discusses rabbinic adaptation to medical and scientific advances and beseeches the rabbis of his time to address the issue of the halachic permissibility of the use of smallpox innoculation.

4. See E. Reichman, "The Halachic Definition of Death in Light of Medical History," *Torah U-Madda Journal 4* (1993): 148–174.

5. See E. Reichman, "The Rabbinic Conception of Conception: An Exercise in Fertility," *Tradition*, 31(1), Fall 1996, 33–36.

Aderet; R. Shimon ben Zemach; R. Isaac Lampronti; R. Yosef Karo; R. Moses Isserles; and R. Jacob Emden, to name a few.[6] However, their medical halachic writings represent only a small part of their respective works and are subsumed under the broader context of the expansive writings of these authors covering all aspects of *halachah*. The importance of the posttalmudic era in medical *halachah*, therefore, lies in the subject matter, for the literature of this vast period reflects the rabbis' responsiveness to the halachic challenges resulting from the continual evolution of medicine and science.

To illustrate the importance of understanding medical history in order to better appreciate the posttalmudic medical halachic literature, we will make a detailed analysis of one topic that would have appeared in a book on medical *halachah* between the sixteenth and nineteenth centuries.

MUMIA: *AN HISTORIC AND HALACHIC OVERVIEW*

In the sixteenth and seventeenth centuries, *mumia* was a commonly prescribed drug for ailments ranging from liver disorders to bone fractures. While in antiquity *mumia* consisted of natural bitumen, at this period in history, the drug called *mumia* was primarily a derivative of parts of ancient Egyptian mummies or other more recently embalmed or desiccated bodies. How this came to be is a tale of mistranslations and transference, as we shall see, and led to some confusion as to the true identity of *mumia*, as well as to questions regarding its therapeutic value.

Throughout this complex history of the origins and uses of *mumia*, the Jews played a prominent role. The fact that Dioscorides (first century C.E.) referred to *mumia*—which in his time consisted

6. Many of the rabbinic figures throughout history who dealt with medical halachic problems were themselves physicians, including Rambam (Maimonides), Ramban (Nachmanides), and R. Isaac Lampronti. See David Margalit, *Chachmei Yisrael k'Rofim* (Jerusalem, Mosad Harav Kook 1962), and idem., *Derech Yisrael beRefuah* (Jerusalem, Academy of Medicine 1970).

of an asphalt-like substance—as bitumen Judaicum (as it derived from the Dead Sea region) is perhaps an historical foreshadowing of the truly important role the Jews would ultimately play in this chapter of medical history.

From the sixteenth century onward, Jews, primarily in Egypt, not only prescribed and imbibed *mumia* but also became heavily involved in the manufacturing and exporting of *mumia*, dominating the international trade. As Jewish law expressly prohibits deriving benefit from a dead body, the fact that the Jews served as both consumers and traders of *mumia*, a substance derived from human corpses, posed serious halachic dilemmas. Some of these issues are preserved in Jewish literature and will be discussed after an overview of the history and origins of *mumia*.

Understanding the history of *mumia* facilitates a greater appreciation of the Jewish, and especially halachic, literature in a number of ways. It explains why the halachic literature is restricted to a certain historical period. It provides an historical context for a selection of sources that reflect not isolated incidents but rather a major historical chapter in both Egyptology and medical history. As a result, secular and Jewish sources work in complementary fashion to provide a more comprehensive picture of the history of *mumia*. This exercise can serve as a paradigm for other writings in medical *halachah* where an appreciation of medical history might supplement our understanding of the rabbinic literature. Finally, and perhaps most important, an appreciation of the medical history of *mumia* illuminates the medical details of rabbinic discussions that may seem enigmatic, at best, to the contemporary reader. By revealing practical or factual background information, we gain insight into the reasons for certain halachic discussions.

MUMIA *(BITUMEN) IN ANTIQUITY*

In antiquity, bituminous or asphalt-like substances were used for multiple purposes.[7] Both Strabo (d. 24 C.E.) and Diodorus Siculus

7. See Charles Singer, E.J. Holmyard, and A.R. Hall, eds., *A History of Technology*, Vol. 1 (New York, Oxford University Press 1954), pp. 250–256.

(50 C.E.) give full accounts of a major source of this bitumen—the Dead Sea area, and each mentions how this substance was exported to Egypt for use in the embalming of human bodies.[8] Josephus attests to the varied uses of the bitumen of the Dead Sea, asserting that it was useful not only for the caulking of ships but also for the cure of men's ailments. Accordingly, it was "mixed in a great many medicines."[9]

Asphalt was used for building in antiquity. The Bible records that Noah's ark[10] and Moses' basket[11] were constructed with the use of asphalt-like substances. The Talmud is also replete with references to the use of asphalt-like materials,[12] reflecting its common usage.

As for the medicinal value of bitumen, Pliny (d. 79 C.E.) hailed its use for cataracts, leprosy, gout, toothaches, coughs, dysentery, and wounds.[13] Galen (ca. 130 C.E.–200 C.E.) considered the asphalt of the Dead Sea to be the most beautiful of bitumens and thought it

---

8. See Menahem Stern, *Greek and Latin Authors on Jews and Judaism* (Jerusalem, Academic Press 1974), Vol. 1, pp. 178, 304. See also p. 181, where Stern comments that since Diodorus and Strabo say the same thing, "It is, therefore, useless to deny that, at least in the Graeco-Roman period, the asphalt of the Dead Sea was used in embalming." See D. Kaplan, "*Al HaTechnologia shel Chomrei Bitumen BiYisrael BiY'mei Kedem*," *Koroth 3*:1–2 (Oct. 1962); ibid., "*HaChomer BiYam HaMelach VhaShimush Bo BiY'mei Kedem*," *Koroth 3*:5–6 (Feb.–March 1964); 230–237; Carl Ritter, *The Comparative Geography of Palestine and the Sinaitic Peninsula* (trans. William Cage) (New York, Haskell House Publishers 1969), pp. 150–158. See also Karl H. Dannenfeldt, "Egyptian Mumia: The Sixteenth Century Experience and Debate," *The Sixteenth Century Journal, 16*:2 (1985): 163–180, esp. 166.

9. *Wars of the Jews*, Book 4, Chap. 8, no. 4.

10. Genesis 5:14. See also D. Kaplan, op. cit.

11. Exodus 2:3.

12. See articles by D. Kaplan, op. cit.

13. *Natural History, 35*, 180–182, quoted in Karl Dannenfeldt, "Egyptian Mumia: The Sixteenth Century Experience and Debate," *The Sixteenth Century Journal, 16*:2 (1985): 163–180. For the subsequent discussion of the mistranslations and transference of the term *mumia*, I am largely indebted to this work.

A general history on the use of *mumia* as a drug is provided by Thomas Pettigrew, *A History of Egyptian Mummies* (London, Longman, Rees,

useful for the closing of bleeding wounds.[14] Dioscorides established the use of bituminous substances in Europe. In his classic work, *Materia Medica*, he refers to the bitumen of the Dead Sea, bitumen Judaicum, as the best bitumen for medicines.[15]

MUMIA *IN THE MIDDLE AGES*

In the Middle Ages, the Dead Sea bitumen was no longer considered the most valuable; rather, the black asphalt from a certain mountain in Persia was considered by the Arabs to be ideal for therapeutic use.[16] The Persians called this substance, as well as the bitumen from the Dead Sea, "*mumiya*," derived from the Persian word for wax, *mum*.[17] The term "mummy" comes from *mumia*, since *mumia* apparently was used in the embalming process in ancient Egypt, as we shall see.

Dannenfeldt states that Rhazes (d. 923 C.E.) was the first to use

---

Orme, Brown, Green and Longman 1834), pp. 1–12. See also Warren R. Dawson, *The Bridle of Pegasus* (London, 1930), pp. 162–173.

For other references to the use of mummy as a drug, see, for example, Warren R. Dawson, "Mummy as a Drug," *Proceedings of the Royal Society of Medicine* (November 1927): 34–39; Howard W. Haggard, *Devils, Drugs, and Doctors* (New York) Blue Ribbon Books, 1929, p. 324; Arno Karlen, *Napoleon's Glands and Other Ventures in Biohistory* (Boston, Little Brown & Co., 1984), pp. 96–119; E.A. Wallis Budge, *The Mummy: A Handbook of Egyptian Funerary Archeology* (New York, Dover 1989), pp. 202–203.

14. See M. Stern, op. cit., Vol. 2, p. 324.

15. Ibid., p. 164.

16. Although medieval Arabic writers like Rhazes and Avicenna make reference to this Persian source of *mumia*, it is not until the early eighteenth century that we find an accurate historical account of the ceremonial collection of *mumia* by the Persian royalty from a remote mountain in the province of Darab. See Robert W. Carrubba, "The First Detailed Report of Persian Mummy," *Physis 23* (1981): 459–471.

17. See Dawson, op. cit.; Carrubba, op. cit., 464; Dannenfeldt, op. cit., p. 463.

the word *mumia* for bituminous substances.[18] A century later, the famous Persian physician Avicenna (d. 1037 C.E.) likewise used the term *mumia* to describe the medicinal bitumen.[19] He refers to the bituminous waters as Judaic waters,[20] likely borrowing the term from Dioscorides.

Thereafter began a transference of the term *mumia* from natural bitumen to an exudate, similar in appearance, derived from the embalmed bodies in the tombs of Egypt. As already mentioned, both Strabo and Diodorus claimed that the bitumen of the Dead Sea, which was later called *mumia* by Arab writers, was used in the embalming process in Egypt. This transference, therefore, seems logical.[21]

Dannenfeldt points out that in the sixteenth century physicians and scholars began to protest the use of *mumia* as a drug. They noted the change in the identity of the drug and attributed the transference to a series of mistranslations of works by Rhazes (d. 923 C.E.) and Serapion the Younger (ca. 1070 C.E.), among others. While these authors were logically referring to the natural bitumen, textual ambiguities led translators to expand on the original texts and identify *mumia* with the exudates of embalmed bodies, an identification common in their day. Furthermore, Dannenfeldt views the transference as occurring in a stepwise fashion. Initially, *mumia* was associated only with the fluids or exudates that flowed from the embalmed body. Ultimately, however, *mumia* became

---

18. Dannenfeldt, op. cit., p. 164.

19. Ibid. See also Pettigrew, op. cit., p. 9.

20. O. Cameron Gruner, trans., *A Treatise on the Canon of Medicine of Avicenna Incorporating a Translation of the First Book* (London, Luzac and Co., 1930), p. 237.

21. Of note, Dawson maintains that bitumen was never used in the embalming process:

> The resin, which was used in large quantities in mummies of late periods, was applied in a molten condition, and in this state often closely simulates both pitch and bitumen, but must not be confounded with these substances as is usually done; there is no evidence as yet that bitumen was ever used.

See Warren R. Dawson, "Making A Mummy," *Journal of Egyptian Archeology, 13* (1927): 40–49, quoted in Carrubba, op. cit., 460, n. 4.

associated with the very flesh of the corpse, for this, too, was impregnated with the valuable bitumen.[22]

THE TRADE OF MUMIA

The first person to prescribe Egyptian mummy, or *mumia*, for medicinal use was the expert Jewish physician named Elmagar.[23] It is recorded in *Les Diverses Leçons de L. Guyon* (1625) that Elmagar lived around 1100 (or possibly 1300, according to some authors), and prescribed *mumia* to the Christians and Moslems then fighting for Palestine. Other physicians followed suit, and so began the widespread use of *mumia*. The Jewish merchants of Egypt soon entered the trade. Some of these merchants, in order to fill the growing demand, took the bodies of executed criminals or others, filled them with inexpensive simple asphalt, bound them up tightly, and exposed them to the heat of the sun for a rapid drying. They then sold these counterfeit mummies in place of genuine, properly

22. Dannenfeldt, op. cit., pp. 164–170.

23. I have found no reference to this physician outside of this statement of Guyon. Regarding medieval Jewish physicians in Arabic countries, see, for example, Max Meyerhof, "Mediaeval Jewish Physicians in the Near East, from Arabic Sources," *ISIS 27–28* (1937–1938): 432–460; idem., "Jewish Physicians Under the Reign of the Fatimid Caliphs in Egypt (969–1171)," *Medical Leaves* (1939): 131–139; S.D. Goitein, "The Medical Profession in Light of the Cairo Geniza Documents," *Hebrew Union College Annual 34* (1963): 177–194; R.Y. Ebied, *Bibliography of Mediaeval Arabic and Jewish Medicine and Allied Sciences* (London, Wellcome Inst Hist Med. 1971); Moshe Perlman, "Notes on the Position of Jewish Physicians in Medieval Muslim Countries," *Journal of Israel Oriental Studies 2* (1972): 315–319; H.D. Isaacs, "Medieval Judaeo-Arabic Medicine as Described in the Cairo Geniza," *Journal of the Royal Society of Medicine 83* (November 1990): 734–737; idem., "A Medieval Arab Medical Certificate," *Medical History 35* (1991): 250–257; idem., *Medical and Para-Medical Manuscripts in the Cambridge Geniza Collections* (Cambridge, Cambridge Univ. Press. 1994).

embalmed ones. These freshly prepared mummies apparently were sold to the Christians.[24]

Although purportedly first prescribed in the Middle Ages, Egyptian *mumia* only became popular in the sixteenth century, when it was widely prescribed by physicians.[25] In 1564, Guy de la Fontaine, physician to the king of Navarre, journeyed to Egypt. While in Alexandria, he sought out the principal Jew in charge of the mummy trade and asked him as to the origin of the supply and the nature of the ancient burial and embalming practices. The merchant showed him some thirty or forty bodies and explained with amusement that all those bodies had been prepared over the last four years. When de la Fontaine asked what nationality they were or whether the bodies were diseased, the merchant said that he cared not, for once the bodies were embalmed, they all appeared the same. The merchant further marveled that the Christians, "so daintily mouthed," could eat of the bodies of the dead.[26]

De la Fontaine related the encounter to his friend Ambrose Paré, the celebrated French military surgeon, who subsequently incorporated the information into his medical works. Paré quotes Louis de Paradis, a French surgeon who visited Cairo, that the Egyptians refused to permit any of their embalmed bodies to be exported, saying that the Christians were unworthy of eating their dead bodies. If the bodies did end up outside the country, he said, it was likely by means of some Jews who smuggled them out by stripping the bodies and packing them with their merchandise.[27] Paré also

24. Cited by Pettigrew, op. cit., pp. 7–8. The anatomist William Williams Keen also mentioned this practice of the Jews in his historical work, *A Sketch of the Early History of Practical Anatomy* (Philadelphia, 1874), p. 37, stating that when the demand for *mumia* exceeded the supply of the real article, a substitute was sold "at enormous profits by avaricious Jews of Alexandria." This passage is quoted in James Moores Ball, *The Body Snatchers* (New York, Dorsett Press 1989), xxiv–xxv.

25. Dannenfeldt, op. cit.

26. Cited by Pettigrew, op. cit., p. 8, without quoting a source, and by Dannenfeldt, op. cit., p. 170 and n. 28.

27. Dannenfeldt, op. cit., pp. 7–8.

wrote an entire treatise, "On Mumia," published in 1582, in which he refers to a Jewish physician prescribing *mumia*.[28]

Regarding the duration of the *mumia* trade, Louis Guyon (1625) relates an anecdote that may account for the diminution of the trade of counterfeit *mumia*, or perhaps even the cessation of the Jewish *mumia* trade altogether. A Jew of Damietta, Egypt, who manufactured counterfeit mummies, had a Christian slave whom he wished to convert to Judaism. When the slave refused to undergo the required circumcision, their relationship turned adversarial, and the merchant began to mistreat the slave. As a result, the slave informed the authorities of his master's illicit practices. The merchant was imprisoned but was able to secure his release with the payment of three hundred sultanins of gold. When the governors of the neighboring cities, including Alexandria, Rosetta, Aleppo, and other Egyptian cities, heard of these events, they delighted in the prospect of easily obtaining money for their respective treasuries. Forthwith, they began collecting ransom from all Jews involved in the mummy trade. Historians recount that from this time onward the trade of *mumia* ceased, since the Jews were fearful of being subjected to further oppression.[29]

Although this account was published in 1625, it is unclear exactly when the trade stopped. In 1718, John Quincy wrote that although *mumia* could still be found in medicinal catalogues, it was rarely prescribed.[30]

Despite this attestation, the use of *mumia* seems to have continued, albeit on a limited basis, into the eighteenth[31] and nineteenth centuries.[32]

In summary, the history of the drug *mumia* is somewhat convoluted, having undergone a transference from the natural bitumen of the Dead Sea and Persia to the embalmed or desiccated bodies of Egypt. This transference resulted in confusion as to the

---

28. Geoffrey Keynes, ed., *The Apologie and Treatise of Ambrose Paré* (New York, Dover 1968), pp. 143–146.

29. Pettigrew, op. cit., p. 11, and Dannenfeldt, op. cit., p. 171.

30. Dannenfeldt, op. cit., p. 179.

31. Pettigrew, whose work was published in 1834, states that in his day Arabs still used mummy powder.

32. Dannenfeldt, op. cit., 179–180.

true identity of *mumia* and led to the questioning of its therapeutic efficacy.

JEWISH SOURCES[33]

With this brief overview, we can now address the Jewish sources on the use of *mumia*. The sources can be divided into two categories: those that simply provide an account of the use of *mumia* and those that address the halachic implications of its use.

ACCOUNTS OF MUMIA *IN EXTRALEGAL SOURCES*

Historians refer to the Jewish physician Elmagar, who is dated between 1100 and 1300 C.E., as being the first to prescribe Egyptian *mumia*. What went unnoticed is the fact that Maimonides, who lived during this very period (1138–1204), includes *mumia* in a list of medications in his medical treatise *Pirkei Moshe*.[34] In this work, Maimonides simply states the term "*mumia*" without qualification, making it difficult to ascertain whether he refers to *mumia* the bitumen or *mumia* the embalmed body. However, in his dictionary of medical terms, Maimonides translates *mumia* as

33. The use of *mumia* in Jewish sources has been dealt with briefly in two previous essays: H.J. Zimmels, *Magicians, Theologians and Doctors* (London, 1952), pp. 126–128, 224–245.; Raphael Patai, "Indulco and Mumia," *Journal of American Folklore, 77* (January–March 1964): 3–11. See also Daniel Sperber, *Minhagei Yisrael 2* (Jerusalem, Mosad Harav Kook 1991), 61, n. 28, where *mumia* is referred to in the context of a discussion on the medicinal use of halachically prohibited substances (e.g., blood).

34. In a personal communication, Dr. Gerrit Bos confirms that the term *mumia* appears in the original Arabic edition (ms. Gotha) of *Pirkei Moshe*, aphorisms, 21:80. See S. Muntner, trans. and ed., *Rambam: Kitvei Refuah 2* (Jerusalem, Mosad Harav Kook 1961), p. 262.

el-k'buria,[35] reflecting *mumia*'s association with graves and, perhaps, with embalmed bodies. Even this term, however, is ambiguous. Is Maimonides referring to the bitumen, which was commonly found in the grave, as it was used in embalming, or is he referring to the corpse itself, which likewise was found in the grave? Maimonides does not explicitly translate the term *mumia* as either bitumen or parts of embalmed corpses.

In any case, this is an important source, for it reflects a step in the transference of the term *mumia*, here being associated, in the twelfth century, with the burial process. In addition, if Maimonides refers to bitumen,[36] this source reflects one of two possibilities. Perhaps Elmagar postdates Maimonides, and Egyptian mummy was only first prescribed after Maimonides' time. Consequently, Mai-

---

35. S. Muntner, ed. and trans., *Biur Shemot HaRefuot* in *Rambam: Kitvei Refuah 4* (Jerusalem, Mosad Harav Kook 1969), p. 71. In Muntner's notes on *Pirkei Moshe*, ibid., n. 385, he translates *el-k'buria* as body parts from ancient corpses. In addition, he states that *mumia* also refers to pissasphalt (bitumen), thereby alluding to the confusion and transference of the term.

The term *el-k'buria* was used in conjunction with the term *mumia* in folk-remedy prescriptions well beyond the time of Maimonides. See Avraham Ben-Yaakov, *HaRefuah HaAmamit Ezel Yehudei Bavel 1* (Jerusalem, Yerid HaSefarim 1991), pp. 533–534.

36. The term *mumia*, as used by Maimonides, more likely refers to bitumen for a number of reasons. *Mumia* is found amongst a list of natural substances; earlier in this list Maimonides cites Avicenna, whom we know to have used the term *mumia* to refer to natural bitumen, and from whom Maimonides may have borrowed some of the terms of this list, including *mumia*; and Maimonides himself acknowledged the medicinal value of asphalt and bitumen elsewhere in his medical works. See Uriel Barzel, trans., *Maimonides' Medical Writings—The Art of Cure: Extracts from Galen* (Haifa, Maimonides Research Institute 1992), p. 176; Fred Rosner, trans., *Moses Maimonides' Glossary of Drug Names* (Philadelphia American Philosophical Society 1979), pp. 99–100, 121–122. (I thank Dr. Fred Rosner for directing me to these sources.)

On the other hand, in his *Glossary of Drug Names,* Maimonides uses the terms *zaft* and *qufr al-Yahud* (bitumen of the Jews) for asphalt and bitumen, rather than the term *mumia*. This may indicate that *mumia* refers to something other than bitumen (i.e., Egyptian *mumia*).

monides, like his contemporaries, prescribed natural bitumen. Alternatively, Elmagar predates Maimonides, and Maimonides continued to prescribe the original *mumia*, being either unaware or disapproving of the Egyptian variety.

If, however, Maimonides refers to Egyptian mummy,[37] then this would represent the earliest primary source on its use, and possibly, depending on the dating of Elmagar, the earliest known prescription of Egyptian *mumia*.

The next account of the use of *mumia* is found in the biblical commentary of Rabbi Eliezer Ashkenazi (1513–1586).[38] God commanded Lot and his wife, when they departed from Sodom, to refrain from looking behind them or standing in the plain. R. Ashkenazi postulates the possible reason for the latter warning:

---

37. If Maimonides refers to Egyptian *mumia*, we might have expected him to deal with, or at least allude to, the halachic ramifications of the use of parts of a corpse for medicinal purposes. In general, however, Maimonides makes no halachic pronouncements in his medical works, and, largely, vice versa. In his *Yad Hachazaka, Hilchot Avel*, where he discusses the laws of impurity as well as the laws regarding deriving benefit from a corpse, he makes no specific reference to *mumia*. There is no discussion of the use of *mumia* in his responsa. This may support the view that Maimonides prescribed *mumia* as bitumen, although it is by no means definitive proof.

R. Judah Rosanes (d. 1727), in his commentary on Maimonides' *Hilchot Avel*, addresses the use of Egyptian mumia from an halachic perspective.

38. *Ma'asei Adoshem* (New York, E. Grossman Publ. House 1962), sect. *Ma'asei Avot*, Chap. 17, 97.

There is also an earlier reference to *mumia* by a physician of the early fourteenth century named Raymund de Tarrega. Like Maimonides, he mentions *mumia* in a list of medications. It is, therefore, impossible to tell whether he refers to *mumia* the bitumen or *mumia* the embalmed body. However, since the list also includes gum arabic, alum, and another clay-like substance, it is likely that de Tarrega was prescribing the bitumen. See Raphael Patai, *The Jewish Alchemists* (Princeton, NJ Princeton Univ. Prėss 1994), pp. 198, 563. Patai, in his footnote, refers to his own article on the topic of *mumia* and assumes that de Tarrega refers to Egyptian *mumia*. Whether or not de Tarrega refers to Egyptian *mumia*, this reference is relevant for the same reasons discussed in the text regarding the reference of Maimonides.

> . . . and furthermore God commanded them not to stand in all the flat plains, for it is known that when snow is blown by the winds, and a man or a tree is standing in its path, the snow will overcome and completely cover them. Such is not the case if a man is running . . . and until today, in the sand-filled deserts, when a strong wind blows the sands, if a man or a tree is in its path, the sand will cover them and form a mound . . . and until today it is known that sometimes it occurs that a man is unable to withstand the force of the wind-blown sands and he is completely covered by them. Subsequently, another wind blows and the body is uncovered. The body, found by desert travelers, is brought to the merchants of medicinal spices. They call it *mumia* and use the desiccated body for the preparation of medical remedies. This is what happened to Lot's wife . . . when she stood still, the wind blew the salt over her and she became a mound of salt.

Rabbi Ashkenazi served as rabbi and judge in Egypt for over twenty years.[39] It is likely that R. Ashkenazi became exposed during this period to the use of desiccated bodies in the production of *mumia*. We know from our earlier discussion that recently deceased, desiccated, unembalmed bodies were used in the manufacture of *mumia*. Such practices, at least initially, were considered fraudulent, as only the genuine embalmed Egyptian mummies were considered to be of medicinal value. R. Ashkenazi attests to this practice but casts no aspersions upon it. Furthermore, he makes no mention of the other kinds of *mumia* or the Jewish involvement in the mummy trade. Neither of these topics is relevant to his biblical commentary. We can, therefore, make no assumptions based on their omission.

The next two sources, which date from the late nineteenth century, prove that *mumia* was still in use at this time.[40] The second source, however, objects to its use, not on halachic grounds, but for medicinal reasons. Both sources refer to the use of *mumia* in Israel, reflecting the fact that the use of *mumia* was not restricted to Egypt.

The first reference is found in the work of Rabbi Moshe Reischer,

---

39. Cecil Roth, ed., *Encyclopedia Judaica*, Keter Publ. House Vol. 3, p. 725, s.v. Ashkenazi, Eliezer.

40. See also Avraham ben-Yaakov, op. cit., n. 35 above.

titled *Sha'arei Yerushalayim* (1870), which details the positive traits of the land of Israel, including the customs of its inhabitants.

> The Sephardim make to this day a remedy, *mumia*, which is prepared from the ground dry bones of dead people found in the desert in the sand. For along the road leading to Mecca there is a big desert, and there is a place full of sand which is called the Sand Sea. And when a storm arises, it lifts up the sand to a height of more than 20 cubits [about 30 feet] and covers everyone who happens to be on the road, for a distance of about a mile. And people go there and, searching diligently, they find these pieces in human form, black and dry as a stone, for even the biggest man who is left lying under the sand dries out and becomes as small as a finger. And they sell it to apothecaries, and they put it into remedies. And the Sephardim, when they have a patient sick for many days, God forbid, take it and grind it well and put a certain amount of it into honey-water which the patient drinks from time to time during three nights. Before he drinks it, they wash him and clothe him in a white robe, and lay him on a bed covered with a white sheet. Menstruating women are not allowed to enter the house as long as the illness of the patient persists, lest this cause harm to the patient and to themselves. The patient lies alone, and nobody else is with him in the house, not even a hen. Moreover, he must beware of the smell of garlic and onions. The only food of the patient throughout the nine days is milk, bread, and butter.[41]

Reischer mentions exclusively the *mumia* consisting of the desiccated bodies found in the desert, especially in the Arabian desert on the road to Mecca. He makes no mention of the *mumia* derived from embalmed Egyptian bodies. While R. Ashkenazi had a particular reason to mention only the desert *mumia*—in order to support his unique commentary of the biblical passage—Reischer had no such agenda. He is simply listing the customs of the land. We can therefore assume that the use of desert *mumia* was the normative practice at this time, perhaps to the exclusion of Egyptian *mumia*. This may reflect yet another form of transference of the

41. The translation is by Patai, op. cit., p. 9. He references the 1870 edition of this work. I consulted the Jerusalem (1967) edition and was unable to find this passage.

term *mumia* from the embalmed Egyptian *mumia* to the more readily obtainable desert *mumia* that, although originally a counterfeit substitute of the former, ultimately supplanted it entirely.

The second source, likewise referring to practices in late-nineteenth-century Jerusalem, seems to corroborate the theory of this transference, as only desert *mumia* is mentioned. This source appears in a journal edited and written mostly by Abraham Luncz, a man who spent most of his life working to perfect his geographical knowledge, especially of Jerusalem.[42] The passage on *mumia* appears under the chapter heading *Emunat Hevel*, translated literally as "belief in nonsense." In a footnote, he states that the following practices have been adopted by women and fools. Wise and intelligent men, however, not only themselves refrain from such practices but castigate others who believe in such nonsense.[43] We know from historical sources that already in the sixteenth century people questioned the value of *mumia*, albeit in reference to Egyptian *mumia*.[44] But despite proclamations against *mumia*, its use continued at least until the end of the nineteenth century, as evidenced by the following passage.

> By this name [*mumia*] is called in Arabic a piece of bone which has become completely black. [Footnote:] According to what the children of the land of the east say, this bone can be found in the sandy desert of Arabia, and it is a part of the bodies of people who were buried among the waves of that sea of sand while on their way to Mecca or to the other cities of that country, and from the great and burning heat their bones hardened, became black and exceedingly small, like the form of embalmed bodies. The mumia is offered for sale in Arab pharmacies of medicine and charms. The price of a dirham [drachma] is about 5 piasters, and those who buy a large quantity of it can see in it the shape of the member from which it is derived [end of footnote]. Its power is such as to heal all illness and disease, and especially sudden and unusual ones.

42. Cecil Roth, ed., *Encyclopedia Judaica*, Keter Publ. House Vol. 11, pp. 564–565.

43. Abraham Moses Luncz, *Yerushalayim 1* (1882): 20, no. 40.

44. See, for example, Lynn Thorndyke, *A History of Magic and Experimental Science, 8* (New York, Columbia Univ. Press 1958), p. 414.

This drug is prepared in the following manner: a certain quantity of mumia—or a part of the black bone—is pounded in a mortar to thin powder—and sometimes they mix some honey and spices into it—and a handful of it is placed on the roof for the night so that the dew descends upon it, or they put it in a coffee cup, and the patient drinks this balsam of Gilead for nine successive nights. On the fifth and ninth day, before he drinks of it they wash his body, wrap him from head to toe in white clothes, and a man or a woman sits next to him all night to watch him—for they believe that the two nights are most dangerous for the patient. The patient's food during this period consists of bread, butter and milk only, and they also take care lest the patient inhale any strong smell, and especially the smell of garlic, onions, and fish. Woman who are in their menses must not enter the house throughout that period, lest they cause damage to the patient and to themselves, and in general, very few people visit them.

The neighbors who live in the same courtyard—and who believe this nonsense—are very much afraid lest the power of the mumia affect them adversely, and they therefore leave their houses for several days, or—if they do not care about the state of the patient and the improvement of his health—they will draw on the door of his house the picture of a hand which is a well known amulet, and then the power of the mumia is broken, and it will neither help nor harm the patient. Therefore, if the patient is apprehensive lest his neighbors perform this contrary act, he will do everything in secret, unknown to anybody.[45]

THE USE OF MUMIA *IN LEGAL SOURCES*

Assuming that Maimonides prescribed bitumen, and that Elmagar lived at the latest possible date, then we find the first prescription of Egyptian *mumia* around 1300. Despite this apparent early usage of Egyptian *mumia*, it is not until the sixteenth century that we find the first recorded reference to *mumia* in rabbinic responsa literature.

45. Translation by Patai, op. cit., pp. 9–10.

Rabbi David ben Abi Zimra (1479–1573), known as Radbaz, served as leader of the Egyptian community for about forty years, until 1553, when he emigrated to Palestine. He was asked the following question: "On what basis do people use as a medicinal remedy the flesh of corpses called *mumia*? They use it even in cases where there is no grave danger . . . and they trade in it as well. This should be forbidden, for as we know, it is forbidden to derive benefit from the flesh of a corpse."[46]

Radbaz justifies the use of *mumia*, despite the biblical prohibition of deriving benefit from a corpse, on a number of grounds. Regarding the ingestion of *mumia*, he states, there is surely no problem, "For *mumia* is the embalmed flesh that is embalmed with many spices . . . and it becomes an asphalt-like substance (*k'ein zephet*). Therefore [since it has lost its original identity] it is permissible to eat." Furthermore, he states, when one eats *mumia* one does not derive benefit from the part of *mumia* that derives from the flesh of the corpse, "for spices are mixed with it [*mumia*]. It is not from the flesh that one obtains [medicinal] benefit, but rather from the spices that are contained therein. Proof of this is that unembalmed corpses are of no [medicinal] value."

The logic of Radbaz is employed to permit the eating of *mumia* for medicinal purposes. In such a case, he argues, there is no benefit derived from the corpse (*shelo k'derech hana'ato*). With regard to selling *mumia*, however, no such leniency exists, since the merchant is profiting from the sale of corpses. As a result, Radbaz uses a different line of reasoning to permit the trade of *mumia*. He concludes that there is no halachic prohibition of deriving benefit from non-Jewish corpses. As *mumia* clearly derives from non-Jewish bodies, there is therefore no prohibition to engaging in the mummy trade.

A number of important points can be gleaned from this responsum. Historical sources indicate that *mumia* was a commonly prescribed drug in Egypt and that the Jews were involved in its trade. As *mumia* consisted partially of the flesh of a corpse, its use and trade presented unique halachic problems. Radbaz, who lived

46. *Teshuvot haRadbaz*, Vol. 3, n. 979 (548).

in Egypt, the center of the *mumia* trade, appears to be the first to address this problem.[47]

Although *mumia* was apparently first prescribed by Elmagar, its use did not become widespread until centuries later. This may explain why it is only in the time of Radbaz that the halachic aspects of the use of *mumia* were addressed. The wording of the question to Radbaz, however, implies that *mumia* had already been in use for some time, and the response reflects a de facto approval of a preexisting practice. It is unclear, however, how long *mumia* was in use before this responsum was written. In any case, it represents the first in a series of halachic discussions that span over one hundred years and that address a contemporary halachic problem.

The resolution of medical halachic problems requires an understanding of the medical realities. Radbaz's decision was partially dependent on his understanding of that reality, as it related to the drug *mumia*. He described the nature of *mumia* as being asphalt-like, and he claimed that the medicinal value of *mumia* lay in the embalming materials (i.e., the asphalt or bitumen) and not in the body of the deceased. As described earlier, *mumia* underwent a gradual transference from bitumen to the embalmed body, for which bitumen was apparently used. Radbaz's understanding reflects a stage in that transference. At this period in history, *mumia* had already become associated with the embalmed body, but it had not completely lost its original association with bitumen, the true medicinal remedy. While Radbaz actually describes the final product of *mumia* as like *zephet*, or bitumen, he does not acknowledge—nor was he likely aware—that originally *mumia* was, in fact, synonymous with *zephet*. He also clearly states that the true medicinal remedy is contained in the embalming materials (i.e., the bitumen or original *mumia*) and not in the corpse, here also reflecting an intermediate state of the transference. With the completion of the transference, the corpse acquires the primary medicinal value, independent of the bitumen or other embalming materials.

47. This is evidenced by the fact that subsequent rabbinic authorities who deal with *mumia* refer to Radbaz, either concurring or disagreeing with his conclusions.

Mumia is next mentioned in a passing reference by Rabbi Jacob Castro (1525?–1610), who permitted the eating and selling of *mumia* based on Radbaz's premise that *mumia* is mere dust.[48] Castro, an Egyptian rabbi, based many of his decisions on his predecessor, Radbaz.[49]

Rabbi Abraham ben Mordechai Halevi (late seventeenth century), also an Egyptian rabbi, treats the topic of *mumia* more extensively.[50] The question posed to him, however, adds a new element to the halachic discussion:

> I was asked regarding the mumia in Egypt, whether the laws of *tum'ah* [ritual defilement] apply to it with respect to a *kohen* [priest], and whether it is permissible to eat it and trade in it.

While Radbaz had alluded to the notion of *tumah* peripherally, for R. Abraham Halevi this issue takes prominence. In order to appropriately address the issue of *tumah* for *mumia*, the author displays an intimate knowledge of its composition in his detailed discussion about whether *mumia* contains the requisite volume of a *kezayit* (size of an olive) of the corpse in order to generate *tumah* (i.e., convey ritual impurity). Mere volume, however, is not sufficient for the prohibition of *tumah*; this *kezayit* must be somewhat solid, so as not to crumble easily. According to R. Abraham Halevi,

---

48. Patai, op. cit., p. 11, n. 21, references Castro's work *Erech Lechem* (Constantinople, 1718), 391:1 as the source for this quote. It should be noted that this is a misprint, as the relevant passage is found at n. 349. R. Abraham Ben Mordechai Halevi also cites R. Castro in his *Ginat Veradim* (Constantinople, 1716), Y.D. 1, n. 4.

Yet another incorrect citation of R. Castro appears in R. Abraham Eisenstadt's *Pitchei Teshuvah*, Y.D., 349:2, where he cites "*BH'T shel ha Maharit*" as the source of a quote that is, in fact, from the aforementioned work of R. Castro. It appears that it should have read Maharik (Moreinu Harav Yaakov Castro) instead of Maharit. The acronym *BH'T* also appears to be a misprint, perhaps intended to be *BH'K* (*B'Hilchot K'riah*), which is where the citation is found.

49. Castro's work, *Sefer Maharikash Hanikra Erech Lechem* (Constantinople, 1718) is replete with references to the responsa of Radbaz.

50. *Ginat Veradim*, op. cit.

mumia fulfills both of these criteria and, therefore, conveys ritual impurity.

> Based on what we have written above . . . the law of *tumah* applies to a *kezayit* of flesh of mumia because it does not crumble unless it is crushed. Even though the mumia only achieves this solid state by virtue of being mixed with spices and salves, without which the mumia would be a pile of dust, still, we are . . . only concerned with its present state.

Like R. Castro, R. Abraham Halevi then quotes Radbaz. However, in contradistinction to R. Castro, he strongly disagrees with Radbaz's conclusions. He enumerates the premises for Radbaz's permissive ruling, then negates them one by one. What is particularly interesting is that the author questions Radbaz's conclusions not only on halachic grounds but on medical grounds as well. Radbaz claimed that the value of *mumia* lies in the embalming spices and not in the flesh of the corpse; hence, one does not, in essence, derive benefit from the corpse itself. R. Abraham Halevi had a different medical opinion:

> Regarding the [Radbaz's] second reason [for permitting mumia], even though there is great value in these spices and salves . . . still, there is medicinal value to the limbs of the corpse. . . . The reason that they do not use the flesh of unembalmed corpses is because the flesh decays and therefore loses its value. The spices that are used in mumia, however, prevent decay and preserve the medicinal value of the flesh of the corpse forever.

R. Abraham Halevi, who lived about a century after Radbaz, attributes medicinal value to the corpse itself.[51] This reflects the completion of the transference, for now it is the body that becomes the primary *mumia*, independent of the embalming materials.

51. In the seventeenth century, many physicians prescribed medicines derived from living human beings (e.g., urine, feces, or saliva), as well as from human cadavers. See Thorndyke, op. cit., Vol. 8, 415. The use of parts of cadavers in medicine cannot be attributed solely to the transference from the use of *mumia*, but in this context it appears to be the case.

Moreover, the embalming process is viewed here as effectively preserving the otherwise temporary medicinal value of the flesh of the corpse.

In addition to the different medical understanding, R. Abraham Halevi also disagrees with Radbaz about two major halachic points. First, he maintains that even if the ingestion of *mumia* is in a manner not involving clear benefit or enjoyment from the flesh of the corpse (*shelo k'derech hana'ato*), as Radbaz claims is the case, it should still be prohibited on halachic grounds. Second, he opines, as opposed to Radbaz, that it is prohibited to derive benefit from a corpse, even if the body belongs to a non-Jew. Consequently, R. Abraham Halevi prohibits both the eating of and trading in *mumia*, for both priest and Israelite alike. He is apparently the first to have so ruled.

Our final primary halachic reference to *mumia* is the commentary of Rabbi Judah Rosanes (1657—1727) to the *Mishneh Torah* of Maimonides. R. Rosanes, unlike the previous discussants, lived not in Egypt but entirely in Turkey. At this period in history, however, Egypt was under Turkish rule, making cultural exchange between these two countries likely.

In three separate places, R. Rosanes addresses the issues related to the use of *mumia*.[52] While he does not directly refer to the previous responsa of Radbaz or R. Abraham Halevi,[53] he discusses the identical issues of deriving benefit from a corpse and whether or not *mumia* constitutes a source of ritual defilement. He addresses these concerns with respect to both Jewish and non-Jewish corpses.

Whereas the question posed to R. Abraham Halevi indicated that priests were somehow involved in the use of *mumia*, he did not stipulate whether they were consumers or traders. The question to R. Rosanes was less ambiguous: "I was asked about the *mumia*

52. *Hilchot Ma'achalot Asurot*, Chap. 8, n. 18; *Hilchot Avel*, Chap. 3, n. 1; ibid., Chap. 14, n. 21.

53. In R. Rosanes' glosses on *Hilchot Avel*, Chap. 3, n. 1, a note in parentheses refers the reader to the work *Ginat Veradim* of R. Abraham Halevi. It is unclear to me, however, whether this note was written by the author or added by an editor. In either case, the works of Radbaz and R. Abraham Halevi, interestingly, are not discussed in the body of the text in any of the three references of R. Rosanes to *mumia*.

which is sold by *kohanim* [priests]. Is it proper for them to do this or not?"

Like his predecessors, R. Rosanes was concerned with the constitution of *mumia*, as it relates to its status of ritual defilement:

> According to what I have heard, this mumia contains no flesh at all, rather just bones covered by skin. [The bones] are very dry with no residual moisture from the flesh. I asked whether these bones crumble spontaneously, and they told me that not only do they not crumble, but it is difficult to break them. Based on this, there is no doubt whatsoever that [mumia] imparts ritual impurity. . . .[54]

R. Rosanes makes no mention of spices or salves intermixed with the *mumia*. As a result, he does not raise the issue, as R. Abraham Halevi had, of whether the spices mixed with the *mumia* affect the measuring of the requisite olive's bulk for ritual defilement. It is possible that the *mumia* he was told about was the desert *mumia*, which contained no spices. This may reflect the transference from Egyptian *mumia* to desert *mumia*.

Unlike his predecessors, R. Rosanes split his decision. Radbaz and R. Abraham Halevi had decided uniformly to either permit or forbid the use of *mumia*, respectively. R. Rosanes, on the other hand, permitted the use and trade of *mumia* by an Israelite, as, like Radbaz, he considered *mumia* to be as mere dust.[55] But with respect to *tumah*, he agreed with the position of R. Abraham Halevi that *mumia* imparts ritual impurity. Consequently, he forbade the handling of *mumia* by priests.[56]

CONCLUSION

Mumia is a chapter in medical halachic history from the sixteenth to the nineteenth centuries that illustrates how an appreciation of

54. Ibid.
55. *Hilchot Ma'akhalot Asurot*, Chap. 9, n. 18.
56. *Hilchot Avel*, Chap. 3, n. 1.

medical history can heighten our understanding of the Jewish sources. It can now be understood why the responsa cover this particular period. Prior to the time of Radbaz, *mumia* was prescribed as the bitumen, but only in the time of Radbaz did the use of *mumia* derived from embalmed or desiccated bodies become widespread. Living in Egypt, the center of the *mumia* trade, Radbaz was the first to address this issue.

The last of the halachic authorities to deal with *mumia* is R. Rosanes, who died in the early eighteenth century. Historical sources state that the *mumia* trade, which was dominated by Jews, either significantly decreased or possibly ceased in the seventeenth century. The work of R. Rosanes confirms that the trade of *mumia* by Jews continued into the late seventeenth and possibly early eighteenth centuries. The absence of any later responsa correlates with the diminution of the *mumia* trade. The two nonhalachic sources from nineteenth-century Jerusalem reflect the residual and peripheral use of *mumia*, relegated at that stage to folklore, as opposed to mainstream medicine.

All the rabbinic figures who grappled with the halachic problems of *mumia* lived in Egypt or in the Turkish empire, of which Egypt was a part. Given the general history of the *mumia* trade and the significant role the Jews played, these responsa, taken collectively, represent an halachic response to a pressing medical halachic dilemma. The testimonies from multiple sources indicate that the livelihood of many Jews in the Egyptian community would likely have been affected by a rabbinic decision on the permissibility of trading in *mumia*.

Despite the fact that each of these rabbinic authorities over a period of roughly two centuries was discussing a drug called *mumia*, the understanding of the nature and constitution of this drug changed from responsum to responsum, influencing the respective decisions accordingly. An appreciation of the evolution and transference of the term *mumia* gives us a better appreciation of the details of the halachic discussions, as well as an understanding of the apparent inconsistencies between them. The historical analysis also reveals that each rabbinic authority was well versed in the practice of medicine of his time.

This approach to the history of *mumia* is but one example of how medical history and medical *halachah* can be integrated in order to provide a more comprehensive understanding of the medical halachic decision-making process throughout the ages.

PIONEERS IN JEWISH MEDICAL ETHICS

Rabbi Moshe Feinstein (1895–1986)

DR. MOSHE D. TENDLER

BACKGROUND

Rabbi (or better, Rav) Moshe Feinstein was born on the seventh day of Adar in the Hebrew year 5655 (corresponding to March 3, 1895) in Uzda, White Russia, of aristocratic ancestors. His father, Rav David, the Rabbi of Uzda, was a direct descendant of Rav Abraham, brother of the *Gaon* of Vilna and author of *Maalot HaTorah*. His mother, Fia Gittel, was the daughter of Rav Yitzchok Yechiel Halevi, Rabbi of Karelitz and direct descendant of the author of *Seder Hadorot*, who traced his lineage to King David.

Rav Feinstein studied Torah in Slutzk, near Luban, with Rav Isser Zalman Meltzer and Rabbi Pesach Pruskin. When Rabbi Pruskin opened his own *yeshiva*, Rav Feinstein went with him and stayed for three years. His primary teacher, however, was his father, Rav David.

At twenty years of age, Rav Feinstein (or Reb Moshe, as he became popularly known) became Rabbi of Uzda and thus escaped the military conscription that was ordered for all nonpracticing *yeshiva* students. After two years, he joined his brother, Rav Mordechai, in establishing a *yeshiva* in Izdarabin. One of their students was Rav Moshe Zvi Neriah, founder of the Bnei Akiba network. Because, in part, of anti-Semitism, Rav Neriah, together with other disciples, was sent by both Reb Moshe and Rav Mordechai to Jerusalem to study with Rabbi Isaac Hakohen Kook.

Rav Feinstein became the Rabbi in Luban and served there until 1936. Growing anti-Semitism led him to obtain a visa to emigrate to the United States with the help of his brother-in-law, Rabbi Nehemiah Katz of Toledo, Ohio, and the intercession of Ohio Senator Taft. Upon his arrival in the United States, Rav Feinstein was greeted by a large contingent of prominent rabbis led by Rabbi Moshe Soloveichik. He was invited by Rabbi Joseph Adler to begin a rabbinical ordination program at the Mesifta Tiferet Jerusalem on the Lower East Side of New York City. Two years later, Rabbi Adler drowned, and Rav Feinstein became the Rosh Yeshiva, a post that he held until his death in 1986.

Reb Moshe was already recognized as the premier rabbinic decisor (*posek*) in Russia. His early responsa were labeled as brilliant by many of his illustrious contemporaries, including Rabbi Chaim Ozer and Rabbi Yechezkel Abramsky. He was a devoted husband, father, and grandfather who took great pride and joy in his family. He gave a disproportionate amount of his income for charity. He was extremely modest, yet no one who met him and knew him could fail to recognize his greatness. He was the rabbinic decisor par excellence for world Jewry for more than seven decades, and for American Jewry for more than half a century.

Rav Feinstein was the moral and halachic conscience of the Torah community. Nowhere was his leadership more keenly felt than in medicine and in medical *halachah*, where his empathy, sensitivity, and intellectual integrity were widely recognized. The study of his famous and now-classic eight volumes of responsa (one published posthumously) will serve to memorialize and eternalize his teachings.

After thirty-six years of personal contact and study with Rav Moshe Feinstein as his son-in-law, I am continually reminded of his greatness as seen in his responsa, whose simplicity and obvious truth represent examples of Torah from Sinai in our daily lives. This chapter is devoted to a select few of his responsa, both medical and nonmedical, that had an enormous impact on contemporary Jewish society.

GENERAL RESPONSA

Many women whose husbands' death in the Holocaust could not be proven by classic laws of evidentiary proof thus became *agunot* (women restrained from remarriage). In a daring responsum that had a major impact on the lives of thousands of people, Rav Feinstein interpreted the rabbinic decree of *mayim she-ein lahem sof* (literally, waters that have no end) to refer to individuals, but not to an entire community. Ordinarily, if a man is lost at sea, his wife cannot remarry because his death has not been absolutely proven. This decree, ruled Rav Feinstein, does not apply to a community of millions of Jews who were exterminated in concentration camps and whose deaths could not be proven with absolute certainty.[1] His responsum is based on his conviction that this was the intent of the talmudic passage that discusses this issue.[2] This responsum may have been the most important one he ever wrote, although it is little known.

Another major responsum that had a major effect on the lives of many people deals with reverse vasectomy.[3] Many of the so-called flower children of the 1950s and 1960s temporarily left society and lived in communes and hippie pads. Some of them were people with hearts and souls who felt deeply that our amoral society was not a decent place in which to live. Many of these young men underwent vasectomy. Through God's compassion, some of these young people became reacquainted with their Judaic heritage and found in Torah the answer for which they had been searching. After their return to Judaism they discovered that, because of their vasectomies, they were not allowed to marry because "one that hath his spermatic cord cut shall not enter into the congregation of the Lord."[4] When they attempted to have their vasectomies reversed, they discovered that there is a prohibition of "castration after castration" or "sterilization after sterilization" (*sirus* after *sirus*). A

1. M. Feinstein, *Responsa Iggrot Moshe, Even Haezer*, part 1, no. 43.
2. *Yevamot* 121.
3. *Iggrot Moshe, Even Haezer*, part 4, no. 30.
4. Deuteronomy 23:2.

reverse vasectomy can be done only by cutting into the vas deferens again to reach live tissue and to then make the anastamosis. The second act of cutting into the vas before its repair is prohibited, just as the initial act of the vasectomy was prohibited. Rav Feinstein interpreted with brilliance that there is a vast difference between the initial prohibited act of vasectomy and the subsequent act of reversal of the vasectomy. God accepts the intent of an act as qualitatively modifying the act. The first act was one of castration, the second an act of curing the illness of infertility. This decision by Rav Feinstein enriched the lives of many hundreds of Jews who returned to their religion to become Orthodox Jews (*baalei teshuvah*).

A third responsum of Rav Feinstein that had universal impact on our society concerns marriage.[5] With absolute conviction, he asserted that a Jewish marriage performed under non-Orthodox auspices is an alternative form of bonding unrelated to the marriage bonds of *kiddushin* (betrothal) and *nesuin* (marriage) as described in Jewish traditional sources. Such a non-Orthodox marriage has no religious import. Our society has proved Rav Feinstein correct on this issue despite opposition by his distinguished colleague, Rav Elijahu Henkin, of blessed memory.[6] The correctness of Rav Feinstein's decision was proven by the development of relationships such as live-ins or trial marriages accepted by our society as alternatives to formal marriage in the traditional manner. His decision allowed hundreds of women to remarry when they were unable to obtain a bill of divorce from their recalcitrant husbands who had drifted away from true Judaism. This decision also permitted thousands of children previously identified as bastards (*mamzerim*) to be reclassified as legitimate (kosher) children. The nullification by Rav Feinstein of the first marriage means that children born from the second marriage were not conceived in sin and are perfectly legitimate Jews. Society is eternally in Rav Feinstein's debt for this and other decisions concerning the Jewish family.

There is another area of *halachah* in which Rav Feinstein

5. *Iggrot Moshe, Even Haezer*, part 1, nos. 76, 77.
6. E. Henkin, *Pirushei Ibra*, responsa 3 and 4.

pioneered a concept that impacted upon thousands of women unable to obtain a bill of divorce from a recalcitrant husband. Rav Feinstein had the strong conviction that marriage under false pretenses (*kiddushei ta'ot*, literally, erroneous marriage) can be annulled if the husband or the wife suffered from an undisclosed defect that would have prevented the marriage in the first place. Many rabbinic decisors accept a declaration from the husband that his wife withheld information about certain diseases or defects from which she suffered. The marriage is then annulled on these grounds. Very few rabbis apply this concept on behalf of a wife who claims that her husband withheld such vital medical information. In three separate responsa, Rav Feinstein states that in our society women refuse to marry men with certain conditions; therefore, if the existence of such a condition in a man is concealed from the woman before the marriage, the woman has the right to demand that the marriage be declared null and void, if and when a bill of divorce cannot be obtained. (In all instances, Rav Feinstein requires that an attempt first be made to obtain a bill of divorce from the husband before consideration can be given to annulment of the marriage.) Rav Feinstein annulled marriages where the husband was unable to perform the marital act,[7] where the husband had serious psychiatric illness and a previous psychiatric hospitalization,[8] and where the husband was bisexual.[9] In all three cases, Rav Feinstein stated that the woman would not have married her husband had she known of his abnormality beforehand. Hence, if a bill of divorce could not be obtained voluntarily, the marriage was declared null and void, since it was undertaken under false pretenses.

One of his earliest responsa is addressed to the community of Luban, which he left because of the coercive influence of the atheistic Communist government. Some Jews supervised the Communist cell that was in charge of Luban. The question posed to Rav Feinstein by the community was whether or not these Communist Jews, children of the old men and women of Luban, could be trusted to provide their parents with kosher food. The Communist

7. *Iggrot Moshe, Even Haezer*, part 1, no. 79.
8. Ibid., no. 80.
9. Ibid., part 4, no. 113.

Jews ate pork and other non-kosher food, but promised to provide strictly kosher food to the elderly Jewish population. Could they be trusted? In this famous responsum, Rav Feinstein rules that there is a level of proof other than the one usually discussed by the Sages in regard to the laws of testimony.[10] Ordinarily, a Sabbath desecrator has no credibility in many areas of law. But there is another level of proof, says Rav Feinstein, a type of intuitive proof based on the concept of "I am certain" (***kim li begavoh***).

The source for this insight by Rav Feinstein is the Talmud,[11] which describes a woman who was once ordered to take an oath at the court of Raba. When Raba's wife said to him, "I know that she is suspected of taking false oaths," he transferred the oath to her opponent. On another occasion, Rav Papa and Rav Adda bar Mattena ate in Raba's presence when a bond was brought to him. Said Rav Papa to him: "I know that this bond is paid up." Raba asked of him, "Is there any other man here to confirm your statement?" "No," he replied. Raba then said to Rav Papa, "Although you are present to give evidence, there is no validity in the testimony of one witness." Said Rav Adda bar Mattena to him: "Should not Rav Papa be deemed as reliable as your wife?" Raba replied, "As to my wife, I am certain of her; I am not sure, however, about Rav Papa." The Talmud concludes that a judge who can assert "I am certain of this person's veracity" may rely upon that person's evidence even though a second witness is not available. This concept was applied by Rav Feinstein to Luban, where he said that there is a level of proof that is above the testimony of witnesses. Raba was certain about the statement of his wife, the daughter of Rav Chisda. She would never tell a lie; it did not fit with her personality. Therefore, if a son who is a Communist says, "I will provide you with kosher food," and the father knows that his son would not lie to him, his statement has credibility and is believed. Thus ruled Rav Feinstein.

10. *Iggrot Moshe, Yoreh De'ah*, part 1, no. 54.
11. *Ketubot* 85a.

MEDICAL RESPONSA

Rav Feinstein believed deeply that *halachah* never backs one into a corner to make one's actions unintelligible or unacceptable to society. A promise from Almighty God is that we are a wise and discerning people.[12] The ways of Torah are acceptable to all intelligent people whose integrity has not been confused by other considerations. This is the background behind Rav Feinstein's responsum allowing the desecration of the Sabbath on behalf of a seriously ill non-Jewish patient.[13] His ruling states that both biblical and rabbinic laws are set aside when a Jewish physician is actively involved in the cure of any patient, Jew or non-Jew. Clearly, any discrimination based on religious affiliation would lead to chaos in the medical profession and endanger the lives of all patients. This rule applies only, of course, in a situation that *halachah* classifies as *pikuach nefesh* (danger to life).

Another important medical pronouncement by Rav Feinstein is that brain death as defined by the President's Commission[14]—when a person has sustained irreversible cessation of all functions of the entire brain, including the brain stem—is an absolutely acceptable definition of death in *halachah.* His several responsa on this subject are discussed in detail elsewhere,[15] and are summarized below.

Rav Feinstein's responsa on organ transplants perhaps give a special insight into his personality. In one of these responsa, he discusses how much one is obliged to save someone else's life.[16] The questioner pointed out that families of a deceased are greatly pained and anguished to consent to have an organ removed for

12. Deuteronomy 4:6.

13. *Iggrot Moshe, Orach Chayim*, part 4, no. 79.

14. President's Commission for the Study of Ethical Problems in Medicine and Biomedical and Behavioral Research, *Defining Death: Medical, Legal, and Ethical Issues in the Determination of Death* (Washington, DC: Government Printing Office, 1981).

15. F. Rosner and M. Tendler, "Definition of Death in Judaism," *Journal of Halacha and Contemporary Society 17* (Spring 1989): 14–31.

16. *Iggrot Moshe, Yoreh De'ah*, part 2, no. 174.

transplantation. According to Jewish law, one is required to expend 20 percent of one's income to perform a righteous deed and all of one's wealth to avoid committing a transgression.[17] Where does anguish fit into this rule? Rav Feinstein answered that if a family is markedly anguished, it is not required to approve the organ donation. However, it is a meritorious act not to be anguished and to find comfort in the fact that the organ transplant may save another life. Therefore, Rav Feinstein ordered the approval of the transplant in question. His unique approach to the question was not to just give a yes-or-no answer. He acceded to the concern of anguish on the part of the family, but said that a Divine command can convert anguish into the joy of saving a life.

Rav Feinstein also clearly enunciated the concept of patient autonomy. He said that the desire of the incurable patient not to persist in a life of pain and discomfort must be accepted.[18] Experimental chemotherapy or other life-prolonging measures that may be associated with significant side effects including pain and suffering can be refused by the patient. Intractable pain is an unacceptable quality of life, according to *halachah*.

Thus, it is not proper to use mechanical restraints to coerce a patient who refuses a nasogastric tube; only sympathetic encouragement and persuasion should be used.

BRAIN DEATH

In a responsum dated 1968, Rabbi Moshe Feinstein declared heart transplantation to constitute double murder,[19] murder of the donor because his heart is removed before he is dead and murder of the recipient because his life is thereby shortened. The dismal results of cardiac transplantation at that time and the high surgical mortality prompted Rabbi Feinstein to consider the procedure as an act of shortening the recipient's life and, therefore, prohibited.

17. J. Karo, *Shulchan Aruch, Yoreh De'ah* 656 and gloss of Rama there.
18. *Iggrot Moshe, Even Haezer*, part 4, nos. 73, 74, 75.
19. Responsa *Iggrot Moshe, Yoreh Deah*, Part 2, #174.

Rabbi Feinstein also condemned the removal of the heart from the donor as murder if the donor suffered from only cerebral death, rather than total brain, including brainstem, death. Neither Judaism nor modern medicine accepts cerebral death as a definition of death. Rabbi Feinstein was clearly writing about cerebral, not total and irreversible brainstem, death because he later reiterates the error of physicians who diagnose death when the patient has no cerebral function but is still breathing spontaneously.

The responsum concludes with the statement that "it is certainly a *mitzvah* for the family of a deceased relative to donate the deceased's organs for transplantation to save the lives of others." Furthermore, even a healthy person asked to donate a spare organ to save someone's life is allowed (but is not required) to donate that organ as a meritorious act (*midat chasidut*). Clearly, Rabbi Feinstein strongly favored organ transplantation such as kidney and corneal transplants because of their high success rate and very low morbidity and mortality in the recipients. At that time, he strongly opposed heart transplantation because of the very poor results.

Two years later, in 1970, Rabbi Feinstein wrote a responsum dealing specifically with "the signs of death."[20] The responsum begins with a condemnation of physicians who diagnose death "when the brain is not functioning . . . even when the patient is still breathing [spontaneously]." Clearly and unambiguously, Rabbi Feinstein is talking about cerebral death, and not brainstem death. The presence of any spontaneous respiratory activity indicates that the patient is still alive, no matter what the clinical neurological picture. Removing an organ from such a patient in a deep coma or in a persistent vegetative state for transplantation is halachically indefensible. The Feinstein prohibition of heart transplantation was clearly related to the lack of success at that time of the procedure prolonging life.

The third widely cited responsum of Rabbi Feinstein is dated 1976.[21] This is the first of the Feinstein responsa that deal with brainstem death and not cerebral death and provides definitive support for the concept of physiologic decapitation. He states that

---

20. Responsa *Iggrot Moshe, Yoreh Deah*, Part 2, #146.
21. Responsa *Iggrot Moshe, Yoreh Deah*, Part 3, #132.

physicians can nowadays test the connection between the brain and the rest of the body by the intravenous injection of a [radioactive] substance. If the substance does not reach the brain:

> . . . it is clear that there is no more connection between the brain and the body. The brain has already completely decayed and it is as if the [patient's] head was forcibly severed.

Nowhere in this responsum does Rabbi Feinstein mention the heartbeat, since in a situation of decapitation, the presence or absence of a heartbeat is irrelevant. In his 1968 responsum, Rabbi Feinstein had already written that "someone whose head has been severed—even if the head and the body shake spastically—that person is legally dead."

Also in 1976, Rabbi Feinstein sent a letter to the Honorable Herbert J. Miller, who was Chairman of the New York State Assembly's Committee on Health, relevant to Assembly Bill 4140/A concerning the determination of death. In his letter, he said:

> The sole criterion of death is the total cessation of spontaneous respiration. In a patient presenting the clinical picture of death, i.e., no signs of life such as movements or response to stimuli, the total cessation of independent respiration is an absolute proof that death has occurred. This interruption of spontaneous breathing must be a sufficient length of time for resuscitation to be impossible [approximately 15 min.].

Clearly, Rabbi Feinstein again supports unambiguously the definition of death as being the complete and irreversible cessation of spontaneous respiration, i.e, brainstem death.

In 1978, Rabbi Feinstein wrote a brief responsum[22] in which he reiterated his 1968 position that heart transplants are double murder. Cardiac transplantation was still in its infancy, and results such as the current 75% five-year survival was still years away. However, already in 1968, Rabbi Feinstein called other standard (i.e., not experimental) organ transplants such as kidney and corneal transplants a *mitzvah*. In fact, in the 1980s, when he

---

22. Responsa *Iggrot Moshe, Choshen Mishpat*, Part 2, #72.

became aware of the markedly improved results of heart transplantation, he sanctioned this procedure, as well as liver and even heart and lung transplants, to a variety of patients and rabbis who sought his counsel on this matter. He insisted, however, that the donor be brainstem dead (not cerebrally dead) at the time the heart or other organ is removed.

Rabbi Shabtai Rapaport, who was in close contact with his grandfather Rabbi Moshe Feinstein during the preparation of the key 1976 responsum, clarified his grandfather's position on this matter as follows.[23]

> The question related only solely to the instance where the heart is still beating and pulsating but the patient is unable to breathe without the artificial respirator. To this question was directed the above responsum which determines that a person who is unable to breathe spontaneously is certainly considered as dead. The only condition which my grandfather imposed is that we are certain that [spontaneous] breathing will not return. Apparently with divine inspiration of a scholar greater than a prophet, my grandfather envisioned the apnea test which came into routine use only years later.
>
> Further, to remove all doubts, I am absolutely certain that this responsum deals with a [patient] situation where the heart is still beating and the patient is breathing on a machine. . . . It is thus clear to anyone who reads his [Rabbi Feinstein's] responsum in *Iggrot Moshe, Yoreh Deah*, Part 2 #174:1 that a decapitated person is considered dead even if his heart is still beating. In the aforementioned responsum in *Yoreh Deah*, Part 3 (#132), he [Rabbi Feinstein] already established that if there is no blood flow to the brain, it is equivalent to a person unable to breathe [spontaneously]. Thus, both [responsa] deal with the situation where the heart is still beating. . . .

The Israeli Chief Rabbinical Council convened in Jerusalem on Rosh Chodesh Cheshvan 5747 (1987) and issued a statement unanimously confirming recommendations of its Transplant Committee dealing with brain death and heart transplants. The statement that accepts brainstem death as halachically valid was

23. Rapaport, S. Z. *Assia, 53–54*, Elul 5755 (August 1994), 29–31.

originally published in Hebrew[24] and later was translated into English and annotated by Yoel Jakobovits.[25]

Thus, a valid definition of death is brainstem death. The classic "respiratory and circulatory death" is, in reality, brain death. Irreversible respiratory arrest is indicative of brainstem death. A brain-dead person is like a physiologically decapitated individual. The requirement of Maimonides to "wait awhile" to confirm that the patient is dead is that amount of time it takes after the heart and lung stop until the brain dies, i.e., a few minutes.

An additional responsum of Rabbi Feinstein concerning brain death recently came to light. This 1985 responsum, addressed to Dr. S.S. Bondi, grandson of Rabbi Joseph Breuer, is dated Kislev 5745. In this responsum, Rabbi Feinstein states that "even though the heart can still beat for several days, nevertheless, as long as the patient has no independent respiration, he is considered dead, as I explained in my responsum in *Iggrot Moshe, Yoreh Deah*, Part 3 #132."[26] He thus clearly and unequivocally reiterates and clarifies his earlier statement on brain death.

Rabbi David Feinstein, in response to a statement attributed to him in *Nishmat Abraham* (*Yoreh Deah* #339), wrote a letter of clarification on November 26, 1992.[27] Rabbi Feinstein's brief letter states the following:

> I have already written that what my revered father [Rabbi Moshe Feinstein] wrote in his *Iggrot Moshe, Yoreh Deah*, Part 3 #132 is a true responsum and one should not question it or think that it may be falsified. Thus, it is accurately his opinion. Some of the details

24. Israel's Chief Rabbinical Council. *Hashtalat Halev—Hachlatat Harabanut Haroshit, Techumin*, Vol. 7, 5746, pp. 187–192. Reprinted in *Assia, 42–43*, Nissan 5747 (April 1987), 70–81. Also reprinted in *Sefer Assia*, Vol. 6 (1989), pp. 27–40. A facsimile of the Chief Rabbinate's statement appeared in *Assia, 47–48,* Kislev 5750 (December 1989), 109–110.

25. Jakobovits, Y. "(Brain Death and) Heart Transplants: The (Israeli) Chief Rabbinate's Directives." *Tradition 24* (4), Summer 1989, 1–14.

26. Facsimile published in *Assia 53–54,* Elul 5755 (August 1994), 24.

27. Reprinted by A. Steinberg in *Assia 53–54,* Elul 5755 (August 1994), 7–8.

therein I heard directly from him. That which I wrote in a letter on 3 Shemot 5750 [1990], I have not retracted. It should not be necessary to repeat this every time a person claims that this responsum [of my father] or that this letter [of mine] is not true. I ask all those who read this letter to not require me to write another.

To clarify the matter: if the patient is lying motionless like a corpse, even if the heart is beating, since he is not breathing [spontaneously], he is completely dead. This additional [statement] to the above is for better clarification.

When life ends is an issue that presently is being actively discussed. The classic definition of death in Judaism is the absence of spontaneous respiration in a patient with no other signs of life. A brief waiting period of a few minutes to a half-hour after breathing has ceased is also required. Brain death is a criterion for confirming death in a patient who already has irreversible absence of spontaneous respiration. Such a patient is figuratively physiologically decapitated. The situation of decapitation, where immediate death is assumed even if the heart may still be briefly beating, is certainly equated with organismal death, as found in classic Jewish sources, as well as the responsa of Rabbi Moshe Feinstein, the Israeli Chief Rabbinate, and other prominent rabbis.

CONCLUSION

The technique of Rav Feinstein should be underscored. He carefully questioned expert physicians, often asking for second or third opinions, before he wrote a responsum on a medical topic. He showed careful concern and asked to see textbooks and diagrams. He studied case histories and considered alternative opinions and medical consensus before he wrote responsa in the sensitive area of human welfare that we call medicine.

The Midrash cites a beautiful exposition on the scriptural verse "Ye shall be holy"[28] as follows:[29]

28. Leviticus 19:2.
29. *Leviticus Rabbah* 24:3.

> Rabbi Berechiah said in the name of Rabbi Simon: it once happened in our town that Abba Jose of Zaythor was sitting and studying at the mouth of a fountain. A certain good spirit that dwelt there appeared to him and said ". . . a certain evil spirit desires to take up his abode here and he will hurt people." Said he to it: "What shall we do?" It answered him: "Go and warn the townspeople and say to them that whoever has a hoe or a shovel or a spade should all come out here tomorrow at daybreak and watch the surface of the water. When they see turbulence on the water, let them strike the irons together and cry out 'we have won' . . ." When they saw the turbulence on the water, they struck the irons together and shouted "we have won, we have won."

The spirit of Torah in our era is being replaced by bad spirits that sadly deny the truth of Torah or are ignorant of the methodology of applying Torah principles to our daily lives. There is only one way to win. The Association of Orthodox Jewish Scientists represents a silent shout of "We have won." Its work, its ideals, its commitments, and its goals are to further true Torah observance through Torah study and practice. The success its members have achieved in transmitting their value system and lifestyle to their own children and to an entire generation is indeed a triumphal shout of victory.

Rabbi Moshe Feinstein (1895–1986)

FRED ROSNER, M.D.

INTRODUCTION

I was privileged to know Rabbi Moshe Feinstein, of blessed memory, personally for many years. He officiated at my wedding. He received my Torah-learning partner, Rabbi Melvin Zelefsky, and me every few weeks for a halachic discussion, or *farher*. He was extremely gracious to me when I called him on the phone and interrupted his *shiur* (Talmud discourse) to ask him about an autopsy consent. He personally offered me halachic (Jewish law) guidance in many areas on many occasions. My task here is to describe Rabbi Feinstein's influence on medical *halachah* as objectively and dispassionately as possible. I will concentrate on thirteen areas in medicine where he had a major influence, including the study and practice of medicine on the Sabbath; Tay-Sachs screening and abortion; contraception; sterilization; artificial insemination; circumcision; dentistry; psychiatry; smoking and *halachah*; visiting the sick; and *kohanim* (priests) studying medicine.

One of my earliest contacts with Rabbi Feinstein was during my first week in medical school. Yeshiva University had just opened its Albert Einstein College of Medicine. The school building was not yet completed, the elevators were not running, the heating and air-conditioning systems were not yet functioning, and we had to walk up to the sixth floor to the anatomy and histology laboratories. Our initial activity was the dissection of a human cadaver. I was chosen by my fellow students to consult with Rabbi Feinstein on this matter. His ruling was that since most cadavers are non-Jewish, it is permissible to dissect a cadaver for the sake of studying anatomy as part of our medical training. Furthermore, since the prohibition of *issur hanaah* (deriving benefit from the dead) does not apply to non-Jewish bodies, it is permissible to perform autopsies on them.[1] The text of Rabbi Feinstein's responsum indicates that he did not arrive at this conclusion lightly and without considerable struggle to reconcile his ruling with the prohibition, enunciated by the author of the *Shulchan Aruch*, of deriving benefit from a gentile cadaver.

THE PHYSICIAN AND THE SABBATH

One of the areas where Rabbi Feinstein made major contributions to medical *halachah* and where he had enormous influence on medical students and physicians alike is the practice of medicine on the Sabbath and on Jewish holidays.

During our third and fourth years in medical school, we served clerkships and subinternships on the wards of various hospitals, and that is when our problems related to the Sabbath and the Jewish holidays came to the fore. In a series of extremely helpful responsa, Rabbi Feinstein detailed for us the laws of healing on the Sabbath and their application to our questions about carrying; writing; using elevators, telephones, beepers, and electric or battery-operated instruments on the Sabbath; turning lights on and off; incising boils and suturing lacerations; scrubbing at surgery; giving injections and infusions and drawing blood on the Sabbath; attending lectures and conferences or delivering a lecture on the Sabbath; traveling by car to the hospital or having to live near the hospital; treating non-Jews on the Sabbath and collecting fees for

1. M. Feinstein, *Responsa Iggrot Moshe, Yoreh De'ah*, part 1, no. 229.

house calls on the Sabbath; training in hospitals without Sabbath obligations; and many more.

I vividly remember my first Sabbath in the hospital as an intern. I was on the seventh floor on a medical ward and heard my name paged over the loudspeaker system. Out of ignorance, I did not pick up the closest phone to answer my page, but ran down eight flights of stairs and through the basement tunnel to the building across the street where the telephone operators were located. To my exasperation I learned that I was needed on the sixth floor of the building I had just come from. I ran up the stairs and took care of the problem for which I was called. This kind of activity continued throughout that Sabbath. On Saturday night, I was totally exhausted and called Rabbi Feinstein, who emphatically told me that I had done the wrong thing; I should have picked up the nearest telephone and answered my page, because it might have been an emergency. "But ninety-nine calls out of a hundred are not emergencies," I protested. "Even if only one out of a hundred calls is a real emergency," replied Rabbi Feinstein, "you must answer all one hundred because you do not know which call will be the emergency. Furthermore," continued Reb Moshe, "if running up the stairs to see your patient takes more time than the elevator or leaves you panting and may thus interfere with your ability to properly evaluate the patient's problem, you have not observed the Sabbath at all but have transgressed the commandment of healing on the Sabbath."

Rabbi Feinstein classified many, if not most, hospitalized patients as dangerously ill (*pikuach nefesh*). Even if a patient brought his illness upon himself through negligence, the Sabbath must be desecrated on his behalf.[2] The codes of Jewish law, including the *Shulchan Aruch*[3] and *Mishneh Torah*,[4] rule that a physician must perform all acts required for the care of his patients and not limit himself exclusively to those things that would remove the danger to life. For a dangerously ill patient, it is permitted to carry through a public thoroughfare the instruments and materials necessary for the

2. M. Feinstein, *Responsa Iggrot Moshe, Orach Chayim*, part 1, no. 127.
3. J. Karo, *Shulchan Aruch, Orach Chayim* 328:4.
4. M. Maimonides, *Mishneh Torah, Shabbat* 2:1.

patient's care. Such items include the stethoscope, keys to narcotics or medication cabinets, radiographs, and the like. Wherever possible, and where no delay in time or loss of efficiency would result, the carrying of these materials should be effected in an unusual manner. Handkerchiefs, house keys, and other nonmedical items may not be carried through the street on the Sabbath, even in an unusual manner.

Writing on the Sabbath is permitted only when absolutely essential to save life, and where no alternative exists. Since writing or typing on the Sabbath is a biblical prohibition, whatever writing can be postponed until after the Sabbath without endangering the proper care of a critically ill patient must be so delayed. A physician is urged, wherever possible, to hire a non-Jewish attendant to do whatever writing is essential and to perform otherwise prohibited acts on the Sabbath, such as driving the car. For a house officer, a nurse, clerk, secretary, or any other non-Jewish person available in the hospital may be asked to write routine histories, physical examination, notes, routine medication and treatment orders, laboratory requisition slips, progress notes, and the like. It is preferable to use the electric nameplate printer on the Sabbath to identify the patient's name and other vital items on a laboratory slip rather than to write out the slip by hand.[5] Where these alternatives are not possible, and where it is essential to the preservation of life that the physician write, he is permitted to do so. Wherever possible, and where no delay in time or loss of efficiency would result, writing should be done in an unusual manner (*shinuy*). Writing with the left hand, in a right-handed person, is considered an unusual manner. What is considered essential to the preservation of life? For example, recording the initial relevant history and physical findings of a critically ill patient (e.g., following a heart attack) admitted to the hospital on a Friday night may be permitted. However, only information that is of significant or perhaps essential value to another physician who may be called upon to assist or take over the care of the patient may be recorded. This Feinstein ruling excludes the writing of social, personal, family, and past medical and surgical histories except where directly relevant to the patient's

5. *Iggrot Moshe, Even Haezer*, part 4, no. 73:4.

present illness. Also excluded is the recording of physical findings that do not bear directly on the patient's immediate problem. Other examples of writing permitted on the Sabbath are the recording of the progress of a woman in labor, vital signs of a postoperative patient, and drug allergies or sensitivities. If the physician's signature is required to obtain needed drugs (e.g., narcotics) or services (e.g., oxygen) for a seriously or dangerously ill patient, he may sign his name. Although this signature is only a legal requirement unrelated to the actual patient care, it is classified as a necessary act if the nurse refuses to provide the essential drugs or services to the patient without it, and thus the signature is permitted. One is not permitted to sign a death or birth certificate on the Sabbath, even with a *shinuy*, since there is no issue of preserving life.

Regarding the use of elevators on the Sabbath, Rabbi Feinstein rules that if delay or loss of efficiency may result from a physician using the stairs, he is obligated to use the elevator to visit his dangerously ill patient. If it is an automatic elevator, the physician may operate it himself. If there is an elevator operator, his religion is irrelevant, since he has the same permissibility as the physician does to help in the care of the patient by transporting the physician there. If no other seriously ill patient is waiting for his services, the physician should walk down the stairs rather than use the elevator.

In regard to the telephone and beepers on the Sabbath, Rabbi Feinstein rules that a house officer may answer all phone calls or paging or beeper messages on the Sabbath, since most, if not all, hospitalized patients are considered to be in the category of dangerously ill. Most, if not all, messages a house officer receives in the hospital relate to his patients. The house officer may make such calls as are required to care for his seriously ill patient. He should not, however, make calls for nonemergency needs. For example, he should not call the laboratory to obtain results of an elective blood test. If the laboratory is nearby, and if no undue delay or loss of efficiency in caring for the patient is involved, then even important blood-test results should be obtained in person, not by phone. A physician in private practice should secure a telephone answering service or an automatic phone recording and answering machine or hire a non-Jewish attendant to receive and make phone calls. A beeper may be hooked onto one's belt and carried on the Sabbath under the license that it is now part of the normal garb of a physician.[6] If the doctor is "beeped" either in the synagogue or at home for an emergency, he should take a taxi to the hospital or the patient's home rather than drive his own car. However, if an undue delay is expected in securing a taxi, the physician may drive his own car. Rabbi Feinstein rules that a physician is allowed to return from the hospital after an emergency call, preferably with a non-Jewish driver.[7] The key consideration in permitting the physician's return is to remove any reluctance to go again in the future for another emergency.[8]

Turning on electrically or battery-operated instruments such as flashlights, ophthalmoscopes, endoscopes, electrocardiogram machines, respirators, pacemaker–defibrillators and the like is not only allowed but mandated where necessary for the proper care of a critically ill patient. For such a patient, the physician is obligated to perform his diagnostic and therapeutic services in the most efficient manner possible, and with adequate illumination and instrumentation. If a non-Jew is available to activate such instruments, he should be asked to do so. The instruments may not be turned off on the Sabbath except by involving non-Jewish personnel, unless it is likely that the instrument will be needed again for the same or another critically ill patient. If the actual working of the instrument requires an on–off cycling by the physician, it is permitted. However, disconnecting the instrument solely to preserve the life of the battery or bulb is not condoned.

Puncturing a boil or abscess and expressing its contents (*mapis mursa*) is permitted on the Sabbath, provided that it is done specifically as a temporary measure to alleviate suffering. Incision and drainage of a boil or abscess that constitutes permanent treatment is prohibited until after the Sabbath. Routine biopsies for diagnostic purposes are also not allowed. Because of the danger of infection or possible infection, traumatic injuries of the skin, i.e., lacerations that are of sufficient magnitude to require stitches, may be repaired by suturing on the Sabbath. Since the natural history of

6. *Iggrot Moshe, Orach Chayim*, part 4, no. 81.
7. Ibid., no. 80.
8. Ibid., part 1, no. 131.

untreated infected wounds is such that septicemia and a potentially fatal outcome may result, lacerations are considered in the category of *pikuach nefesh* (danger to life). Although the prophylactic use of antibiotics might eradicate any infection that might develop, these considerations do not remove the laceration from the category of *pikuach nefesh*, and thus it may be sutured on the Sabbath.

Rabbi Feinstein never hesitated in giving us his time, his guidance, and his expert rulings. No question was rejected by him as too simple or self-evident. He listened carefully as we presented to him question after question, week after week, month after month, year after year. He made life bearable for us when we served in the hospital on the Sabbath caring for patients. His answers were practical, helpful, and clearly geared to our needs as Torah-observant Jewish physicians. He told us that the drawing of blood for tests should be viewed as involving biblical prohibitions on the Sabbath and that it therefore should be limited to critically ill patients. The necessity of administering blood, blood products, antibiotics, chemotherapy, glucose, or other solutions usually means that the patient is classified as critically ill by halachic standards. Therefore, all activities necessary for the most efficient method of accomplishing this act must be undertaken for the benefit of the patient.

Thus, tearing tape, opening the box containing the infusion set, tearing gauze paper containers, applying antiseptic to the area of injection before and after injection or infusion, and the like are all permitted on the Sabbath. If possible, and if no loss of time or efficiency is involved, the Sabbath violations should be minimized. If it is possible to tear tape and make other preparations before the Sabbath, this should be done. If feasible, the antiseptic swab or medication should be applied in a hemostat-held gauze pad so as to approximate the situation referred to in Jewish law as a "sponge with a handle."

Rabbi Feinstein ruled that it is the responsibility and duty of a physician to treat his patients with consummate skill and competence. Any failure to achieve this competence disqualifies the individual from continuing in his role as a physician. Therefore, within the framework of halachic permissibility, the medical student or house officer must sacrifice some of the "spirit" of the Sabbath in order to obtain the maximum training in his chosen profession.

With the clear understanding that there will be no violation of Sabbath law such as taking notes, operating laboratory equipment, etc., the student should attend those lectures and conferences that will add significantly to his mastery of the art and science of medicine. The same principle applies to the physician in practice who may attend certain vitally important conferences on the Sabbath to maintain or improve his level of competence in medical practice, provided that no Sabbath laws are violated. The availability of tapes now partially obviates the need to attend general conferences. However, where personal contact with the lecturer is critically important, it may be permitted on the Sabbath. Similarly, if a physician or dentist is invited to deliver an important paper or lecture on the Sabbath, he is permitted to do so, provided that he does not desecrate the Sabbath in any way. Hence, he must be within walking distance and may not ride the elevator to the lecture room. He may not use a microphone or other amplifying device, or use audiovisual material such as slide or movie projectors, and he may not write on a blackboard. The appearance of the physician's or dentist's name on the printed program does not violate any Jewish law.

One of the most controversial rulings of Rabbi Feinstein in regard to the Sabbath is his strong position in regard to the obligation of a Jewish physician to treat a non-Jewish patient. Reb Moshe said that the Sabbath laws, both rabbinic and biblical, are set aside when a Jewish physician is actively involved in the care of a patient, Jew or non-Jew.[9] Where the doctor is present, he cannot refuse to treat a patient because he is not Jewish. Nowadays, physicians can find colleagues to cover for them on the Sabbath. This rule applies, of course, only in a medical situation that Jewish law (i.e., *halachah*) classifies as *pikuach nefesh*. Rabbi Feinstein's position is based on the ruling of Rabbi Moshe Schreiber.[10] The impact that failure to treat a non-Jew would have on the safety of all Jews was a key consideration in Rabbi Feinstein's ruling. His opinion was that, under present-day societal ethics, even the author

9. Ibid., part 4, no. 79.

10. *Responsa Chatam Sofer, Yoreh De'ah*, no. 131; abstract printed in the margin of Karo's *Shulchan Aruch, Orach Chayim*, 329.

of *Mishnah Berurah* would concur. Rabbi Feinstein also rules that if a physician knows beforehand that he will have to be in the hospital on the Sabbath, he should arrange to sleep over in or near the hospital on Friday night.[11] Many more responsa deal with the physician's conduct on the Sabbath, and with *pikuach nefesh* and the Sabbath.[12]

THE PATIENT AND THE SABBATH

Rabbi Feinstein was concerned just as much about the patient as about the physician, and he issued a variety of rulings regarding the patient and the Sabbath. He allows a hearing-impaired person to wear a hearing aid on the Sabbath.[13] He also allows a disabled person who cannot walk without a cane, crutches, a walker, a wheelchair, or the like to go out on the Sabbath using these mechanical aids. They are considered in Jewish law like his own legs. If, however, they are used only to steady the gait of someone who can walk unaided, then their use on the Sabbath is prohibited.[14]

Rabbi Feinstein also allows the measurement of body temperature with a thermometer on the Sabbath, even for a patient who is not dangerously ill, since this act involves no prohibition.[15] The degree of fever for which the Sabbath may be desecrated on behalf of a patient varies. Certainly, for 102°F, one sets aside the Sabbath. Even if someone feels ill at 101°F and asks that one desecrate the Sabbath for him, one should do so, because it is no worse than any external injury for which one desecrates the Sabbath if the patient so requests. In the case of a child who cannot describe a sensation of fever, continues Rabbi Feinstein, if one observes that the child is extremely uncomfortable or gives other signs of illness, even if the

---

11. *Iggrot Moshe, Orach Chayim*, part 1, no. 131.

12. *Iggrot Moshe, Choshen Mishpat*, part 2, no. 79; *Orach Chayim*, part 4, no. 79.

13. *Iggrot Moshe, Orach Chayim*, part 4, no. 85.

14. M. Feinstein, personal communication, based on *Shulchan Aruch, Orach Chayim*, 301:15–17.

15. *Iggrot Moshe, Orach Chayim*, part 1, no. 128.

temperature is only 100°F or above, one desecrates the Sabbath. If the fever is due to an illness of the lungs or any other internal organ, one desecrates the Sabbath even if there is only low-grade fever. But if a person has low-grade fever due to an ordinary cold, one should not desecrate the Sabbath on his behalf.[16]

For the comfort of a critically ill patient, one is allowed to turn lights on and off either to perform diagnostic or therapeutic procedures or purely for the patient's comfort. A sleep-disturbing lamp may be turned off to give the critically ill patient much-needed rest. If no direct benefit to the patient would result, turning a light off on the Sabbath is prohibited. Rabbi Feinstein also allows the husband or mother of a woman in labor to accompany her in a taxi or car to the hospital on the Sabbath to avoid the potential danger to her life because of her fear of traveling alone.[17] Food consumed on the Sabbath even for medicinal purposes is permissible.[18] Mixing medicines with foods to disguise them from recognition is permissible if the medication needs to be taken on the Sabbath.[19] If a patient who is allowed to take medication on the Sabbath for a serious illness also suffers from another minor ailment for which one is not allowed to take medication on the Sabbath, the patient is not permitted to take the latter medication. In the preparation of the medication for the minor ailment, one has to be concerned about biblical prohibitions such as pounding medicines, cooking, and carrying on the Sabbath. However, if the minor ailment does not require another medication but can be treated by increasing the dose of the medication for the serious illness, the use of such an increased dose is permitted.[20]

THE PATIENT AND JEWISH HOLIDAYS

For a patient who must eat on Yom Kippur, Rabbi Feinstein rules that the patient need not recite the Kiddush (sanctification of the

16. Ibid., no. 129.
17. Ibid., no. 132.
18. Ibid., no. 130.
19. Ibid., part 2, no. 86.
20. Ibid., part 3, no. 53.

Festival) over a cup of wine or other beverage, since he fulfills the obligation with the Kiddush in the prayer service of Yom Kippur.[21] If a patient is not dangerously ill on Yom Kippur but needs to swallow pills without water to prevent another serious illness from occurring, he is permitted to do so.[22] Rabbi Feinstein quotes Rabbi Yisroel Salanter, who, during a cholera outbreak, instructed all the healthy townspeople to eat on Yom Kippur because hunger makes one more susceptible to cholera. If physicians state that a woman who had two postpartum psychoses may have another nervous breakdown if she fasts, that woman must eat on Yom Kippur.[23] In two separate responsa, Rabbi Feinstein also rules that a patient who is not allowed to fast on Yom Kippur should not have an intravenous feeding line inserted to avoid oral feeding, since the insertion of the needle into the vein solely for that purpose constitutes the infliction of a wound (*chavalah*), which is prohibited on Yom Kippur as it is on the Sabbath.[24] Finally, in regard to Yom Kippur, Rabbi Feinstein allows the use of vitamin suppositories for a patient who becomes so weak from fasting that he nearly faints.[25] Another lengthy responsum deals with the oral consumption of vitamins by healthy people on the Sabbath. Obviously, on Yom Kippur, these are prohibited.[26]

In regard to Passover, if a patient following surgery has to take pills that may contain *chometz* (leaven, which is prohibited on Passover), he is permitted to do so. In fact, Rabbi Feinstein rules that the patient is obligated to take the pills, even if they definitely contain *chometz* and even if the patient is not now dangerously ill, since the pills became nullified as a food before Passover and constitute necessary medicine.[27]

21. *Iggrot Moshe, Choshen Mishpat*, part 1, no. 39.
22. *Iggrot Moshe, Orach Chayim*, part 3, no. 91.
23. *Iggrot Moshe, Even Haezer*, part 1, no. 65.
24. *Iggrot Moshe, Orach Chayim*, part 3, no. 90; part 4, no. 101:3.
25. Ibid., part 4, no. 121.
26. Ibid., part 3, no. 54.
27. Ibid., part 2, no. 92.

KOHANIM *(PRIESTS) AND MEDICINE*

The problem of whether or not a *kohen* (priest) is permitted in modern times to study and practice medicine has been debated in the rabbinic responsa literature for over a century.[28] The majority of rabbis answer in the negative. Rabbi Feinstein states that there is no obligation for a *kohen* to study medicine.[29] He strongly rejects the permissive rulings of some rabbis, based on the *kohen*'s strong desire to study medicine, on the basis that most corpses nowadays are non-Jews, which, according to some authorities, do not defile by overshadowing (*tumat ohel*), and because a *kohen* physician would later save lives. Rabbi Feinstein states that one is not obligated to study medicine to become a physician any more than one is obligated to conduct a lot of business to become rich in order to give charity. Feinstein disapproves of such permissiveness, stating that "it is foolish and vain and should not be articulated by any intelligent person." Feinstein also strongly denounces *kohanim* (priests) who rely on this opinion and attend medical school:

> It is clear to me that if the *kohanim* who study medicine and ritually defile themselves through contact with corpses would really wish to know the true law in this regard, they would know who to ask . . . rather, they are not at all concerned about this prohibition and delude themselves . . . by claiming to have found [a lenient ruling in] some pamphlet upon which they rely.
>
> . . . It is absolutely clear that it is prohibited for a *kohen* to ritually defile himself through contact with a corpse and this fact is well known throughout the world. Therefore, it is absolutely clear that even if the most learned rabbis in the world would be lenient [and say otherwise], one should not listen to them. . . .
>
> . . . It is prohibited for *kohanim* to study medicine in medical schools in countries where it is necessary to have contact with corpses. One should not point to some of our ancient Sages who

28. F. Rosner, "Priests (*Kohanim*) Studying and Practicing Medicine," *Journal of Halachah and Contemporary Society 8* (Fall 1984):48–61.
29. *Iggrot Moshe, Yoreh De'ah*, part 2, no. 155.

> were both *kohanim* and physicians and were able to learn all of medical science by oral teachings without any observations on or physical contact with corpses. In our times, this is impossible and therefore it is prohibited.

Rabbi Feinstein permits a *kohen* to work in a hospital if he can leave the hospital when a death occurs and if most patients are non-Jews.[30] Rabbi Feinstein allows *kohanin* who are not physicians to visit patients in the hospital to fulfill the commandment of visiting the sick (*bikur cholim*) because of "great need" such as emotional pain and anguish.[31] He thus permits such visits to a parent, child, or spouse or to one's wife's relatives because we assume that most patients are non-Jews and that any corpses or parts thereof in the hospital at any given time are those of non-Jews and do not impart ritual defilement by being in the same room or building with a Jew.

Rabbi Feinstein discusses whether or not a *kohen* is permitted to travel on an airplane in which a Jewish corpse in the baggage compartment is being transported to Israel for burial, since the entire plane is made of metal other than the six types of metal specified in the Torah that transmit defilement: gold, silver, copper, iron, tin, and lead.[32] Since the plane is made primarily of metals such as aluminum and magnesium, it may not transmit defilement. Rabbi Feinstein concludes that the matter requires further study. In another responsum, Rabbi Feinstein rules that if an autopsy is performed on a *kohen*, his immediate family may arrange and implement his burial without concern about ritual defilement.[33] Finally, in regard to a *kohen*, Rabbi Feinstein wrote a very long responsum about a *kohen* who needs to receive an organ or flesh from a cadaver.[34]

The topics of organ transplantation and the use of organs for

---

30. Ibid., part 1, no. 248.
31. Ibid., part 2, no. 166.
32. Ibid., no. 164.
33. Ibid., no. 165.
34. Ibid., part 1, no. 230.

medical research are discussed by Rabbi Feinstein in numerous responsa.[35]

DENTISTRY

Several of Rabbi Feinstein's responsa deal with dentistry. One lengthy responsum deals with temporary fillings and dental prostheses and ritual immersion (*tevilah*).[36] In brief, all permanent bridgework, or cemented or wired (i.e., permanent) braces do not constitute an interposing barrier (*chatzitzah*) and therefore do not hinder the regular process of *tevilah.* However, removable dentures, removable braces, removable bridges, and the like must be removed before *tevilah.* All fillings, whether temporary or permanent, that were fashioned by a skilled dentist are not a *chatzitzah. Tevilah* may be performed without their removal unless they have been improperly placed and must be removed and corrected by the dentist, in which case *tevilah* must be postponed until such correction is made. For example, a filling that is interfering with chewing and must be corrected by the dentist, or a bridge that is painful because further correction must be made on the device, should be fixed before *tevilah.*

The application of a surgical dressing on the gums during extensive gum work may require delay in the time of *tevilah.* However, says Rabbi Feinstein, if stitches in the mouth are deeply embedded in the gums and are not readily visible, they are not considered an interposition.[37] Plastic coverings on the teeth, however, that are only temporary in nature, must be removed before *tevilah.*[38] In another responsum on dentistry, Rabbi Feinstein rules that if a person has pain, it is permissible to fix the teeth

35. Ibid., nos. 229, 230, 231, 232; part 2, nos. 150, 174; part 3, nos. 140, 141; *Choshen Mishpat*, part 2, no. 72.

36. *Iggrot Moshe, Yoreh De'ah*, part 1, no. 97.

37. Ibid., part 2, no. 87.

38. Ibid., part 2, no. 88.

even on Chol Hamoed (intermediate days of festivals).[39] Obviously, if there is no pain and if no harm will come from waiting, the patient should postpone the visit to the dentist until after the holiday. A patient with false dentures need not secure a separate set for Passover.

SMOKING AND JEWISH LAW

For many years, I have had numerous intensive discussions with prominent rabbis about smoking and *halachah*. It has been my personal opinion as a non-rabbi that, in the light of the overwhelming medical evidence proving the causal relationship of cigarette smoking to cancer of the lung; heart disease; chronic bronchitis; bladder, head and neck cancer and other ailments, Jewish law should absolutely prohibit this practice.[40] Yet, very few rabbis prohibit smoking, although most condemn the practice as foolhardy and dangerous.

In his first brief responsum on this subject in 1964, the year of the first Surgeon General's report on smoking, Rabbi Feinstein asserts that although it is proper not to begin smoking because of the possibility of becoming ill therefrom, one cannot say that it is prohibited because of the danger, since many people smoke, and the Talmud states that "the Lord preserveth the simple." Furthermore, continues Rabbi Feinstein, many rabbinic scholars from previous generations, as well as from our own era, smoke. In addition, even to those who are strict and do not smoke because of their concern about possible danger to health or life, there is no prohibition in lighting the match for those who smoke.[41]

Rabbi Feinstein reconfirmed his opinions in a later responsum addressed to me dated 1981 and published in the seventh volume

---

39. *Iggrot Moshe, Orach Chayim*, part 3, no. 78.

40. F. Rosner, *Modern Medicine and Jewish Ethics* (Hoboken, NJ, and New York: Ktav and Yeshiva University Press, 1986), pp. 363–375.

41. *Iggrot Moshe, Yoreh De'ah*, part 2, no. 49.

of his responsa.[42] The explanation of his view is that "the Lord preserveth the simple" is a concept that is applied to low-incidence natural dangers. The phrase *doshu bo rabim* (the multitude are accustomed to it) means that society recognizes and accepts the risk, similar to flying on an airplane or walking across a busy boulevard. Although many people may develop lung cancer from smoking, it represents a very small fraction of the many millions of people who smoke. Overeating or failure to exercise properly may involve a far greater risk to health than smoking, yet no rabbi prohibits overeating or sedentariness.

I still do not fully understand this reasoning and continue to press my personal views about the dangers of smoking and my conviction that it should be halachically prohibited. Nevertheless, I accept Rabbi Feinstein's ruling unhesitatingly. He was my *posek* (rabbinic decisor). He was the *posek* for the Association of Orthodox Jewish Scientists. He was the *posek hador*, the rabbinic decisor for the entire Jewish world during the generation in which he lived. His written responsa and other writings are sacrosanct and accepted as authoritative by all Jews.

On the other hand, in view of the deleterious effects of exhaled smoke on others in close proximity to the smokers, Rabbi Feinstein prohibits such passive smoking. He rules that even if the exhaled smoke is only annoying to others, smokers are obligated to smoke in private or far removed from other people. Those whose smoking causes discomfort, headache, or harm to the health of nonsmokers are considered as *mazikin*, people who inflict damage on others. Therefore, concludes Rabbi Feinstein, smokers are prohibited from smoking in the *beit hamidrash* (house of Torah study) or *beit haknesset* (synagogue) if there is even one person who objects.[43]

Rabbi Feinstein also prohibits the smoking of marijuana because it is harmful to the body.[44] Even those people who suffer no physical damage may suffer mental harm in that marijuana confuses the mind and distorts one's abilities of reasoning and comprehension. Such a person is thereby preventing himself not only from

---

42. *Iggrot Moshe, Choshen Mishpat*, part 2, no. 76.
43. *Iggrot Moshe, Yoreh De'ah*, part 3, no. 35.
44. Ibid.

studying Torah but also from performing other precepts. Marijuana use, continues Feinstein, can also bring on extreme and uncontrollable lusts and desires. Furthermore, since the parents of marijuana users are usually opposed to its use, the users violate the biblical commandment of honoring one's father and mother. Other prohibitions may also be involved in marijuana use, and therefore, concludes Feinstein, one must use all one's energies to uproot and eliminate this pernicious habit.

PSYCHIATRY

Rabbi Feinstein wrote several responsa dealing with psychiatric issues. In one case he rules that a psychotic patient who was healed but still hospitalized for observation need not be removed from the hospital against medical advice in order to hear the blowing of the *shofar* (ram's horn) on Rosh Hashanah.[45] He permits a woman who has had two postpartum psychoses to use contraception, since another pregnancy would be a serious threat to her mental health.[46] In another case, Rabbi Feinstein allows the institutionalization of an uncurable psychotic girl although she will be fed nonkosher food there.[47] He also permits the sterilization of this girl to prevent her from engaging in promiscuous sexual behavior. Rabbi Feinstein expresses disapproval of hypnosis in general but permits it for medical purposes.[48]

Finally, Rabbi Feinstein discusses the use of irreligious or agnostic psychiatrists to treat mental illness in Jews.[49] He expresses concern that psychologists and psychiatrists whose entire therapy consists of verbal analyses and analytical deductions may speak words of agnosticism or impose their value systems on their patients. But if they are expert physicians and promise that they will not speak

45. *Iggrot Moshe, Orach Chayim*, part 1, no. 172.
46. *Iggrot Moshe, Even Haezer*, part 1, no. 65.
47. *Iggrot Moshe, Orach Chayim*, part 2, no. 88.
48. *Iggrot Moshe, Yoreh De'ah*, part 3, no. 44.
49. Ibid., part 2, no. 57.

words that are contrary to the tenets of our faith or the commandments of the Torah, one may be able to rely upon them, because experts do not lie. Therefore, one should certainly try to locate a psychiatrist who is an observant Jew. If none is available, concludes Rabbi Feinstein, one should arrange with the therapist that he not speak on matters relating to the Jewish faith or the religious lifestyle.

In a related responsum, Rabbi Feinstein was asked about a patient who has a choice between two physicians, one who is Torah observant but not a specialist and another who is an atheist but a specialist.[50] He answered that one should go to the most expert physician, even if he is an atheist, since the overwhelming majority of physicians, whether gentiles or irreligious Jews, perform their healing tasks appropriately and have nothing to do with religious heresy.

BIKUR CHOLIM *(VISITING THE SICK)*

In a responsum about visiting the sick by telephone, Rabbi Feinstein points out that the precept of visiting the sick is more than just paying a social call but includes helping the patient in some tangible way and praying on his behalf.[51] One cannot provide this help over the telephone. Nevertheless, if someone is unable to visit the patient at the bedside, that person partially discharges his obligation of visiting the sick by telephoning because he at least performs one of the three parts of the precept, i.e., comforting the patient. Prayers may be recited on behalf of a seriously ill patient even on the Sabbath and Jewish holidays, says Rabbi Feinstein in another responsum.[52] A personal visit to the patient's bedside may also stimulate the visitor to pray more intensely for the patient.

---

50. M. Feinstein, in M. Hershler, ed., *Halachah Urefuah*, Vol. 1 (1980), p. 130.

51. *Iggrot Moshe, Yoreh De'ah*, part 1, no. 223.

52. *Iggrot Moshe, Orach Chayim*, part 1, no. 105.

Perhaps, continues Feinstein, prayers are more readily answered in the patient's room because the *Shechinah* (Divine Presence) is said to rest at the head of the patient's bed. Finally, in yet another responsum, Rabbi Feinstein says that a person cannot delegate his obligation of visiting the sick to another person; even a prominent individual should visit a simple person.[53]

CIRCUMCISION

When I was in postdoctoral training as a fellow in hematology in 1962, I took care of many hemophiliac patients. At that time, I asked Rabbi Feinstein whether it is permissible to circumcise a hemophiliac boy by infusing blood products to reduce the risk of bleeding. He said no and gave me a single-word explanation: *lechesheyerapeh*—when he is healed, then one can perform the circumcision. I told Rabbi Feinstein that hemophilia is a genetic disorder for which there is no cure. His answer, again, was *lechesheyerapeh*—when he is healed. His first responsum concerning a boy whose brothers died following circumcision is dated 1947.[54] His logic is that even with the advent of blood products to replace the missing clotting factor, the risk of bleeding following circumcision is still substantially greater in a hemophiliac child than in a normal infant. This logic is based on the ruling enunciated by Maimonides in his *Mishneh Torah*.[55]

> One may circumcise only a child that is totally free of disease, because danger to life overrides every other consideration. It is possible to circumcise later than the proper time when the perinatal period is over and the danger of prolonged bleeding of the otherwise healthy child is no longer viewed as potentially life-threatening, but it is impossible to restore a single [departed] soul of Israel forever.

---

53. *Iggrot Moshe, Yoreh De'ah*, part 1, no. 222.
54. Ibid., no. 154.
55. M. Maimonides, *Mishneh Torah, Milah* 1:18.

In 1969, I published an article on hemophilia in the Talmud and talmudic writings.[56] I again asked Rabbi Feinstein whether a hemophiliac boy can be circumcised. His answer was the same: *lechesheyerapeh.* In more recent years, with the availability of blood-clotting hemophilic factor concentrates, the risk of circumcision decreased significantly, so that Rabbi Feinstein permitted it. An underweight baby may be circumcised as soon as he reaches adequate weight. For a baby who had an exchange transfusion, an additional seven-day waiting period is required before circumcision may be allowed.[57]

In another responsum, Rabbi Feinstein rules against the use of the *Mogen* (Bronstein) circumcision clamp, because if the clamp is left on for more than a minute or so, complete hemostasis results so that no drop of blood flows freely, thereby invalidating the circumcision.[58] He also expresses concern that the use of clamps in general might lead to circumcision becoming a surgical procedure rather than a ritual procedure, performed by non-orthodox physicians, clergymen, or laymen rather than by Orthodox Jews. He also says that the baby suffers more when a clamp is used.[59] He therefore recommends a simple shield or butterfly as a guard for ritual circumcision. Numerous other Feinstein responsa deal with technical aspects of circumcision.[60]

TAY-SACHS DISEASE AND ABORTION

One of the controversial areas where Rabbi Feinstein's opinion was sought is Tay-Sachs screening, amniocentesis, and abortion of Tay-Sachs-affected fetuses. In 1973, the Association of Orthodox

---

56. F. Rosner, "Hemophilia in the Talmud and Rabbinic Writings," *Annals of Internal Medicine 70* (1969):833–837.

57. *Iggrot Moshe, Yoreh De'ah*, part 2, no. 121.

58. Ibid., no. 119.

59. Ibid., part 3, no. 99.

60. Ibid., part 1, nos. 155, 156, 157, 158; part 2, nos. 118, 120, 123; part 3, nos. 97, 98, 100, 101, 102, 105.

Jewish Scientists sent a delegation, of which I was a member, to ask Rabbi Feinstein about the advisability of a boy or girl being screened for Tay-Sachs disease, and, if it is proper, at what age should the test be performed. We further asked him whether screening should be performed as part of a publicized screening program or only as a private test. His answer was:

> . . . It is advisable for one preparing to be married, to have himself tested. It is also proper to publicize the fact, via newspapers and other media, that such a test is available. It is clear and certain that absolute secrecy must be maintained to prevent anyone from learning the result of such a test performed on another. The physician must not reveal these to anyone . . . these tests must be performed in private, and, consequently, it is not proper to schedule these test in large groups as, for example, in Yeshivas, schools, or other similar situations.[61]

Rabbi Feinstein also points out that most young people are quite susceptible to nervous tension or psychological stress and that, therefore, young men (below age twenty) or women (below age eighteen) not yet contemplating marriage should not be screened for Tay-Sachs disease. Finally, Rabbi Feinstein strongly condemns abortion for Tay-Sachs disease and even questions the permissibility of the amniocentesis that proves the presence of a Tay-Sachs fetus, since amniocentesis is not without risk, albeit small.[62]

Rabbi Feinstein was also asked about the use of contraceptives by a woman who gave birth to two Tay-Sachs babies, both of whom died in infancy. In that case, he disallowed the use of a contraceptive diaphragm but permitted the use of spermicidal foams and jellies.[63] Rabbi Feinstein also allows the use of spermicidal foams and jellies by a woman who should not become pregnant because of danger to life.[64] However, he does not allow sterilization of a woman with mental anguish who had previously given birth to two physically

61. *Iggrot Moshe, Even Haezer*, part 4, no. 10.
62. *Iggrot Moshe, Choshen Mishpat*, part 2, no. 71.
63. *Iggrot Moshe, Even Haezer*, part 1, no. 62.
64. Ibid., part 3, no. 21.

defective children[65] or for a woman who gave birth to two blind children.[66] He suggests, instead, that she practice contraception.

The objections to amniocentesis and abortion in Jewish law are predicated on considerations surrounding the fetus. Extreme emotional stress in the mother leading to suicidal intent might constitute one of the situations in which abortion would be sanctioned. If a woman who suffered a nervous breakdown following the birth (or death) of a child with Tay-Sachs disease becomes pregnant again and is so distraught with the knowledge that she may be carrying another child with the fatal disease that she threatens suicide, Jewish law might allow amniocentesis. If this procedure reveals an unaffected fetus, the pregnancy continues to term. If the result of the amniocentesis indicates a homozygous fetus with Tay-Sachs disease, rabbinic consultation regarding the decision of whether or not to perform an abortion should be obtained. No general rule of permissiveness or prohibition can be enunciated in regard to abortion in Jewish law. Each case must be individualized and evaluated on the basis of its merits, taking into consideration all the prevailing medical, psychological, social, and religious circumstances. Two lengthy responsa on abortion were published in the seventh volume of Rabbi Feinstein's responsa.[67]

CONTRACEPTION

There are at least twenty-five responsa in *Iggrot Moshe* that deal with contraception. Most methods of contraception are discussed. For example, Rabbi Feinstein allows the use of a diaphragm in a case where pregnancy would be dangerous.[68] If there is a great danger, he even allows the use of a condom by the man, if other methods of contraception cannot be used.[69] Rabbi Feinstein was very

65. Ibid., no. 12.
66. Ibid., no. 13.
67. *Iggrot Moshe, Choshen Mishpat*, part 2, nos. 69, 70.
68. *Iggrot Moshe, Even Haezer*, part 1, no. 63.
69. Ibid.

concerned that his lenient rulings in these cases should not be widely applied. He writes that he thoroughly investigates not only the medical danger of pregnancy but also the character of the married couple as to their level of Jewishness, Jewish practice, and God-fearing nature. He gave lenient rulings for finite periods of time and asked couples to return to him to periodically reassess the situation.[70] In the case of a man who wanted to marry a woman with serious kidney disease, Rabbi Feinstein allowed the use of a diaphragm until the renal disease improved. He asked that his ruling not be widely publicized. He also said that if bed rest throughout pregnancy removes the danger, then the diaphragm is not allowed. Since Rabbi Feinstein himself decided to publish his views in his responsa, it is not contrary to or disrespectful of his wishes to discuss them here.

Rabbi Feinstein's first responsum on the oral contraceptive pill, written in 1962, allowed the temporary use of the pill by a woman who already had two children, a boy and a girl, and would have a difficult time raising more children until the first two were somewhat older. The pill does not violate the prohibition of emitting semen for naught.[71] Rabbi Feinstein voices concern about vaginal bleeding and spotting from the pill. He also allows the pill to be used by a woman who is weak and would find pregnancy difficult, even if she has not yet had two children. After three years, when she has regained her strength, she should stop using the pill.[72]

In another responsum, he writes that temporary sterility in a man for about six months following a contraceptive injection does not violate the prohibition against castration.[73] The intrauterine device (IUD) should not be used to prevent pregnancy in a woman with varicose veins who cannot take the pill, because the IUD causes bleeding and may be an abortifacient. Rather, Rabbi Feinstein suggests the use of the diaphragm where pregnancy would constitute a danger to the mother.[74] He also allows the use of spermicidal

70. Ibid., no. 64.
71. Ibid., part 2, no. 17.
72. Ibid., part 3, no. 24.
73. Ibid., no. 15.
74. Ibid., no. 21.

jellies but claims that they are unreliable and that, therefore, the diaphragm is preferable. There is no permissibility, however, for the man to use a condom, and the case must be reassessed in two years because the danger of pregnancy may no longer be present.[75] The pill is discussed in several additional responsa.[76]

In the case of a man who was angry when he learned that his wife, who had already given him five children, was using a diaphragm because of mental illness, Rabbi Feinstein ruled that the husband should not be upset and should continue living with her.[77] He suggested, however, that the wife's illness be reevaluated after a few years to determine whether the danger of pregnancy has receded. He also asked that his ruling not be widely publicized, lest people apply leniencies in other cases where such may not be allowed.[78] The rhythm method is also discussed by Rabbi Feinstein.[79] He allows this method of contraception only after the couple has already had two children and only if it would be difficult for them to have and raise more children.

Rabbi Feinstein allows a woman to use contraception following a cesarean-section delivery until the danger from another pregnancy passes, even for up to a year or more, depending on the medical circumstances.[80] In another responsum, he reiterates the permissibility of the use of either the diaphragm or the pill by the woman—but not the condom by the man—where pregnancy might be dangerous.[81] A couple that was guilty of child abuse was temporarily allowed to use the diaphragm for two years as a method of contraception because of the mother's mental illness.[82] Similarly, Rabbi Feinstein allows the use of the diaphragm because of depression in the mother.[83] He again advises against the pill and the IUD because they cause vaginal bleeding and spotting.

---

75. Ibid.
76. Ibid., part 4, nos. 72, 74.
77. Ibid., part 3, no. 22.
78. Ibid.
79. Ibid., part 1, no. 102; part 4, no. 32:3.
80. Ibid., part 4, no. 62:2.
81. Ibid., no. 67.
82. Ibid., no. 68.
83. Ibid., no. 69.

If a woman insists on using a diaphragm to prevent pregnancy, even though she does not suffer from any medical or psychiatric illness, the husband is allowed to remain with his wife and cohabit with her.[84] Rabbi Feinstein disallows a sick man who wished to marry a woman who would use a diaphragm to prevent pregnancy from marrying her.[85] Only maternal illness can allow the use of contraceptives. Finally, Rabbi Feinstein discusses the use of contraception to enable the woman to care for a sick child[86] and the obligation of a man with Marfan's syndrome to marry a fertile woman who can become pregnant and give birth to his children.[87]

In summary, Rabbi Feinstein rules that in Jewish law contraceptive methods and devices cannot be used except for specific medical indications such as rheumatic heart disease, severe renal disease, and similar situations where pregnancy may constitute a serious threat to the health of the mother. Jewish law requires that the marital act be as normal as possible. When medical indications, which include psychological factors, necessitate the use of a contraceptive technique, Jewish law grades methods of contraception techniques from least to most objectionable in the following order: oral contraceptives; chemical spermicidals; diaphragms and cervical caps to be used by the wife; condoms; and coitus interruptus. The most objectionable methods, and those that are least often permitted under Jewish law, are the husband's use of the condom and withdrawal (i.e., *coitus interruptus*).

STERILIZATION

Surgical or physical impairment of the reproductive organs of any living creature violates Jewish law, except in cases of urgent medical necessity. In the case of men, upon whom the biblical commandment to be fruitful and multiply rests, only a risk to life (e.g.,

84. Ibid., no. 70.
85. Ibid., no. 71.
86. Ibid., no. 73:1.
87. Ibid., no. 73:2.

cancer), can justify such procedures. Hence, unless medically demanded, the ligation of the vas deferens during prostatectomy should be avoided. The prohibition against impairing the male reproductive organs and functions is unrelated to man's fertility. It applies even to a man known to have become sterile or impotent whether by reason of age or of anatomic or physiologic aberration that occurred after birth. If he was born sterile, this prohibition may not apply. Vasectomy as a "population control" technique is not condoned in *halachah*. It is forbidden to assist at such surgery, in any way, on man or animal.

Rabbi Feinstein permits surgery on a child with an undescended testicle even if the testicle may have to be totally removed.[88] He disallows hysterectomy in a case where the woman has mental illness, renal disease, and varicose veins. He suggests that she use a diaphragm, since another pregnancy might be dangerous for her life.[89] As mentioned earlier, he also disallows sterilization of a woman who gave birth to defective children,[90] or in another case, to two blind children.[91] Even reversible Fallopian tube tying or cutting is not permissible because this constitutes a forbidden act of castration.[92] Rabbi Feinstein is strongly opposed to vasectomies even in men who are already infertile.[93] He also objects to the cutting of the vas deferens during prostate surgery unless it is absolutely essential medically.[94]

Rabbi Feinstein disallows the sterilization of a woman following several cesarean sections[95] or in other cases where pregnancy would be dangerous, unless no other method of contraception can be used.[96] Fear of pregnancy by a woman is not sufficient reason to

88. *Iggrot Moshe, Even Haezer*, part 1, no. 12.
89. Ibid., no. 13.
90. *Iggrot Moshe, Even Haezer*, part 3, no. 12; part 4, no. 35.
91. *Iggrot Moshe, Even Haezer*, part 3, no. 13.
92. *Iggrot Moshe, Even Haezer*, part 4, no. 32.
93. Ibid., nos. 30, 31.
94. Ibid., nos. 28–29.
95. Ibid., no. 33.
96. Ibid., no. 34.

allow sterilization; only if her life is in danger is this procedure permitted.[97]

ARTIFICIAL INSEMINATION AND FERTILITY TESTING

Artificial insemination using the semen of a donor other than the husband (AID) is considered by most rabbis to be strictly prohibited for a variety of reasons, including the possibility of incest, confused genealogy, and problems related to inheritance. However, without a sexual act involved, the woman is not guilty of adultery and is not prohibited from living with her husband.[98] The child born from AID does not carry any stigma of illegitimacy. In an extremely controversial ruling in 1959, Rabbi Feinstein permitted the use of semen from a gentile for insemination into a Jewish woman because all the technical problems of AID do not exist in such a case.[99] Although he was strongly criticized for this ruling, he reiterated its correctness in a much later responsum dated 1981.[100]

The use of the husband's sperm for artificial insemination is certainly permissible.[101] If the husband happens to be a physician, it is preferable that he perform the insemination.[102] If a woman has a short menstrual cycle, Rabbi Feinstein allows her to be inseminated with her husband's sperm even during her *niddah* period.[103] Similarly, he allows such a woman to shorten her *niddah* period and begin counting her seven "clean days" immediately upon complete cessation of her menses, even before day six, to allow her to cohabit with her husband to coincide with early ovulation to permit a

---

97. Ibid., no. 36.
98. Ibid., part 1, no. 10.
99. Ibid., no. 71.
100. Ibid., part 4, no. 32:5.
101. Ibid., part 2, no. 18.
102. *Iggrot Moshe, Yoreh De'ah*, part 3, no. 54.
103. *Iggrot Moshe, Even Haezer*, part 2, no. 18.

pregnancy to result.[104] Sperm analysis and sperm procurement for fertility testing are permissible, according to Rabbi Feinstein, and do not violate the prohibition of emitting semen for naught, since the semen may be used to fulfill the commandment of procreation.[105] Preferably, the sperm should be obtained by a method other than masturbation. Rabbi Feinstein also wrote a lengthy responsum on testicular biopsy as part of fertility testing.[106]

MISCELLANEOUS RESPONSA

Many other medical and medically related topics are discussed in the hundreds of responsa in the eight volumes of *Iggrot Moshe*. A small sampling is all that space will allow. A blind man is allowed to be accompanied by his guide dog into the synagogue.[107] It is preferable that he sit with his dog near the door so as not to disturb those congregants who fear animals. A patient with a paralyzed left arm still dons phylacteries on that arm.[108] A patient with an indwelling catheter may recite his prayers if he covers the catheter and collection bag.[109] Rabbi Feinstein prohibits a man from taking medication to dye his hair.[110] He allows a person to donate blood for financial compensation.[111] He allows people to be professional ballplayers to earn a livelihood, even though there is a chance they may be injured.[112] He prohibits the elective consumption of vitamins on the Sabbath by healthy people.[113] Labor should not be

104. *Iggrot Moshe, Yoreh De'ah*, part 2, no. 84.

105. *Iggrot Moshe, Even Haezer*, part 1, no. 70; part 2, no. 16; part 3, no. 14, part 4, no. 27.

106. Ibid., part 2, no. 3.

107. *Iggrot Moshe, Orach Chayim*, part 1, no. 45.

108. Ibid., no. 8.

109. Ibid., no. 27.

110. Ibid., no. 82.

111. *Iggrot Moshe, Choshen Mishpat*, part 1, no. 103.

112. Ibid., no. 104.

113. *Iggrot Moshe, Orach Chayim*, part 3, no. 54.

induced purely for the sake of convenience.[114] Rabbi Feinstein is not critical of people who suffer hunger by going on a strict diet to lose weight in order to improve their appearance.[115] He also discusses cosmetic surgery for girls concerned about finding a mate.[116] There is even a very unusual responsum, dated Purim 1981, on the death penalty in response to an inquiry by the Governor of the State of New York.[117]

CONCLUSION

How does one assess the influence of this humble man—Reb Moshe, as he was known by everyone? One book on the life and ideals of HaGaon Rabbi Moshe Feinstein[118] states that, for half a century in America, these two words—Reb Moshe—were synonymous with Torah greatness, encyclopedic knowledge, compassion, generosity, piety, faith, and countless other precious and sacred concepts. He left us many legacies: He was a giant in *halachah*. He was a giant in the fear of God. He was a giant in prayer. He was a giant in modesty. He was a giant in humility. He was a giant in kindness. He was a giant of inspiration to his countless students and disciples, among whom I was privileged to be one.

But he was also the rabbinic decisor (*posek*) for the medical students and physicians of the Association of Orthodox Jewish Scientists. He answered hundreds of our questions, some in writing, many more orally. He gave us the ability to practice medicine as Torah-observant Jews, and he told us how to do so. He was decisive and pragmatic, understanding and sensitive, knowledgeable and down-to-earth. He was never timid. His answers to us were clear, concise, precise, and to the point. His answers adhered

---

114. *Iggrot Moshe, Yoreh De'ah*, part 2, no. 74; *Orach Chayim*, part 4, no. 105:6.

115. *Iggrot Moshe, Choshen Mishpat*, part 2, no. 65.

116. Ibid., no. 66.

117. Ibid., no. 68.

118. S. Finkelman, *Reb Moshe. The Life and Ideals of HaGaon Rabbi Moshe Feinstein* (New York: Mesorah Publications, 1986).

scrupulously to the laws of the Torah but also were in keeping with high standards of medical practice. He was for us, for all those years, our guide and our inspiration, and his memory lives on in our hearts and in our minds.

Rabbi Shlomo Zalman Auerbach (1910–1995)

AVRAHAM STEINBERG, M.D.

INTRODUCTION

Rabbi Shlomo Zalman Auerbach was born in Jerusalem on July 30, 1910 (23 Tamuz 5670, in the Hebrew calendar) and died on February 20, 1995 (20 Adar 5755). He lived his entire life in the Shaare Chesed neighborhood of Jerusalem, where he raised his ten children. He never left the Holy Land, lived a simple and spartan life, and devoted himself entirely to the study of the Torah and the performance and fulfillment of biblical and rabbinic commandments and precepts.

Rabbi Auerbach began teaching Torah at the rabbinical seminary Yeshiva Kol Torah in 1949. Three years later he became the Dean, or Rosh Yeshiva, a position he held until his death. He refused offers to become a judge in the Supreme Rabbinical Court and declined to become Jerusalem's or Israel's Chief Rabbi. Nevertheless, he was recognized as one of the greatest rabbinic decisors of the twentieth century. He was loved and admired not only for his erudition in rabbinics and theology but also for his impeccable integrity and modesty. Throughout his life he was unpretentious and actively engaged in acts of charity and psychological support for the needy.

Rabbi Auerbach was totally free of politics. He had no material ambitions, did not seek power and glory, and shunned the limelight. He was punctilious in his observance of obligations and commandments between himself and God, and between himself and his fellow human beings. He attended rigorously to his Torah studies. He showed love and affection to every man, woman, and child. He respected every Jew, religious and secular alike, and he was accessible to anyone who needed his guidance and advice. Rabbi Auerbach's rabbinic rulings were based on strict halachic principles, not on intuition. His advice and personal actions and behavior were refined by *halachah* and Jewish thought.

Rabbi Auerbach's last will and testament typifies his humble character and his respect and consideration for others. He entitled it *Bakashah*, meaning request, rather than using the conventional term *Tzavaah*, meaning instruction. He asked that his tombstone not be larger than those of his parents, that it not be inscribed with titles or praises, and that it indicate only that he taught Torah at Yeshiva Kol Torah in Jerusalem. He requested that eulogies delivered at his funeral be brief, so as not to burden the assembled people, and that the speakers endeavor to stimulate the spiritual and religious feelings of the people in attendance. He asked emphatically that eulogizers refrain from speaking words of lavish praise, since he was greatly pained by such introductions during his lifetime and wished to be spared them at his funeral. He forgave all who committed an offense against him during his lifetime and asked forgiveness of anyone who felt that he had offended him. Finally, he asked his family to live together in peace and harmony.

These qualities, combined with enormous Torah knowledge and erudition, allowed Rabbi Auerbach to analyze and define halachic concepts as they apply to modern issues in medicine, technology, agriculture, economics, and other areas. He never issued a ruling without a thorough investigation of the subject matter. He consulted with experts to obtain a detailed and comprehensive understanding of the relevant facts before issuing his ruling. The sum of these characteristics, personal qualities, and halachic abilities made Rabbi Auerbach the widely recognized Torah giant and *posek hador* (rabbinic decisor of the generation) that he was.

Although Rabbi Auerbach never wrote or compiled a book of his rabbinic responsa, he authored and published several books and many articles in halachic periodicals. His books are: *Interpretations on Shev Shemateta* (1932; 2nd edition, 1991, Shaare Ziv Institute, Jerusalem); *Meorei Aish* (1935, Jerusalem); *Kovetz Maamarim Be'inyanei Chashmal Beshabbat* (1978, Institute for Science and Halacha, Jerusalem); *Maadanei Eretz*, Part 1, *Shevi'it* (1944; 2nd edition, 1992, Moriah, Jerusalem); and *Maadanei Eretz*, Part 2, *Terumot* (1952, Jerusalem).

A compilation of some of his articles from various Hebrew periodicals was published as *Responsa Minchat Schlomo* in 1986 by the Shaare Ziv Institute in Jerusalem. Some medical halachic articles by Rabbi Auerbach were published in various Hebrew periodicals, such as *Noam, Sinai*, and *Moriah*. Some of his medical halachic rulings are quoted by other authors in various articles in Hebrew periodicals such as *Assia* and *Hamayan*.

Most of Rabbi Auerbach's medical halachic rulings, as well as other rulings in all spheres of human life, were rendered orally and never formally published by him in a volume of responsa. However, many of his rulings involving medical subjects have been summarized by three of his outstanding disciples, Rabbi Joshua J. Neuwirth, Rabbi Dr. Abraham S. Abraham, and Rabbi Dr. Avraham Steinberg, in their renowned multivolume works. These are, respectively, *Shemirat Shabbat Kehilchatah* (3 volumes, new and enlarged edition, Moriah, Jerusalem, 1979–1993); *Nishmat Avraham* (5 volumes, 2nd edition, Schlesinger Institute, Jerusalem, 1984–1993); and *Encyclopedia Hilchatit Refuit* (6 volumes, Schlesinger Institute, Jerusalem, 1988–1997). This chapter is based primarily on these sources and is the first attempt to collect and summarize Rabbi Auerbach's medical halachic rulings. I was privileged to have spent many hours with Rabbi Auerbach discussing a wide variety of issues in medicine and *halachah*. In this essay, I summarize only those rulings published by his disciples in authorized sources and which he personally reviewed and approved. Additional oral rulings on medical halachic questions were undoubtedly rendered by Rabbi Auerbach. This essay does not address or summarize his numerous rulings on nonmedical issues. The reader is strongly encouraged, wherever possible, to directly consult the original Hebrew sources just cited.

The various medical halachic rulings of Rabbi Auerbach are summarized in subject categories relating to the beginning of life (contraception, fertility testing, artificial insemination, surrogate motherhood, abortion, anencephalics and other defective newborns, redemption of the firstborn, and circumcision) and to the end of life (terminally ill, brain death and organ transplantation, and autopsy).

Also summarized are rulings about the practice of medicine on the Sabbath, Festivals, and fast days; medicine and the priest (*Kohen*); malpractice; confidentiality; surgery; informed consent; medical experimentation; smoking; triage; and dietary laws. Also presented are rulings by Rabbi Auerbach concerning patients reciting blessings and prayers, and medical questions relating to the disabled, a menstruant woman, and seclusion.

THE BEGINNING OF LIFE

Contraception

Rabbi Auerbach allows a Jewish bride to use contraceptive pills prior to her marriage to ensure that she not menstruate on her wedding day (*Nishmat Avraham, Yoreh Deah* 193:1). It is preferable that she take the pills up to three weeks before the scheduled wedding. After she stops, she has her regular menstruation and should count five "unclean" and seven "clean" days (*Encyclopedia Hilchatit Refuit*, Vol. 5, pp. 12–13). A Jewish physician ordinarily is not allowed to prescribe contraceptive pills for a sexually active unmarried woman (*Nishmat Avraham*, Vol. 4, *Even Haezer* 5:1). In situations where Jewish law permits the use of contraceptives, the minipill is as acceptable halachically as regular contraceptive pills (ibid., 5:13:2:3). A woman who feels very weak after childbirth is permitted for a limited time to use contraceptive pills, even if her husband has not yet fulfilled the precept of procreation (ibid., 5:13:1).

Rabbi Auerbach also allows a woman who is fearful of having another episode of postpartum depression to use contraceptives, even over the objections of her husband (ibid., 5:13:2:8:4). If she chooses to become pregnant again, she may do so, since effective treatment is available for postpartum depression; she is not considered to be violating the prohibition against self-endangerment (ibid.). Where contraception is halachically permissible, the diaphragm is preferable to spermicides (ibid., 5:13:2:1). In a case where a baby may be born with a serious and even lethal genetic defect causing much suffering to the parents, it is permissible for the woman to use a diaphragm; the couple is not obligated to separate or divorce (ibid., 5:13:2:8:5). A woman who was raped is permitted to use the "morning-after pill" or to have an emergency intrauterine device inserted within 72 hours, to avoid pregnancy (ibid., *Choshen Mishpat* 425:1:20).

Fertility Testing, Artificial Insemination, and Surrogate Motherhood

Rabbi Auerbach allows the provision of sperm by a man for fertility testing, even if a couple has already sired a son and a daughter (*Nishmat Avraham, Even Haezer* 22:9). It is preferable, if possible, to obtain the sperm sample from a method other than masturbation, such as retrieval of sperm from the wife following cohabitation, or even by the use of a condom by the man (ibid., 23:2). If an unmarried man with cancer is told by his physicians to freeze some of his sperm for possible future use if he is cured because the chemotherapy or radiotherapy may make him sterile, he should not do so. It is not prohibited for him to do so, however, whether he is single or married (ibid., Vol. 4, 23:1).

Rabbi Auerbach rules that artificial insemination using the husband's sperm (AIH) is permissible, provided that there is no other alternative for the couple to have a child and provided that the sperm is not mixed with donor sperm (*Noam*, 1958, Vol. 1, pp. 155–166). Such AIH is permissible even during the period when the woman is ritually unclean (*niddah*) and forbidden to cohabit with her husband, if it is impossible to perform AIH at another time (ibid.). The introduction of semen into the woman's vagina during AIH does not render the woman ritually unclean (ibid.). A child born following AIH is considered to be the son of the sperm donor, i.e., the husband, in all respects (ibid.).

Rabbi Auerbach also rules that it is forbidden to inseminate a woman with sperm from a Jewish donor who is not the husband. If it was nevertheless performed, the woman may continue to live with her husband, even if he is a *Kohen*. The child born from this procedure is a doubtful bastard (*mamzer*) in Jewish law (ibid.). If no other method is available to help a couple have children, it is permissible to use the sperm from a non-Jewish donor, and the child born is a full Jew and requires no conversion (ibid.).

In Rabbi Auerbach's view, it is forbidden for a single woman to become pregnant by artificial insemination, even if the sperm is obtained from a Jew who donated sperm anyway (*Nishmat Avraham*, Vol. 4, *Even Haezer* 1:3). It is also forbidden to separate male-producing sperm from female-producing sperm in order to choose the sex of one's offspring. However, in the case of x-linked diseases such as hemophilia, it is permissible to separate sperm to try to ensure the birth of girls who are clinically unaffected (ibid., 1:1).

Rabbi Auerbach was opposed to surrogate motherhood a priori. If, however, it was performed, both the genetic mother (i.e., egg donor) and the birth mother are considered mothers for halachic purposes (*Nishmat Avraham*, Vol. 4, *Even Haezer* 5:2). If either the surrogate mother or the genetic mother is non-Jewish, the child must undergo full conversion to Judaism even if the surrogate mother converted to Judaism during the pregnancy (*Emek Halakhah*, Vol. 2, 1989, p. 170). A firstborn male born following artificial insemination or in vitro fertilization requires redemption like any other firstborn son (*Nishmat Avraham, Even Haezer* 1:2).

Abortion

Rabbi Auerbach prohibits the abortion of even a Tay-Sachs fetus (*Nishmat Avraham, Choshen Mishpat* 425:1:15), but allows the abortion of an anencephalic fetus (ibid., *Orach Chayim* 330:5). In cases of multifetal pregnancy such as quadruplets or more, he permits the selective abortion of some of the fetuses to save the mother and the other fetuses (ibid., *Choshen Mishpat* 425:1:21). Rabbi Auerbach rules that an anesthesiologist is forbidden to give anesthesia to a woman for an abortion that is halachically prohibited, even if he may lose his job (*Nishmat Avraham*, Vol. 4, *Orach Chayim* 656:2). An expert in ultrasound should not perform this procedure for a forbidden abortion, but need not lose his job because of it (ibid.). Finally, Rabbi Auerbach permits an autopsy of an abortus after repeated miscarriages in order to determine the reason for the repeated miscarriages (ibid., *Yoreh Deah* 349:2:4).

Anencephalics and Other Defective Newborns

Although Rabbi Auerbach permits the abortion of an anencephalic fetus, he forbids the removal of organs for transplantation from an anencephalic newborn as long as the baby breathes spontaneously. To do so constitutes an act of murder (*Emek Halakhah*, Vol. 2, 1989, pp. 207ff). An anencephalic baby should be treated even on the Sabbath, but there is no obligation to resuscitate it. It may even be forbidden to prolong its dying process (*Nishmat Avraham*, Vol. 4, *Orach Chayim* 390:5).

Spina bifida in a baby should be surgically corrected, if possible (*Encyclopedia Hilchatit Refuit*, Vol. 3, s.v. *yilod*, p. 130, n. 390). A baby with major physical defects need not be operated on if the result may be significant suffering such as paralysis and the chances of surviving the surgery are doubtful (*Responsa Minchat Shlomo* #91:24). One should not desecrate the Sabbath for a prematurely born baby who also suffers from one or more lethal defects. However, in a hospital, one should do everything possible to save even such a baby so that people should not neglect appropriate treatment for a future baby who may have a chance, however slim, to survive. If there is doubt as to whether or not the defect is lethal, or if the baby was born at term with a lethal defect, everything necessary should be done on the Sabbath except for resuscitation (*Shemirat Shabbat Kehilchatah* Chap. 36, n. 24; *Nishmat Avraham*, Vol. 4, *Orach Chayim* 330:3).

The laws of mourning apply to prematurely born babies, even those born after only five or six gestational months, provided that they survive for more than thirty days after discharge from an incubator (*Nishmat Avraham, Yoreh Deah*, end of 374). However, if a baby dies within a few days after discharge from an incubator in which it lived for more than thirty days, or if it has lethal defects in the respiratory or cardiac systems, the laws of mourning do not apply (ibid., Vol. 4, *Yoreh Deah* 305:1).

Redemption of the Firstborn

According to Rabbi Auerbach, a premature newborn baby boy should be redeemed, if he is a firstborn, thirty days after his discharge from the incubator. A term firstborn baby boy should be redeemed on time, even if he is still in an incubator (*Otzar Pidyon Haben*, Chap. 3, n. 32). A baby boy born with lethal defects should not be redeemed, even if he survived for more than thirty days because of medical interventions (*Nishmat Avraham*, Vol. 4, *Yoreh Deah* 305:1). A baby boy born with a defect halachically classified as *terefah* (nonviable) should nevertheless be redeemed, with the recitation of the appropriate blessings, if he was medically treated and he recovered (ibid., 305:3).

Further concerning the redemption of a firstborn son, Rabbi Auerbach rules that a boy born after an abortus up to forty days of conception should be redeemed as the firstborn (*Nishmat Avraham, Yoreh Deah* 305:4). After three months of gestation, a fetus is considered formed, and a baby boy born after such an abortus should not be redeemed. However, if the first fetus was found to be underdeveloped by ultrasound examination, the next newborn boy should be redeemed as a firstborn (*Otzar Pidyon Haben*, Chap. 1, n. 19).

Circumcision

Rabbi Auerbach rules that a baby with physiological jaundice should be circumcised as soon as he no longer appears jaundiced to the naked eye (*Noam*, Vol. 10, 1967, pp. 168ff). A newborn baby boy with 38°C temperature or above is considered ill, even if the fever is due to dehydration. Circumcision, therefore, should be postponed until seven days after recovery (*Nishmat Avraham, Yoreh Deah* 262:6:3 and Vol. 4, *Yoreh Deah* 262:1). The requirement to wait seven days after complete recovery from an illness also applies to adults who have to be circumcised (ibid., *Yoreh Deah* 262:4). An anemic baby can be circumcised as soon as he recovers from the anemia; but if he required treatment such as blood transfusion, one must postpone the circumcision until seven days after complete recovery (*ibid.*, 262:2:1). A baby who is born circumcised and who requires only the extraction of a drop of blood can have this done without waiting seven days, if the baby was ill (ibid., 263:4). A baby treated with antibiotics for an infection should be circumcised seven days after recovery from the infection, irrespective of when the antibiotics were discontinued (ibid., Vol. 4, *Yoreh Deah* 262:1).

Nowadays, asserts Rabbi Auerbach, it is permissible to circumcise a hemophiliac boy on the eighth day of life because of the availability of efficacious treatment to replace the missing clotting factor (ibid., *Yoreh Deah* 263:4). A baby born with incurable severe cyanotic congenital heart disease should be circumcised thirty days after birth, if there is no medical contraindication (ibid., 262:6:2). If a small piece of foreskin can be excised on the eighth day of life in a baby with hypospadias, leaving the remaining foreskin for later urological correction of the defect, this should be done. If not, the *mohel* or ritual circumciser should be present at the corrective surgery, uncover the foreskin, and recite the appropriate blessings (*Assia*, Vol. 3, 1983, p. 389).

A boy born following artificial insemination or in vitro fertilization should not be circumcised on the Sabbath or a Festival, if the eighth day of life occurs on the Sabbath or a Festival (*Noam*, Vol. 1 (1958), pp. 156–166). In a case of suspected acquired immunodeficiency syndrome (AIDS), the *mohel* is allowed to perform the *metzitzah* or sucking part of the circumcision ceremony using a glass tube or the back of a 5-cc syringe (*Nishmat Avraham*, Vol. 4, *Yoreh Deah* 264:1).

THE END OF LIFE

Terminal Illness

Rabbi Auerbach rules that there is no obligation to actively prolong the life of a suffering terminally ill patient (*Responsa Minchat Shlomo* #91:24) even if the patient is in a coma (*Encyclopedia Hilchatit Refuit*, Vol. 4, s.v. *noteh lamut*, pp. 402–403). The talmudic and rabbinic term *goses* (traditionally referring to a person who will live no more than 72 hours) cannot be precisely defined in modern medical terms for halachic purposes (ibid., p. 371). Nevertheless, one should not move a *goses* unnecessarily, but one may touch him to provide for the patient's needs (ibid., p. 374). A *goses* may be moved in order to save another patient's life; for example, if the *goses* lies in an emergency room, thereby interfering with access for another very seriously ill patient, the *goses* may be carefully moved (*Assia*, No. 55, 1994, 43). It is forbidden, however, to disconnect or remove equipment from a *goses* even for the sake of saving someone else (ibid.).

According to Rabbi Auerbach, nutrition and hydration (i.e., food and fluids) should be given to a terminally ill patient, even against the patient's wishes (*Responsa Minchat Shlomo* #91:24)—if necessary, by a nasogastric tube or gastrostomy. There is no obligation to supply hyperalimentation to such a patient (*Encyclopedia Hilchatit Refuit*, Vol. 4, s.v. *noteh lamut*, p. 405). Specific medical treatments for the terminal illness or its complications, such as chemotherapy, hemodialysis, and mechanical ventilation may be withheld. However, general supportive and comfort measures such as nutrition, hydration, oxygen, and antibiotics should be administered (ibid., p. 403).

A suffering, terminally ill patient with three or more failing organs who is expected to die soon may have all further treatments and laboratory evaluations withheld. It is also permissible to gradually reduce current treatments, such as lowering the respirator settings, decreasing the oxygen concentration, and discontinuing further use of drugs to maintain blood pressure, provided that these maneuvers do not cause immediate death (ibid., p. 404). A patient in a permanent coma or persistent vegetative state should receive routine care and treatment but should not be resuscitated (*Nishmat Avraham* Vol. 4, *Yoreh Deah* 339:2). Pain-relief medications, including opiates such as morphine, should be given to all patients with pain, including the terminally ill, even if there is a risk of depressing respiration and thereby hastening death (ibid., 339:4). It is permissible for a patient with amyotrophic lateral sclerosis (ALS) to request not to be connected to a respirator when the disease progresses to its late states, and this request should be honored (*Responsa Yachel Yisroel*, Part 2, #62).

Brain Death and Organ Transplantation

There is presently an intense rabbinic debate about whether or not total brain death, including brainstem death, is a valid halachic definition of death, irrespective of cardiac activity. Rabbi Auerbach's view was that complete irreversible brain death, namely death of all the cells of the brain, constitutes death according to *halachah*, even if the heart is still beating, and even in the case of a brain-dead pregnant woman whose baby is delivered alive. This fact has to be medically established with certitude; brainstem death alone is insufficient to determine death (*Assia, 53–54*, 1994, 5ff). Nowadays, since physicians cannot establish the abovementioned criteria with absolute certainty, a brain-dead person is considered doubtfully dead, and the halachic rules pertaining to a *goses* apply to him as long as the heart beats. Accordingly, it is forbidden to move such a patient or to inject into his body any material to verify whether or not the brain is completely dead. Theoretically, if one could establish brain death by applying highly reliable tests that would not require moving the patient at all, it would be permissible (ibid.).

Rabbi Auerbach also ruled that if a patient is diagnosed as brain-dead by routine criteria, it is permissible to disconnect the respirator even though the patient has not been proven absolutely to be brain-dead as required by *halachah* (ibid.). If the heart stops for thirty seconds in a clinically diagnosed brain-dead patient, the patient is dead according to *halachah* (ibid.). A patient who, following open-heart surgery, cannot be weaned off the heart–lung machine is considered halachically dead and may be disconnected from the machine (*Nishmat Avraham*, Vol. 4, *Yoreh Deah* 155:1). It is forbidden to disconnect a terminally ill patient from a respirator unless the patient is clinically diagnosed as brain-dead (*Encyclopedia Hilchatit Refuit*, Vol. 4, s.v. *noteh lamut*, p. 407).

These pivotal rulings by Rabbi Auerbach concerning brain death are consistent with his views on organ transplantation. Since the determination of total brain death nowadays is inadequate according to halachic criteria, it is forbidden to use a brain-dead person as an organ donor. Rabbi Auerbach also forbids a Jew in Israel to be enrolled as a potential organ recipient but allows it abroad (*Assia 53–54*, 1994, 5ff). Theoretically, if new medical tests ascertain with absolute certainty the complete and irreversible cellular death of the brain, it will be permissible to use such a patient as an organ donor even if the heart is still beating (ibid.). In the meantime, since Rabbi Auerbach allows the removal of a respirator from a clinically diagnosed brain-dead person, when that person's heart stops for thirty seconds, if he can then be successfully resuscitated, his organs can be removed for transplantation (ibid.).

Heart transplantation is not considered murder of the recipient at any stage of the operation. The patient does not assume the halachic categorization of a *nevelah* (corpse) or *tereifah* (nonviable) after the old heart is removed and before the new heart is implanted (*Nishmat Avraham, Yoreh Deah* 155:2:1). It is permissible to obtain skin from a dead person in order to treat a severely burned patient (ibid., 349:3:2:2).

Regarding the donation of organs by live donors, Rabbi Auerbach states that it is permissible to be a live kidney donor, but there is no obligation to do so (ibid., 157:4:2). There is no prohibition barring a live kidney donor from receiving payment; nor is it forbidden for a middleman to receive payment for his services in matching a donor with a recipient. In either case, one still fulfills the *mitzvah* of saving the recipient's life (ibid., Vol. 4, *Choshen Mishpat* 420:1).

According to Rabbi Auerbach, a live bone-marrow donor for a needy relative is performing a *mitzvah* (ibid., *Yoreh Deah* 349:3:3:2). Every suitable bone-marrow donor should be encouraged to donate marrow to save life. He should not, however, be pressured to do so if he is afraid of the discomfort and the minimal danger involved in the procedure (ibid., Vol. 4, *Even Haezer* 80:1). A child can serve as a bone-marrow donor only if he understands the meaning of being a donor and can consent thereto; otherwise, it is doubtful that he can serve as a donor (ibid., *Choshen Mishpat* 243:1). It is permissible to donate blood to a blood bank, even for a fee, and even if the blood eventually may be discarded (*Nishmat Avraham, Yoreh Deah* 349:3:3:3).

Autopsy and Post-Mortem Tests

In Judaism, autopsies are permitted (and perhaps are required) only when the results of the autopsy may immediately save the life of another extant patient dying of the same disease. Since biopsies are performed on living patients, Rabbi Auerbach permits post-mortem biopsies even if no patient is at hand who may directly benefit from the results of such biopsies (*Nishmat Avraham*, Vol. 4, *Yoreh Deah* 349:2). On the Sabbath, however, a post-mortem biopsy is allowed only if there is a patient at hand who may benefit from the results (ibid., *Orach Chayim* 316:12).

Rabbi Auerbach allows the performance of tests on a dead body in order to identify the deceased so that the family can mourn and the wife remarry (ibid., *Yoreh Deah* 349:1). He also allows the removal of a pacemaker from a deceased person; if the relatives object, they must pay for the pacemaker (ibid., *Yoreh Deah* 349:3:1 and *Choshen Mishpat* 235:2). He also forbids a person from selling or donating his body after death to a medical school (ibid., *Yoreh Deah* 349:2:3). Finally, he permits physicians to perform endotracheal intubation on the recently deceased to develop expertise with which to save future patients (ibid., Vol. 4, *Yoreh Deah* 349:2).

THE PRACTICE OF MEDICINE

Confidentiality

Rabbi Auerbach rules that whoever knows of a significant defect or illness in a bride or a groom may, but is not obligated to, disclose the information to the other side. (*Nishmat Avraham, Even Haezer* 2:1). The affected future spouse may also withhold disclosure of the defect or illness at the first or second meeting but should do so before the engagement is announced (*Encyclopedia Hilchatit Refuit*, Vol. 5, s.v. *kiddushin vegerushin*, p. 484). Failure by a woman to disclose that she suffers from a disease like severe heart disease, diabetes mellitus, or infertility may be grounds for nullification of the marriage, unless these abnormalities developed after the marriage (*Nishmat Avraham, Even Haezer* 154:3, and Vol. 4, *Even Haezer* 68:1). The same rule applies for a significant blemish or disease in a man (ibid., *Even Haezer* 39:1:5).

If a woman with a venereal disease asks her physician not to disclose to her husband that she had an affair with a stranger, the physician is not obligated to do so (ibid., Part 4, *Even Haezer* 115:1). A man is obligated to disclose to his spouse that he is suffering from AIDS; if he refuses to do so, the physician should do so, even against the patient's wishes (ibid., 2:1:1). If one spouse suffers from AIDS, the man may not use a condom, the couple cannot live together, and their only recourse, rules Rabbi Auerbach, is divorce (ibid., 2:1:2).

One is obligated to report child abuse to the authorities. It is forbidden to return a battered child to his parents. It is preferable to find an observant Jewish foster or surrogate family for such a child; if it is not possible, the child may be placed with a nonobservant family. These rules apply irrespective of whether the child is physically battered, raped, or otherwise seriously abused (ibid., Vol. 4, *Choshen Mishpat* 388:1).

Informed Consent

There is no need, according to Rabbi Auerbach, to obtain specific informed consent for routine blood-drawing in a hospital, even if it is done by students and resident physicians (*Nishmat Avraham, Yoreh Deah* 155:2:4). It is permissible for a resident surgeon to operate upon patients, even if a more qualified surgeon is available, unless the patient specifically demands the more experienced physician (ibid.). A pregnant woman cannot be coerced into undergoing a cesarean section, even if there is an increased risk to the fetus by vaginal delivery (*Shemirat Shabbat Kehilchatah*, Chap. 36, n. 4).

Medical Experimentation and Genetic Manipulations

A healthy person may participate in a medical experiment only if there is no danger or suffering involved other than minor discomfort, such as blood drawing. If a dangerously ill patient is in need of a lifesaving treatment, a healthy person is allowed to expose himself to some danger or suffering to save the patient's life, i.e., to donate a kidney (*Nishmat Avraham, Yoreh Deah* 157:4 and 349:3:3:4). A non-seriously ill patient without pain or suffering should not participate in potentially dangerous experiments (*Assia*, Vol. 5, 1986 18ff). For medical studies or medical experiments, it is forbidden to castrate animals of either sex (*Nishmat Avraham, Even Haezer* 5:9).

Genetic material may be transferred from one species to another by means of bacteria or viruses, and the resultant species is not considered to be *kilayim* (forbidden mixtures) (*Nishmat Avraham,*

Vol. 4, *Choshen Mishpat* 425:1). The transfer of genetic material that creates a significant change in the characteristics of the species is permissible in animals but not in plants (ibid.). If genetic manipulation of a tree induces it to produce vegetables such as tomatoes, the blessing to be recited when eating the "fruit" is *boreh peri ha'etz*, which is the usual blessing for fruits of a tree (ibid.). If genetic manipulation of nonkosher fish causes it to grow scales, it is still considered nonkosher (ibid.).

Malpractice and Physicians' Strikes

Rabbi Auerbach rules that if a patient dies during surgery because of the surgeon's error, the surgeon may have to be exiled to a city of refuge (*galut*). If the patient dies after the surgery, the surgeon is exempt from *galut* (*Nishmat Avraham, Yoreh Deah* 336:7). If the patient had chosen the surgeon, the surgeon is exempt from *galut*, unless he was negligent in performing the surgery (ibid.).

Physicians and nurses are forbidden to strike in order to improve their salaries or working conditions if any patient might thereby be endangered (ibid., *Choshen Mishpat*, 333:1).

Surgery

Rabbi Auerbach is of the opinion that it is permissible to remove one or both undescended testicles from their intraabdominal location because of the danger of malignant transformation (*Nishmat Avraham, Even Haezer* 5:5). A patient with metastatic cancer who requires bilateral orchiectomy to palliate his disease is not halachically considered to have been castrated and may continue to live with his wife (ibid.). An enlarged clitoris in a chromosomal and phenotypic baby girl may be surgically corrected (ibid., 44:3).

Triage

It is axiomatic in Judaism that one may not sacrifice one life to save another life. Therefore, Rabbi Auerbach rules that one may not hasten the death of any person—even a dangerously ill patient close to death—in order to save another person, even if the latter is a great Torah scholar (*Encyclopedia Hilchatit Refuit*, Vol. 5, s.v.

kedumiyot, p. 532; *Nishmat Avraham, Yoreh Deah* 252:2). Thus, it is forbidden to disconnect a patient from a respirator, even if he is close to death and has no chance to survive, in order to provide that respirator to another needy patient who has a curable illness (*Encyclopedia*, p. 533).

Priority considerations are invoked only if two people need a treatment that is sufficient only for one (ibid.). In such a case, priority should be given to the patient in whom the medical chances for success are greatest, irrespective of the social status of the two patients (*Nishmat Avraham, Yoreh Deah* 252:2). If the chances for success are equal, the priorities enumerated in the Talmud (*Horayot* 13a) should be followed (ibid., 252, n. 5). It is preferable not to connect a patient who has only a slim chance of survival to a respirator that probably will be needed by another dangerously ill patient with a curable illness (*Bishvilei Harefuah 8,* (1987), 16ff).

Dietary Laws (Kashrut)

Rabbi Auerbach rules that a non-seriously ill patient need wait only one hour after eating a meat meal before consuming dairy products (*Nishmat Avraham, Yoreh Deah* 89:3). A hospitalized patient may eat kosher food from dishes that were not ritually immersed prior to their first use as required by *halachah* (ibid., 120:1). It is forbidden to desecrate the Sabbath to bring a patient special kosher food if reliably kosher food is provided to the patient by the hospital (*Shemirat Shabbat Kehilchatah*, Chap. 40, n. 48). A person is not obligated to give his kosher food to a patient who is allowed to eat a nonkosher product (*Nishmat Avraham, Choshen Mishpat* 340:1).

Even a non-dangerously ill patient is allowed to swallow pills containing nonkosher products (*Shemirat Shabbat Kehilchatah*, Chap. 33, n. 19). Swallowing pills is not considered eating (*Responsa Minchat Shlomo* #17), although consuming any substance contained in a capsule is considered eating (*Bishvilei Harefuah* 2 (1979), 27ff.).

Priests (Kohanim)

In Judaism, a *kohen* (priest), even nowadays, is warned against becoming ritually defiled. The highest grade of such defilement occurs if a *kohen* touches a dead body or is present in the same room with a dead body. Therefore, a *kohen* should not study to become a male nurse [or physician]. However, rules Rabbi Auerbach, if he did so, he is permitted to do whatever is needed for the care of his patients, including their excretory functions (*Nishmat Avraham, Orach Chayim* 128:6). A *kohen* who is a male nurse may work in a hospital provided that he is able to leave the room in which a patient dies. If he is caring for other patients in another room, he should close the door and continue treating his patients (ibid., *Yoreh Deah* 370:2:2). A *kohen* should leave a dying person and not stay in the same room with him unless the patient is conscious and afraid to be alone; then the *kohen* should remain with the patient (ibid., Vol. 4, *Yoreh Deah* 339:4).

A *kohen* may visit hospitalized patients as long as he is unaware that there is a dead person in the hospital (ibid., *Yoreh Deah* 335:4). A hospitalized *kohen* may go to the hospital synagogue for services. If he learns that there is a dead body in the hospital, he should go to the nearest room and close the door until the deceased is removed to the mortuary or out of the building (ibid., 372:1). In order to minimize halachic problems pertaining to a *kohen* in a hospital, Rabbi Auerbach recommends that a special closed stretcher be constructed according to halachic specifications in which deceased patients can be transported without their imparting ritual defilement (*Responsa Minchat Shlomo* #72).

A pregnant woman in her ninth month of pregnancy whose husband is a *kohen* should not enter a house in which there is a dead body, lest she deliver her baby there and her *kohen* son become ritually defiled (*Nishmat Avraham, Yoreh Deah* 37:1:1). A newborn *kohen* should be discharged from the hospital as soon as medically permitted, even after only 24 hours (ibid., *Orach Chayim* 343:2).

The Sabbath

General Rules

Rabbi Auerbach enunciates the principle that one is obligated to desecrate the Sabbath for a dangerously ill patient. If one did so and it turned out to be an error, the person is exempt and is considered to have acted properly (*Shemirat Shabbat Kehilchatah* 32:19). For a non-seriously ill patient, one may violate only rabbinic prohibitions on the Sabbath. Thus, one may ask a non-Jew to perform necessary tasks for the patient, or one may perform such tasks oneself in a manner different than usual (*shinuy*) in order to convert a biblical violation into a rabbinic violation (ibid., 32:17). Following the completion of lifesaving activity on the Sabbath, one may violate only rabbinic prohibitions. Thus, a physician returning from a medical emergency should ask a non-Jew to drive his car home (*Responsa Minchat Shlomo* #8).

Rabbi Auerbach rules that one is not obligated to take burdensome preventive steps before the Sabbath in order to avoid possible permissible Sabbath desecration (*Shemirat Shabbat Kehilchatah* 32:104). For example, a physician who is on call does not have to leave his family before the Sabbath and stay in the hospital in order not to have to travel on the Sabbath if he is called (ibid., 40:64). One may call an ambulance on the Sabbath; one is not obligated to ask a neighbor to drive the patient to the hospital, since the neighbor will have to stay there until the Sabbath is over (ibid., 40:72). A pregnant woman in her ninth month is not required to stay close to the hospital before the Sabbath in order to avoid the need to travel on the Sabbath if labor begins then (*Nishmat Avraham, Orach Chayim* 330:2). One may cook on the Sabbath for a dangerously ill person even if other people have cooked food, if by their giving the patient their food they are left without cooked food on the Sabbath (*Shemirat Shabbat Kehilchatah* 32:74). Left-over food cooked for a dangerously ill patient may not be eaten by healthy people or even by non-seriously ill patients (*Nishmat Avraham, Yoreh Deah* 155:6:7). One may turn on a light to treat a dangerously ill patient even if a light near the next patient could be moved but might wake him up (*Shemirat Shabbat Kehilchatah* 32:65).

Nowadays, according to Rabbi Auerbach, it is permissible to violate even biblical Sabbath prohibitions to treat a non-Jew on the Sabbath (ibid., 40:14). One is not obligated to spend one's money to avoid Sabbath desecration on behalf of a dangerously ill patient (*Responsa Minchat Shlomo* #7:1). One should not desecrate the Sabbath to contact one's Rabbi to ask him to pray on behalf of a patient (*Nishmat Avraham, Orach Chayim* 301:14).

Dangerously Ill Patients

In Jewish law, all biblical and rabbinic commandments are suspended in order to try to save a human life. The only exceptions are the prohibitions against idolatry, murder, and forbidden sexual relations such as incest and adultery. Thus, the Sabbath laws are waived or disregarded if any lifesaving action is needed. Rabbi Auerbach rules that one should desecrate the Sabbath even to save the life of an unborn fetus (*Nishmat Avraham*, Part 4, *Orach Chayim* 330:4). All efforts should be made on the Sabbath to treat a prematurely born baby or a baby born with one or more disabilities, such as Down's syndrome, if there is any hope for survival. A full-term baby with a life-threatening condition should be treated aggressively even if the baby can live for only a short while (*Shemirat Shabbat Kehilchatah* 36:24).

A patient who suffers cardiopulmonary arrest may be resuscitated on the Sabbath even if the chances for success are deemed slim (ibid., 32:20). A patient who may have suffered a heart attack may be transported to the hospital on the Sabbath even if he looks well (*Shemirat Shabbat Kehilchatah* 32:14). A seriously ill patient may receive injections of medications on the Sabbath (ibid., 32:57). High fever of undetermined cause is considered a situation for which the Sabbath may be desecrated (ibid., 32:11). One desecrates the Sabbath even for a person who endangered his own life (*Moriah*, Sivan 5731 (1971), 32ff).

A tooth may be extracted on the Sabbath if the patient might otherwise be endangered (*Nishmat Avraham, Orach Chayim* 328:12). Wounds should not be sutured on the Sabbath unless possible danger to life might otherwise ensue (ibid., Vol. 4, *Orach Chayim* 340:2). Battery-operated medical equipment may be switched off after use on the Sabbath because it may be needed later for other dangerously ill patients (*Shemirat Shabbat Kehilchatah* 40:91). Medication or food for a dangerously ill patient may be removed from a refrigerator on the Sabbath even if by doing so the light will go on (ibid., 32:71). After using the phone on the Sabbath for a dangerously ill patient, one should not replace the receiver on the hook, unless the phone may be needed again during that

Sabbath for the same or other dangerously ill patients (ibid., 32:41).

Non-seriously Ill Patients

According to Rabbi Auerbach, intravenous injections may not be given on the Sabbath to non-seriously ill patients (*Nishmat Avraham, Orach Chayim* 316:2). A diabetic patient, however, is allowed to check his blood sugar by taking a drop of blood and testing it on a suitable paper (ibid., Vol. 4, *Orach Chayim* 316:1). A needle and syringe may be connected on the Sabbath to inject a medication subcutaneously or intramuscularly or to draw blood, provided that they are separated again before being discarded (*Shemirat Shabbat Kehilchatah*, Chap. 33, n. 43).

Rabbi Auerbach allows the measuring of body temperature on the Sabbath (ibid., 40:2, and n. 3 and 8). He also permits the use of suppositories (ibid., 33:11) and ophthalmic ointment (ibid., 34:8) on the Sabbath. One may, on the Sabbath, extract ointment from a tube, apply it to a wound, and cover the wound with a bandage (ibid., 33:14).

An insomniac is allowed to take sleeping pills on the Sabbath (ibid., 33:16). A patient prescribed a several-day course of medication is allowed to take it even on the Sabbath, provided that any interruption of medication use may harm the patient or that the efficacy of the medication depends on its uninterrupted use (*Nishmat Avraham, Orach Chayim* 321:2). One may tear the paper cover of a medication on the Sabbath even if one thereby tears the letters or writing on the cover (*Shemirat Shabbat Kehilchatah* Chap. 33, n. 29). A patient with a minor ailment should take medication on the Sabbath in a manner different than usual (i.e., without water) (ibid., 34:5). One may use drops for a common cold on the Sabbath if one is otherwise embarrassed by the runny nose (ibid., 34:10, and n. 52). A woman permitted to use contraceptive pills may take them on the Sabbath (ibid., 34:19).

A variety of additional rulings by Rabbi Auerbach concerning non-seriously ill patients on the Sabbath include the following. One may apply an elastic bandage on a dislocated ankle on the Sabbath (*Nishmat Avraham, Orach Chayim* 301:15). One may not fasten a bandage with adhesive tape (*Shemirat Shabbat Kehilchatah* 35:25). Although one may tear cotton wool on the Sabbath (ibid., Chap. 35, n. 48), it is forbidden to use alcohol-wet cotton to clean a wound or to disinfect the skin before an injection (ibid., 35:11). One may wear orthodontic devices on the Sabbath, even in a public domain (ibid., 34:29). A patient with an ileostomy, colostomy, or urinary-drainage bag should empty the bag before going out into a public domain (*Nishmat Avraham, Orach Chayim* 301:4).

A nursing woman with excess milk may extract it on the Sabbath, even using a mechanical pump (ibid., 278:4). One may extinguish a light if it disturbs the patient (ibid., 278:4). It is preferable to schedule elective surgery for the beginning of the week, so as to minimize the need for postoperative Sabbath desecration. If the surgeon's schedule does not allow that or if the patient is in pain, the elective surgery may be performed at any time (*Shemirat Shabbat Kehilchatah* 32:33).

The Physician and the Sabbath

Rabbi Auerbach allows a physician, but not a medical student, to study medicine on the Sabbath (*Nishmat Avraham, Orach Chayim* 307:5), provided that the physician does not desecrate the Sabbath in any way (*Responsa Tzitz Eliezer*, Vol. 9, #17:2:9). An observant Jewish physician should take his "on call" duty on the Sabbath and not switch with a nonobservant Jew (*Shemirat Shabbat Kehilchatah*, Chap. 32, n. 125) or a non-Jew (ibid., Chap. 40, n. 65). A physician may carry a beeper on the Sabbath if he may be called to care for dangerously ill patients (*Nishmat Avraham*, Vol. 4, *Orach Chayim* 201:1). It is preferable for a physician to use a calculator on the Sabbath to calculate the dose of a medication rather than to do so in writing (*Assia 57–58* (1996) 17–61).

A physician may write on the Sabbath using ink that disappears in three to four days (*Nishmat Avraham, Orach Chayim* 340:6). It is forbidden to write a discharge summary on a patient on the Sabbath, but it may be dictated to a non-Jew (ibid.). A death certificate may not be signed on the Sabbath; if delay might cause dishonor to the deceased, it is permissible to ask a non-Jewish physician to sign it (ibid.).

Festivals and Fast Days

It is permitted to telephone the physician or hospital on a Festival, even for a non-dangerously ill patient (*Nishmat Avraham, Orach Chayim* 502:1). During the intermediate days of Passover or Tabernacles (Chol Hamoed), one should not schedule elective visits to a physician (ibid., 532:1). A physician who cares for a patient during Chol Hamoed is allowed to receive his usual fee (ibid.).

A dangerously ill patient who needs a medication containing *chometz* (leavened bread) on Passover should obtain it before the holiday but defer taking possession of it until after the holiday by paying for it after the holiday (ibid., 550:1). If *chometz*-free medications are not available, even a non-seriously ill patient may use his regular medications that are usually bitter (*Moriah, 147–148* (1984), 61ff) even if they are coated with a sweetener (*Shemirat Shabbat Kehilchatah*, Chap. 40, n. 163).

On Yom Kippur, it is preferable for a patient to stay home in bed rather than go to synagogue if bed rest will allow the patient to fast (ibid., Chap. 39, n. 94). A non-seriously ill patient who needs to take a medication on Yom Kippur should wrap it in a thin piece of paper and then swallow it (ibid., 39:8). A nursing woman should fast on Yom Kippur, unless she feels that she has inadequate milk for her baby (*Assia 53–54* (1994), 208). A patient who must eat on Yom Kippur should eat very small amounts beginning in the morning, rather than eating a larger amount later in the day (*Shemirat Shabbat Kehilchatah*, Chap. 39, n. 69). A patient who eats less than the amount for which one is culpable (*shiur*) is as if he fasted, and he may be called up to the Torah reading on Yom Kippur (ibid., Chap. 39, n. 115). A patient who must eat on Yom Kippur may eat regular food and drink regular beverages (*Nishmat Avraham*, Vol. 4, *Orach Chayim* 612:1). However, he should not eat sweets just for the enjoyment (*Otzar Habrit*, Part 1, p. 17). A healthy person who feels sick on Yom Kippur and claims that he must eat should not be fed, but he may feed himself. If a pregnant woman feels a need to eat, she may be fed on Yom Kippur (*Moriah*, Sivan 5731 (1971), 31ff). A patient who needs to eat bread on Yom

Kippur should wash his hands and recite the appropriate blessings before and after (*Shemirat Shabbat Kehilchatah* 39:31).

On the Ninth of Av (Tisha B'Av), a patient who needs to eat may do so and consume normal amounts of food (*Nishmat Avraham*, Vol. 4, *Orach Chayim* 554:1). Such a patient should don phylacteries in the afternoon like all fasting people (ibid., *Orach Chayim* 555:1). If he eats only after midday, he should don phylacteries before eating and again in the afternoon (*Shemirat Shabbat Kehilchatah*, Chap. 62, n. 108).

MISCELLANEOUS PATIENT ISSUES

The Disabled

Rabbi Auerbach answered many inquiries about Jewish law and the disabled. A deaf-mute who can understand and "speak" in sign language is considered as a normal person for all halachic purposes (*Responsa Minchat Shlomo* #34). A deaf-mute who can hear with a hearing aid is considered as a hearing person for the purpose of marrying a wife (*Nishmat Avraham, Even Haezer* 44:1). It is permitted to use a hearing aid on the Sabbath provided that it was activated before the Sabbath. One may adjust the volume, and one is permitted to wear the hearing aid in a public domain on the Sabbath (*Shemirat Shabbat Kehilchatah* 34:28). One may fix a broken hearing aid on Chol Hamoed (ibid., Chap. 66, n. 88). A deaf person who hears with a hearing aid cannot read the Scroll of Esther (Megillah) on Purim and certainly should not recite the blessings (*Sinai, 22* (1948), 139).

A blind person can be called up to the Torah reading and may recite the appropriate blessings (*Nishmat Avraham, Orach Chayim* 139:2). Nowadays, a blind man can also serve as a rabbinical judge in a Beit Din (Jewish court of law) (ibid., *Choshen Mishpat* 7:2). It is doubtful whether a blind person can go into a public domain with a seeing-eye dog on the Sabbath, since the dog's leash may not be carried in a public domain on the Sabbath (*Shemirat Shabbat Kehilchatah*, Chap. 18, n. 62).

A father is obligated to educate his mentally retarded son

according to the son's ability, provided that he functions cognitively at least at a level of a four- or five-year-old who can understand that God gave us the Torah. When he becomes thirteen years of age, he is considered to be an adult and is obligated to fulfill all commandments but is exempt from punishment (*Responsa Minchat Shlomo* #34). The communicative method used for severely mentally retarded or autistic people (facilitated communication) should be used as a limited clinical tool but should not be abused for mystical purposes (*Assia, 57–58* (1996), 17–61). Finally, Rabbi Auerbach rules that a mentally retarded child may be placed in an institution where he will be fed nonkosher food provided that there is hope that he might improve (*Nishmat Avraham, Yoreh Deah* 81:2).

Blessings and Prayers

A variety of medical situations arise that involve questions about the recitation of prayers and blessings. Rabbi Auerbach's view is that a patient with an indwelling urinary catheter with continuous urinary flow should recite the *asher yatzar* blessing only once daily (*Nishmat Avraham, Orach Chayim* 7:1). If a person provides a urine sample for examination and testing, he should recite the *asher yatzar* blessing (ibid.). A patient with an ileostomy or colostomy may recite the daily prayers or study Torah after cleaning the bag and covering it. A patient with an indwelling urinary catheter need not cover the bag when he prays or studies Torah (ibid., 76:6).

A person with a paralyzed right arm should use his left arm to don phylacteries on the paralyzed arm. If, however, he has no sensation in that arm, he should put the phylacteries on his left arm (ibid., *Even Haezer* 169:5). A hospitalized bedridden patient may don phylacteries even if his room is not clean. It is preferable, however, to do so after the room is cleaned (ibid., *Yoreh Deah* 19:1).

A patient unable to eat the amount of bread needed for hand-washing, i.e., the bulk of two olives, should wash his hands, without reciting the blessing *al netilat yadayim*, before eating the bread (ibid., *Orach Chayim* end of 210). One may feed a patient even if the patient does not recite the appropriate blessings before and after the meal (ibid., 163:2).

After recovering from a serious illness, one recites the *hagomel* blessing of thanksgiving. This rule applies even to a potentially dangerous diagnostic procedure. Thus, a patient who underwent cardiac catheterization, even without ballooning or angioplasty, should recite the *hagomel* blessing (ibid., Vol. 4, *Orach Chayim* 219:2). If an adult is circumcised, he should recite this blessing (ibid., 219:4). Women do not recite the *hagomel* blessing except after childbirth (ibid., *Orach Chayim* 219:1).

A Menstruant Woman (Niddah)

A menstruating woman is ritually impure and is not allowed to cohabit with her husband until she undergoes ritual purification culminating in immersion (*tevilah*) in a ritual bath (*mikvah*). The same rule applies in regard to any uterine bleeding but not for bleeding due to a vaginal lesion or wound. Thus, Rabbi Auerbach rules that a woman who has an intrauterine device removed is considered *niddah* and must undergo full ritual purification, including the counting of five "unclean" and seven "clean" days followed by ritual immersion, unless a physician diagnoses a wound as a result of the IUD (*Nishmat Avraham, Yoreh Deah* 196:2). If a woman bleeds following a cytologic examination of the vagina, she is also considered *niddah* since such bleeding cannot be considered as due to a wound (ibid., Vol. 4, *Yoreh Deah* 194:1). A woman whose hymen is surgically incised is not considered *niddah* and is permitted to cohabit with her husband immediately after surgery (ibid., *Yoreh Deah* 193:2).

The "breaking of the waters" in a pregnant woman does not necessarily render her *niddah*. Hence, if there is no bleeding after the breaking of waters, she remains ritually pure (ibid., 194:1). Technically, there is no inherent prohibition for a husband to be present in the delivery room when his wife is giving birth to a baby, but it is not proper for him to do so. However, if his wife requests her husband's presence to comfort her, it is permissible, provided that he does not touch her or look at her private parts during the delivery (ibid., 193–195).

During the immersion of a *niddah* in a *mikvah* as part of her ritual purification, no interposing object (*chatzitzah*) may be present on her body that separates her from the water. Rabbi Auerbach, however, rules that an intrauterine device (IUD) is not considered a *chatzitzah* for a ritual immersion (*Shaare Tevilah* #40). A woman with a perforated eardrum may put fish oil in her ear to prevent water from entering it during her ritual immersion (ibid., #4). A woman with a permanent catheter in her urinary bladder is permitted to undergo ritual immersion with the catheter in place (*Nishmat Avraham, Yoreh Deah* 298:12:5).

Sutures in a woman's mouth following oral surgery are not considered as a *chatzitzah*, since they are only temporary. However, it is preferable to delay her ritual immersion until after their removal (*Shaare Tevilah* #35:4). A temporary tooth filling that is expected to remain in place for at least a week is not considered as a *chatzitzah* (ibid., #34:4). Loose orthodontic devices are not considered as a *chatzitzah*; even if they are tight but inserted for medical rather than esthetic reasons, they are also not considered as a *chatzitzah* (ibid., #35).

Seclusion

It is prohibited in Jewish law for a man to be secluded in a room with a woman. A male physician alone in an examining room or consultation room with a female patient is not considered to be secluded with her, because nurses or other staff members frequently enter the room. Rabbi Auerbach describes various leniencies in the physician–patient relationship in regard to the prohibition of seclusion (*Nishmat Avraham, Even Haezer* 22:1). The leniency of "the husband is in town" does not apply in the case of a female patient repeatedly examined by the same physician (ibid.).

The prohibition of seclusion also applies in regard to a woman in labor before giving birth (*Responsa Minchat Shlomo* #91:21). There is no prohibition of seclusion in an automobile, even at night (ibid.), or in an elevator, even on high floors (*Devar Halakhah*, beginning of the book). The prohibition does apply, however, to an old man secluded with a woman other than his wife or daughter (*Nishmat Avraham, Even Haezer* 22:2).

Other Topics

Rabbi Auerbach issued rulings in response to many other inquiries involving various medical topics. For example, although he does not prohibit smoking as a biblical law violation, he strongly advises people not to smoke (*Nishmat Avraham, Orach Chayim* 511:1 and *Choshen Mishpat* 155:2). A widowed woman must wait ninety days before remarrying in order to differentiate a pregnancy and baby between the deceased husband and her new husband. This law applies even to a woman who used contraception and even to a woman who had a hysterectomy (ibid., 13:3).

EPILOGUE

Rabbi Emanuel Feldman, editor of *Tradition*, the Rabbinical Council of America's journal of Orthodox Jewish thought, wrote a eulogy about Rabbi Auerbach titled "A Death in Jerusalem: The Real World" (*29*, 3 (Spring 1995), 1–4). Rabbi Feldman eloquently captured the essence of Rabbi Auerbach when he wrote, in part:

> Here was a man who shunned all publicity, had no official titles, never granted media interviews, had no PR office, issued no bulletins or journals, assiduously discouraged any view of himself that might tend to ascribe anything but ordinary human abilities to him, was not even mentioned in Jewish encyclopedias, and had never left the borders of the Holy Land—and yet the myriads of religious Jews around the world felt so intimately connected to him that hundreds of thousands spontaneously flocked to pay him a last tribute on just a few hours' notice.
>
> Clearly, it was more than prodigious scholarship that was being honored here; it was what lay beyond that learning. The people were responding to qualities which have grown increasingly rare; genuineness, wholeness, straightforwardness, impeccable integrity—what our tradition calls an *ish emet* [man of integrity]. What touched them was the awareness that not only were his halakhic rulings avidly sought out and followed by believing Jews, but that this quiet, self-effacing man was the embodiment of this *emet*. . . .
>
> In him there existed a remarkable fusion of the rigorous intellectual discipline of the *talmid hakham* [Torah scholar] and the fatherly love for his people. The emotional outpouring of respect and

affection for him was an echo of his respect and affection for each of them.

For it was not only halakha that occupied his days. It was the people to whom it applied. They were instinctively drawn to a man whose primary goal was to understand God's will as reflected in the Torah, whose life was free from the dross of politics, power, and material ambition, who had no personal agenda, who was open and accepting of various points of view within the halakhic framework, and who gave them warmth and attention while asking nothing in return. He was wise and witty, possessed of an incisive mind and an unerring insight into people. Both world-class scholars and ordinary *amkha* [our people] felt that few if any were better equipped to guide them both on arcane halakhic matters and on the mundane issues which beset every human being. Inundated with inquiries from everywhere, he was nevertheless accessible to anyone who knocked at his door and needed face-to-face counsel or comfort.

He was, in a word, the embodiment of Torah; majestic yet simple, transcendent yet worldly, old yet profoundly new, rigorous yet compassionate, multi-faceted yet natural and artless. Whatever advice he would offer was inevitably refined through the purifying filter of his learning, piety, love, and halakhic discipline. . . .

Lord Immanuel Jakobovits (1921–)

YOEL JAKOBOVITS, M.D.

INTRODUCTION

When testimony rests on facts, and when these are of public record, even one with strong emotional links may be a reliable source. As a son, I am, of course, not expected to be altogether impartial. It is with these recognized limitations that I agreed to undertake the task of writing this chapter; not as an evaluator or a judge, but merely as an observer, albeit a biased one, presenting the record as I have been especially privileged to see it. On the other hand, the reader may find some special worth in my presentation, allowing strictly legal disabilities to be outweighed by the advantages of intimateness and familiarity that I can claim over any other less partial attestants.

Many aspects of this challenge made me very uncomfortable. Standing back a bit from the subject, as one must, to write such an evaluation implies that the subject's work is complete and ready for an overall assessment. Fortunately, this is not true here. Although he has published only one book entirely dedicated to Jewish medical ethics, my father continues to enrich the field by a constant stream of lectures and articles in numerous formats and publications. Although my father's "pulpit" has changed enormously over the years, his message and approach have remained remarkably even and consistent.

A second introductory point concerns the choice of subjects for this book. The author has chosen four commanding figures whose works have reflected their tremendous contributions to contemporary Jewish medical ethics. He believes that these four contributors have added important and crucial dimensions to the ever-burgeoning discipline of Jewish medical ethics in unique and definable ways. Mindful of these aims, I have tried to portray the ways in which my father has aided in developing the field from its earliest days to the widely recognized and much discussed area of study and wider interest it has become today.

BIOGRAPHICAL HIGHLIGHTS[1]

My father was born in Koenigsberg, Germany—now Kalinigrad, after its annexation by Russia—on February 8, 1921. His father was Dayan Dr. Julius Jakobovits, who was then serving as the Orthodox rabbi of Koenigsberg. Schooled in the Hungarian *yeshivot* (rabbinic academies), my grandfather was also a great admirer of Immanuel Kant. This admiration was not unique among rabbinic thinkers of that time and place.[2] In fact, although my father's Hebrew name is Yisrael, he was civilly named in honor of the great philosopher who lived all his life in Koenigsberg, which also was known as the "Kantstadt" in reverence to this distinguished thinker. Nevertheless Kant, who, along with the contrasting views of Steward Mills, contributed greatly to the fundamentals of modern secular medical ethics, does not figure anywhere in my father's writings.

---

1. Some more details are found in Lionel Swifts' brief "The Chief Rabbi—An Appreciation" in Jonathan Sacks, ed., *Tradition and Transition: Essays Presented to Chief Rabbi Sir Immanuel Jakobovits to Celebrate Twenty Years in Office*, London Jews' College Publications, 1986.

2. For example, Rabbi Isaac Breuer is reported to have had two portraits above his study desk: one of his maternal grandfather, Rabbi Samson Raphael Hirsch and the other of Immanuel Kant! "Breuer and Kant," W.S. Wurzburger, *Tradition 26*, 2 (1992), 71.

My paternal grandfather hailed from a family of eight: six brothers and two sisters. Of the men, three became rabbis and three became physicians. Of the women, one married a rabbi and the other married a physician. With this strikingly even distribution in the genes, it is not surprising that my father intertwined the two traditions, rabbinic and medical. Of course, the alliance of rabbinics and medicine is nothing new; many leading medieval Sages earned their way in this world by practicing medicine and in the next world by practicing rabbinics.

Fearing the rising Nazi menace, my grandfather arranged with the help of the late Rabbi Dr. Solomon Schonfeld, who saved so many lives, for his eldest son—my father—to escape to England. He arrived in London late in 1936, at the age of sixteen, two years before the rest of the family joined him there. My father entered Yeshiva Etz Chaim to study with such masters as R. Eliyohu Lopian, R. Nachman Greenspan, and R. Leib Gurwicz, from whom, after eight years of learning, he obtained *smichah* (rabbinic ordination). During this period he also developed a lifelong admiration of, and relationship with, R. Yechezkel Abramsky, then the chief *dayan* of the London Beth Din. My grandfather was the junior *dayan* on the Beth Din at that time. Concurrently, my father obtained ministerial training at Jews' College. Actually, he had at first registered as a student at Queen's College, London, intending to undertake a career in mathematics. However, my grandfather insisted that his eldest son follow in the family tradition of rabbinics.

INTEREST IN MEDICAL ETHICS

Although my father had already delved into medical ethics in the late 1940s,[3] it was not until he arrived in Ireland that the idea of dedicating his academic career to medical ethics began to take

3. "Medicine in the Talmud and Rabbinic Literature: Based on a Paper Read Before the Jewish Literary and Social Club," *Chayenu 14*, 7–8 (1950), 4–7. All citations are by Immanuel Jakobovits, unless otherwise indicated.

shape. By the early 1950s he had already published several seminal articles: an edited transcript[4] and a series of articles in Hebrew[5,6] on halachic problems at life's beginning, and an early review of the history of medical practice in Jewish law and literature.[7] Contributions to the literature continued to appear throughout the mid-1950s. Articles appeared regarding autopsies[8] and vivisection,[9] and, in Hebrew, regarding duchaning by a *kohen* (the priestly benediction) who had inadvertently killed someone,[10] abortion,[11] and euthanasia.[12] These were written in the classic *sheilah v'teshuvah* (question-and-answer) style. Besides addressing these concrete halachic questions, several essays were also devoted to more general abstract issues like irrational medicine[13] and, in French, the history of biblical medicine.[14]

A landmark article appeared in 1958 in the first issue of

---

4. "Problems of Jewish Family Life, with Special Reference to the Jewish Attitude Towards Artificial Insemination and Birth-control," reprint of a paper read before the Ninth Conference of Anglo-Jewish Preachers, London, on May 17, 1951 (1953), 1–26.

5. "Artificial Insemination, Birth-control and Abortion," *The Hebrew Medical Journal Semi-Annual Publication 26*, 2 (1953), 169–183, translated from Hebrew.

6. "Sterilization and Eugenics in Jewish Law," *The Hebrew Medical Journal 27*, 2 (1954), 173–186, translated from Hebrew.

7. "The Physician in Jewish Law and Literature," *The Hebrew Medical Journal Semi-Annual Publication 29*, 1 (1956), 156–169, translated from Hebrew.

8. "Dissection in Jewish Law," *The Jewish Chronicle*, 4487 (1955), 13.

9. "The Medical Treatment of Animals in Jewish Law," *The Journal of Jewish Studies 7*, 3–4 (1956), 207–220.

10. "Whether a [Kohen] Physician Who [inadvertently] Killed a Patient May *Duchan*," *HaMoar 6*, 5 (64) (1956), 10–12.

11. "Abortion for the Sake of the Mother's life or Health," *HaPardes 30*, 7 (1956), 20–23.

12. "Mercy Killing to Spare Overwhelming Terminal Suffering," *HaPardes 31*, 1 (1956), 28–31, and *31*, 3 (1956), 16–19.

13. "Irrational Medical Beliefs in Jewish Law," *The Hebrew Medical Journal Semi-Annual Publication 30*, 1 (1957), 166–177, and *31*, 1 (1958), 187–201.

14. "La Bible et la Medecine," *Trait d'Union 6*, 50 (1957), 27–28.

Tradition[15]—itself a landmark rabbinic journal. This article not only presented the halachic attitudes to autopsies but did so in the context of a comparative and historical analysis, thus presaging the subtitle of my father's magnum opus published the next year.

At first my father thought he would devote his doctorate dissertation to examining the rationale of the *mitzvot* (commandments). For several reasons, however, medical ethics in the Jewish tradition ultimately became the major focus of his academic attention. After all, many had already written on the rationale of the *mitzvot*; characteristically, my father sought other, less-well-cultivated areas for research. Aside from the rich historical association of rabbinics with medicine throughout the ages, as noted in my father's Introduction to this book, and to the familial influence alluded to earlier, there was a uniquely Irish factor that led to this pioneering undertaking.

Ireland is, of course, a predominantly Roman Catholic country. It was estimated that, during those years, 97 percent of the population was Roman Catholic, 3 percent was Protestant, and the Jews—they were a fraction of a percent. The widespread public influence of the Church and its teachings prompted examination of practically all issues through the prism of religion. The Church had a ready answer for virtually every question, and, as Chief Rabbi, my father was frequently consulted regarding the parallel Jewish opinion. As questions arose, the immense mass of original sources had to be consulted again and again in order to clarify the authentic Jewish attitudes. By contrast, the Catholics already had many readily available books that collected their teachings on medico-moral matters. Thus, medical ethics from the Jewish perspective became my father's primary interest for both rabbinic and academic reasons. Even then, he hoped to position Jewish medical ethics prominently on the rabbinic map, the medical map, and the academic map.

As Chief Rabbi of Ireland, my father felt it only proper to obtain his doctorate from an Irish university. To this end, he approached Trinity College, Dublin. The faculty at Trinity decided not to

15. "The Dissection of the Dead in Jewish Law—a Comparative and Historical Study," *Tradition 1*, 1 (1958), 77–103.

accept his candidature because of the invidious position they would be in were they to reject the country's Chief Rabbi's dissertation! More seriously, Trinity could provide scholars neither as competent referees nor as adequate literary resources in this still-nascent discipline. Consequently, my father had to turn to the University of London, and he made many a trip across the Irish Sea to consult that institution's vast literary holdings. Moreover, London could provide qualified mentors, though it took three who between them had the necessary credentials. The three were: Rabbi Dr. Isidore Epstein, Principal of Jews' College, chosen for his rabbinic scholarship; Prof. Charles Singer—son of the Singer of *Singer's Prayer Book* fame—the leading general medical historian of his day in England; and Dr. Siegfried Stein, a widely recognized expert of medieval Hebrew literature. The Wellcome Historical Medical Library, the collections at Jews' College and the British Museum in London, and those at the Bibliothèque Nationale in Paris and Trinity College in Dublin, provided abundant and indispensable literary resources. Years later, the Wellcome's location across the street from Adler House, the seat of the British Chief Rabbinate at that time, prompted my father to say that the story of his rabbinic career stretched across the width of the intervening street!

The volume was first submitted to the University of London in 1955 and was subsequently published in 1959.[16] In 1966, a Hebrew edition titled *HaRefuah v'Hayahadus*[17] appeared, and, in 1975, a forty-page chapter on recent developments was added. The first edition is graced by a Foreword by my late sainted maternal grandfather, Rabbi Dr. Elie Munk of Paris. Alas, my paternal grandfather died in 1947, and though he had, and continues to have, a profound influence on my father, he was not spared to see my father's literary or other rabbinic achievements. On the other hand, my maternal grandfather lived until 1983 and provided

16. *Jewish Medical Ethics—a Comparative and Historical Study of the Jewish Religious Attitude to Medicine and Its Practice* (New York: Philosophical Library, 1959) (New York: Bloch, 1975).

17. Translated by Geulah bas Yehuda, Mossad HaRav Kook (Jerusalem, 1966). My father has noted his debt to the translator, who enhanced the book by checking numerous references in their original texts, correcting several of them.

guidance and encouragement over many years. In his Foreword, my grandfather underscores several critical points that retain their truth concerning this book specifically and my father's overall outlook more generally:

> The present work of our author, whose purpose is a detailed treatment of "Jewish Medical Ethics," is . . . a timely one. Keeping theoretical speculation to a minimum, he records the great problems of medical practice by analyzing the position of the Jewish doctrine with regard to them. Each subject is introduced by a historical and comparative study in order to permit the solutions inspired by Jewish ethics to appear in their true light. Thus, the vast subjects of medico-moral conflict . . . which have not ceased, over the generations, to beset the moral conscience of humanity, are treated in the light of the eternal truths whose authentic source is the biblical revelation. The positions taken are clear; they are not the result of personal or sentimental considerations, always subject to caution, not to systematic philosophy, a product of the human spirit and, consequently, always relative in value; they are based, in the final analysis, on the solid foundations of universal morality whose charter is contained in the Decalogue. In practical life, man, faced with a crisis of conscience, can give it his confidence. It is the wisdom of Israel, derived from the most venerable sources of the history of our civilization, which raises its voice in the midst of the mental confusion of our epoch, an epoch of which Paul Valery said: "We no longer know how to collect all our gains in the lottery of experience. All the results speak at once. And the mental confusion confounds itself with the confusion of reality."

And this was already true nearly half a century ago!

ETHICS OR LAW?

To its enduring credit, the book's title, *Jewish Medical Ethics*, has been universally adopted as the appellation of the specialty to which it gave birth. An argument can be made that the term "law" should have been used in place of "ethics." After all, it is hard even to find an exact rabbinic Hebrew equivalent of the term "ethics." There are no distinct Jewish ethics altogether; these are incorporated wholly within the rubric of Jewish law, *halachah.* Comprising civil and ritual law, morals, and ethics, the *halachah* does not recognize any substantial difference between these categories and legislates for each in conjunction with the others. In the Jewish view, as emphasized in the passage from the Foreword just cited, ethical and moral choices are always made in the light of specific legal—that is, halachic—precedents. The ethical underpinnings can usually be extrapolated from the halachic norms. By contrast with general secular medical ethics in which the *principles* are crucial, in Jewish law the detailed *applications* are crucial. In the secular view, general ethics guidelines beget specific practical rulings; in Jewish thinking, the reverse obtains: Specific applications shed light on underlying ethical considerations.

The use of the term ethics, however, may reflect a crucial dimension of the book and of its role in the development of Jewish medical ethics. My father's contribution cannot be subsumed under the same rubric as that of the sainted Rabbis M. Feinstein and S.Z. Auerbach, or, *l'havdil bein chaim l'chaim* (may he live and be well), Rabbi E. Waldenberg. This undisputed preeminent halachic trio contributed primarily to the legal aspects of medical *halachah.*

By training, background, and scholarship, my father can be readily distinguished from the other three figures in this section. Each of the others is recognized as a world-class halachist who has made major and indispensable contributions to modern applied *halachah* generally, and to medical *halachah* specifically. Their works, written in Hebrew, are in the classic tradition of the great rabbinic decisors of earlier generations. Their medium of communication is almost exclusively written in the *sheilah v'teshuvah* (question-and-answer) model, where specific questions are submitted for adjudication. Striking originality marks these *teshuvot,* known as responsa, in terms of the analysis of the crucial elements of the question, the applicability of the sources marshaled, and the application of earlier principles to novel situations and circumstances. No attempt is made by any of these scholars to present an organized or comprehensive code for medical conduct.

Classical *sheiloth v'teshuvot* are primarily written for, and directed toward, other rabbinic scholars. While, in general, an effort is made by the author to *convince* the reader, as opposed to merely *informing* him, this effort is largely confined to the intricacies of the halachic process itself. It is assumed that the reader accepts the philosophical principles and theologic postulates upon which the halachic discourse is predicated. The historical and broader sociologic factors involved in, and the consequences of, the *halachah* are generally not directly addressed by these master halachists.

In contrast with Rabbis Feinstein, Auerbach, and Waldenberg, my father's main attention was directed at moral problems raised by medicine, as opposed to those raised by Jewish law. That is to say, many widely recognized inherent ethical dilemmas exist in medical practice today, beyond the exclusive interest or concern of Jewishly observant practitioners or patients. Problems of abortion, experimental surgery, life support, and euthanasia, just to name a few, fall within this category. On the other hand, difficulties in medical practice sometimes arise because of Judaism: Sabbath, Yom Kippur, *kashrut* (dietary regulations), and autopsies fall under this heading. Except for autopsies, and except for *Jewish Medical Ethics*, which has several chapters on ritual problems in medical practice, my father's involvement has been almost exclusively in the arena of problems prompted by medical practices. Several other exceptions include articles on circumcision,[18] priests (*kohanim*) in medicine,[19] *anninut* (laws pertaining to the preburial period),[20] mourning,[21] and *pikuach nefesh* (danger of life) on the Sabbath.[22]

My father's penchant for focusing authentic Jewish teachings on the complexities of modern life is evident throughout his career, beyond the confines of medical *halachah* as well. In articles on abortion[23] and contraception,[24] as well as in more general re-

18. "Medical Aspects of Circumcision in Jewish Law," *The Hebrew Medical Journal Semi-Annual Publication 34*, 1 (1961), 258–270.

19. "May a Kohen study medicine?" *Tradition 4*, 2 (1962), 262–264.

20. "*Aninut*, mourning, and priestly defilement at autopsies," *Hadarom 11* (1960), 9–12, in Hebrew.

21. "Mourning Laws for Babies," *Tradition 8*, 3 (1966), 57–58.

22. "A Modern Blood Libel—l'Affaire Shahak," *Tradition 8*, 2 (1966), 58–65, and "Sabbath and the Non-Jew," *The Sabbath in Modern Times* (Manchester: Sabbath Observance League, 1967), 92–97.

23. "Jewish Views on Abortion," *Western Reserve Law Review 17*, 2 (1965), 480–497, reprinted numerous times.

views,[25] he repeatedly underscores the relevance of Jewish teachings to modern Jewish—and, indeed, general—society. My father has honed the ability to analyze difficult questions through the prism of halachic ethics and to express his thoughts in language that projects the sublime beauty of our heritage and its transcendent applicability across time and cultures. This has been a constant theme in all the many facets of his literary and pastoral career. Numerous speeches, and the essays[26] that have preserved them, resonate with this purpose. Even in personal and familial settings, he frequently gauges his reactions and conclusions against the measuring rod of halachically derived moral sensitivity and insight.

My father's chief focus, then, is to proclaim Torah values in contemporary language and current frames of reference in ways that are convincing and attractive to modern men and women, whether committed to Jewish practice or not. In this respect he does not distinguish between Orthodox and non-Orthodox.[27] All

24. "The 'Pill' and Jewish Law," *Jewish Digest 11*, 9 (1966), 57–60, and "Population Explosion—the Jewish Attitude to Birth-control: Edited and Annotated Transcript of the Jewish Marriage Education Council Annual Lecture, delivered on October 28, 1968," (1969), reprinted in *Child and Family 9*, 3 (1970), 241–251.

25. "A Modern Doctor's Dilemma," *The Jewish Chronicle 5*, 108 (1967), 7; "Halakhah in Modern Jewish Life: Transcript of Presentation at the Symposium Held at the Conference of the Memorial Foundation for Jewish Culture, Geneva, July 10, 1973," printed in *Halakha in Modern Jewish Life—proceedings of a Symposium* (New York: Memorial Foundation for Jewish Culture, 1973), 4–12, excerpts in *Judaism 29*, 1 (1980), 5–8; "The Jewish Contribution to Medicine: Presented at the Eighth International Conference of the Israeli Medical Society," in *Shanah B'Shanah . . . 5733* (Jerusalem: Heikhal Shlomo, 1973), 203–211, in Hebrew; and "Jewish Medical Ethics: St. Paul's Lecture Delivered . . . on November 23, 1976 in the Crypt of St. Paul's Cathedral" (London: London Diocesan Council for Christian–Jewish Understanding, 1976).

26. Ruth P. Goldschmidt-Lehmann, "Bibliography of the Published Works of Immanuel Jakobovits," in Jonathan Sacks, ed., *Tradition and Transition: Essays Presented to Chief Rabbi Immanuel Jakobovits to Celebrate Twenty Years in Office* (London: Jews' College Publications, 1986).

27. My father frequently stresses his dislike of the term "Orthodox." There is only one body of Jewish law. The different "branches" within

Jews have the obligation to accept, and to become familiar with, our heritage. Furthermore, a recurrent theme in his *Weltanschauung* stresses the overarching obligation to project Jewish teachings in a way that attracts the attention and respect of society at large. The ultimate goal of the Jewish experience and its teachings is to heighten the moral standards of *all* men. The application of many medical halachic principles should be seen in their universal context, as well as in their more confined Jewish sphere. As one of his critics writes: "One can say without a doubt that Immanuel Jakobovits was the first really to begin to systematically address the varied and challenging elements of Jewish medical ethics in a way intended for both scholar and lay-person, for both Jew and Gentile. Every Jewish scholar of medical ethics will be eternally in his debt for his pioneering work."[28]

Jewish Medical Ethics is unique and pioneering in three fundamental respects. It was the first book to review and organize the diverse sources and opinions regarding Jewish views of medical practice. Second, it was written in English. Finally, it repeatedly stresses the ethical dimensions embedded in these rulings. These last two features are combined to project a general ethical view that often speaks beyond the Jewish community in universal tones as well.

ETHICS: THE SPIRIT OF THE LAW

A particularly penetrating analogy explains the relationship of the ethics, or spirit, of the law with the legality, or letter, of the law.[29]

Judaism more properly classify Jews in accordance with their varying shades of belief in the enduring, binding character of the law and their differing degrees of fastidiousness in the application of its principles in the modern era.

28. Marc A. Gellman, "On Immanuel Jakobovits: Bringing the Ancient Word to the Modern World," in Allen Verhey and Stephen E. Lammers, eds., *Theological Voices in Medical Ethics* (Grand Rapids, Mich: Wm. B. Eerdmans Publishers, 1993).

29. "The Letter and the Spirit of Jewish Law," *Tradition* 4, 2 (1962), 257–260.

With some justification, religiously fastidious people are often thought of as being overly concerned with the letter of the law at the expense of the law's spirit. In this respect, it is useful to consider the investment made when constructing a new home. Enormous energy and resources are expended at every stage of the enterprise, from the architect and license fees to the interior decorating costs. Yet, in spite of this colossal expenditure, the tangible elements—the bricks, the plumbing, the landscaping—are all merely secondary to the principal purpose of the house: the space inside. The living space is the essential intention of the house. The walls, ceiling, and so on merely fulfill secondary roles in order to define the space—that is, to demarcate the property limits—and to protect the space from the ravages of inclement weather and unscrupulous neighbors. Similarly, although the effort invested in the letter of the law sequesters the vast bulk of energy and preoccupation, the significance of the centrality of the spirit of the law must not be overlooked. The principles of morals and ethics that imbue the law must also imbue its practitioners, raising their moral sensitivity and ethical deportment.

Collecting, organizing, and explaining philosophical and halachic concepts requires multiple skills. Jewish medical ethics requires special skills in law, medicine, philosophy, and—in our case—*halachah*. Because of its many diverse ramifications, medical ethics regularly attracts experts from many different fields. Men like Fred Rosner, Abraham Steinberg, and Abraham S. Abraham are professional physicians with significant knowledge of Jewish law. Others are primarily philosophers who have adapted their skills to the interplay of *halachah* and medical ethics. But the main experts in the halachic field are unquestionably those who speak as rabbis. It is largely due to the groundwork laid by my father that rabbis, and not Jewish physicians or philosophers, have defined and retained the field as it is today.

Returning for a moment to the "ethics" in *Jewish Medical Ethics*, I believe that the use of this term rather than "*halachah*," or even "law," has also contributed significantly to the development of Jewish medical ethics as a recognized autonomous academic discipline. By employing terminology akin to that which describes the prevailing discipline of general medical ethics, many who are more secularly inclined have also come to regard the Jewish enterprise with similar seriousness. Consequently, the subject has grown immensely since the seeds were first planted by *Jewish Medical Ethics*, in parallel with the now widely accepted programs of secular medical ethics. Continuing evolution is evidenced by the burgeoning literature, including books and periodicals in several languages, by the establishment of university chairs, and by regular international meetings. All of this must have been impeded—if not rendered impossible altogether—were the language of academia and that of Judaic scholarship to have been fundamentally strange to one another.[30] The term "ethics," though perhaps not entirely correct in the Jewish context, is the single crucial term that has made these parallel developments possible by bridging the halachic world with its outside counterpart.

My father never attempted, however, to erect the bridge in the other direction, to bring secular ethical concepts into the language of Jewish conceptualization. Currently popular terms such as autonomy, beneficence, maleficence, or distributive justice never figure in his writings or speeches.

NEW YORK

In 1958, my father accepted a call to become the first rabbi of the newly founded Fifth Avenue Synagogue of New York. In sharp contrast with Ireland, this brought him to the very heart of one of the world's largest Jewish communities. In addition, New York was home to many Orthodox Jewish physicians and scientists and to many Jewish hospitals. This stimulating environment provided my father with many opportunities to further develop the still-fledgling field of Jewish medical ethics.

During this period, he continued to lecture widely, locally and

30. The problem of bridging religious and secular ethical systems has been reviewed by B. Newman, "Talking Ethics with Strangers: A View from Jewish Tradition," *Journal of Medical Philosophy, 18* (1993) 549–567.

throughout the country. Among my warmest childhood memories are those special evenings when I would accompany him to a lecture within driving distance from home. I still recall how invigorating he found these interchanges, especially the question-and-answer periods that followed the main presentation. I remember being struck by the broad similarity in the questions asked by the varied audiences. Notably, there was always at least one questioner whose agenda focused primarily on attacking the supremacy of the Torah, the authority of the rabbis—particularly the Orthodox ones—and the relevance of religion altogether to modern medical practice. It amazed me to hear how many people seemed to know of Hillel's *pruzbul* device, and how many used it as the paradigm of rabbinic flexibility. These challenges offered my father ready opportunities to expand his discussion by emphasizing the broad moral and ennobling doctrines of Judaism as applied to the contemporary scene.

I also recall that many medical ethics lectures in those days began with a plea that ethical decision making in medicine be seen as a discrete and necessary subspecialty. Just as a nonspecialist physician would turn to a specialist cardiologist or neurologist for help with a difficult cardiac or neurologic problem, physicians ought to seek help from ethics specialists when faced with moral dilemmas. Frequently, these arguments prompted vigorous resistance by physicians who regarded their professional training and experience as license to pronounce on the ethical as well as the technical nature of their ministrations. These attitudes reflected the generally unchallenged paternalistic posture of physicians in those days. A measure of the enormous change that has occurred in this regard is indicated by the currently widespread acceptance of ethics programs, and even ethics departments, in medical schools and university medical centers as compared with the entire absence of—nay, resistance to—"outside" expertise in those early days.

The Fifth Avenue Synagogue provided a venue for my father to develop important medical relationships over many years. During these years, he conducted a biweekly *shiur* (class) attended by dozens of physicians, nurses, and allied medical personnel. This *shiur* has had a reincarnation in recent years in London, where my father meets every month or two with about twenty doctors and allied professionals. The purpose of these encounters is to support bidirectional flow of information. My father gains updated information about current medical advances and problems; the audience gains by hearing authentically Jewish insights and evaluations directly related to their practices.

In New York, prominent regular participants included Dr. Shimon Glick, now of Ben-Gurion Medical Center in Beersheva, and the late *mohel* (ritual circumciser) Rabbi Z. Krohn. The cross-fertilization of ideas and concepts bore numerous fruits. One was the development, for the first time, of a practical guide for Jewish doctors and the institutions in which they work.[31] The guide was designed to help doctors deal with the ritual and the medical ethical problems arising in the care of observant Jewish patients. By now, over 100,000 copies of the *Hospital Compendium*—now in its sixth edition—have been distributed. It continues to serve as a model of the application of traditional sources to modern medical perplexities. Similarly, the committee in which my father brought together rabbis, attorneys, physicians, and philosophers remains a paragon of interdisciplinary approaches to vexing societal difficulties.

In spite of increased rabbinic and communal responsibilities, the early 1960s continued to see literary activity. Articles on the history of *halachah* in medicine,[32] pain control,[33] and medical aspects of circumcision[34] and *kohanim* (priests)[35] in medicine appeared in various formats.

---

31. *A Hospital Compendium: a Guide to Jewish Moral and Religious Principles in Hospital Practice* (New York: Commission on Synagogue Relations, 1963). Reprinted under the title "Medicine and Religion—the Jewish View," *Nu Sigma Nu 48* (1963), 48–56.

32. "The Inexhaustible Wealth of the Bible—and Medicine," in Jacob B. Glenn, ed., *The Bible and Modern Medicine* (New York: 1959), 47.

33. "The Consideration of Human Pain in Jewish Law," in *The Hebrew Medical Journal Semi-Annual Publication 32*, 1 (1959), 161–168, translated from Hebrew; and "Human Pain in Jewish Law" (Hebrew), in M.M. Kasher, N. Lamm, and L. Rosenfeld, eds., *Sefer HaYovel in Honor of Rabbi Dr. L. Jung* (New York: 1962) 133–141.

34. See note 17.

35. See note 18.

AUTOPSY

One of the major points of divergence between halachic and general medical ethics pertains to the attitudes to autopsy. In Jewish circles, the debate was greatly exacerbated by the battle that raged in Israel over the last several decades. The autopsy issue became one of the flashpoints that characterized the strained and often bitter relationships between the observant and nonobservant camps in Israel, and between the rabbinic and medical professions. Thus, the issue became one of more than only technical halachic interest. In Israel, government coalitions were threatened and political pacts were secured in relation to attitudes on this divisive issue.

Over the years, my father had discussed and documented the traditional attitudes to autopsy in several comprehensive articles,[36] in addition to the chapter in *Jewish Medical Ethics.* Taken together, these analyze the history and development of the traditional opposition to routine autopsies. However, my father went beyond the halachic details by also stressing an overall appreciation of Jewish sensitivity and thinking as reflected in this apparently narrow ritualistic area of concern. He argued that the opposition to autopsies should be seen as something more than merely an ancient restrictive regulation. Rather, it demonstrates in a powerful way the high standards of humane care that Judaism demands of its practitioners. The law's ultimate goal should not be obscured by attention to detail, no matter how important such scrupulous attention is. Judaism's overriding interest is to promote dignified

---

36. "The Dissection of the Dead in Jewish Law—a Comparative and Historical Study," *Tradition 1*, 1 (1958), 77–103; "The Dissection of the Dead in Jewish Law," in *The Hebrew Medical Journal Semi-Annual Publication 33*, 1 (1960), 210–222, and *33*, 2 (1960), 212–221, translated from Hebrew; "The Religious Problem of Autopsies in New York Jewish Hospitals: a Preliminary Report," *The Hebrew Medical Journal—Annual Combined Israel Edition 34*, 2 (1961), 262–267, and *The Hebrew Medical Journal Semi-Annual Publication 34*, 2 (1961), 233–238; "Regarding Autopsies in Jewish Law," *Torah Sh'ba'al Peh: Presentations at the Sixth National Conference for Torah Sh'ba'al Peh* (Jerusalem: Mossad Harav Kook, 1964), 61–66, in Hebrew; and "Autopsies," *Tradition 7*, 1 (1965), 88–92.

care and respect for people even in death, thereby underscoring the even higher standards of dignified and considerate care owed to the living. The frequently encountered medical attitude that views patients as cases and relates to them merely as scientific challenges and curiosities would be largely dispelled were the profession to insist on dignified and thoughtful approaches to even the most defenseless—the deceased—in its care. The Torah expresses its concern for the respect of the deceased in two contexts. First, even the High Priest, normally prohibited from defiling himself even for his own parents, must do so by personally attending to the burial of an unclaimed body. Second, the corpses of criminals executed by the state must be buried by nightfall. The Torah chooses to teach the high regard that obtains to the human body even in death by insisting on the respect owed to the most defenseless members of society, the vagabond and the criminal. Note how sharply this approach contrasts with that of many Christian European centers, where the most likely cadavers for medical-school instruction were unclaimed bodies and the corpses of executed criminals!

Characteristically, my father often developed these points as examples of how the Orthodox camps in Israel, in particular, could transmit its values in such a way as to have a reinforcing influence, as opposed to merely a restraining one, on the wider society. My father always encourages Orthodox groups to vocalize the broader overarching socioethical consequences of adhering to the authentic values of our faith with as much vigor as they defend their civil rights in protecting their traditions.

PROCREATION

My father devoted many articles to clarifying the halachic attitude to contraception,[37] population control,[38] and the problems of

37. "Birth-control," *Tradition 3*, 2 (1961), 224–226; "The 'Pill' and Jewish Law," *Jewish Digest 11*, 9 (1966), 57–60; "Artificial Insemination," *Tradition 8*, 2 (1966), 81–83.

38. "Population Explosion—the Jewish Attitude to Birth-control: Edited and Annotated Transcript of the Jewish Marriage Education Council Annual Lecture, delivered on October 28, 1968" (1969), reprinted in *Child and Family 9*, 3 (1970), 241–251.

abortion.[39] As in the case of autopsy, he frequently stressed the wider social implications of halachic guidelines in addition to the more narrowly focused legal aspects. He often argued that the ready availability of contraceptive and abortion services gave birth to the age of "credit-card morality," enabling people to "enjoy now and pay later." Regarding abortion, especially in Israel's current liberal social environment, he emphasized the enormous aggregate losses to the population because of widespread birth control. These losses, which now account for many tens of thousands, if not millions, would have matured into homegrown *sabras* (native-born Israelis), obviating the need for the vast financial and human resources expended over the years in promoting immigration and facilitating absorption. The demographic and geopolitical implications of these losses can only be guessed at. These arguments, which he also made in many personal representations to Israel's leadership, demonstrate in a concrete way how the application of authentic Jewish values has broad positive significance to contemporary society at large.[40] Reasoning cast in this language is more likely to persuade those who do not share the commitment to, and understanding of, our Torah-based beliefs.

Limitations on Jewish procreation have great implications beyond the boarders of Israel, too. My father often says: "Nothing is more indispensable to the strengthening of our people and the

---

39. "Abortion," *Tradition 6*, 2 (1964), 114–115; "Jewish Views on Abortion," *Western Reserve Law Review 17*, 2 (1965), 480–497, reprinted numerous times.

40. My father's elevation to the House of Lords reflects the esteem in which his views were held by the then-Prime Minister, Margaret Thatcher. My father once observed that though the conservative social agenda is often in striking agreement with our Torah-based timeless values, the ultimate driving concern of the secular approach is their analysis of the economic—not moral—consequences of their platform. Economic vitality can only be fostered in a secure, wholesome, and healthy society, free of drugs and other socially detrimental disorders such as rampant crime, alcoholism, and sexual licentiousness that have such demonstrably devastating effects on the stability of families—the basic social building block—and on the integrity of individuals, namely, AIDS and alcohol-related disease.

assurance of its continuity than having children."[41] Clearly, segments of our people who have adopted Western standards by having 1.7 children per couple will contribute to significantly diminishing demographics. If it takes two people to reproduce less than two children, our members can only dwindle with each generation. Greatly accelerated shrinkage can be anticipated if one adds the tremendous losses owing to assimilation and intermarriage. This sets the stage for asking with real fear whether Jews are a disappearing people, a notion which, even in the darkest days of our people's persecution, when our total numbers were estimated at less than a million people over many centuries, never crossed anyone's mind! If present trends continue, the only Jews left will be the strictly observant ones. Alarm over the repercussions of curtailed propagation to Jewish national survival recalls Rachel's lament to her husband, Jacob: "Give me children, for otherwise I am dead."[42]

TRADITION

A particularly original and enduring literary enterprise during the New York years was my father's founding editorship of the column titled "Review of Recent Halakhic Periodical Literature." This ongoing commentary, which he began in the Fall 1961 issue of *Tradition*, was a digest of rabbinic responsa and other articles on a wide range of issues.

Topics were varied and included items from all areas of rabbinic interest. Among the medical entries are sections on birth control[43]; corneal transplants[44]; medical experimentation on animals[45]; *kohanim* (priests) studying medicine[46]; deformed and Thalidomide

41. "Large Jewish Families," *Midstream 29*, 8 (The Theodore Herzl Foundation, 1983), 39–43.

42. Genesis 30:1.

43. "Birth-control," *Tradition 3*, 2 (1961), 224–226.

44. "Corneal Transplants," *Tradition 4*, 1 (1961), 97–99.

45. "Medical Experiments on Animals," *Tradition 4*, 1 (1961), 101–102.

46. "May a Kohen Study Medicine?" *Tradition* 4, 2 (1962), 262–264.

babies[47]; prayers for the sick[48]; abortion[49]; circumcision of proselytes[50]; autopsy[51]; oral contraception[52]; circumcision by nonobservant *mohelim* (ritual circumcisers)[53]; accompanying women in labor on the Sabbath[54]; the blind in Jewish law[55]; artificial insemination[56]; mourning for deceased babies[57]; and experiments on humans.[58] Somewhat more general, but equally important, reviews discuss rabbinic decision making[59] and objectivity in *halachah*.[60] Ultimately, the competing pressures of the British Chief Rabbinate, which he assumed in 1967, forced my father to relinquish the column, which he bequeathed to the notably adept and versatile pen of Rabbi J. David Bleich.

THE MATURATION OF JEWISH MEDICAL ETHICS

Since the appearance of *Jewish Medical Ethics*, several developments confirm the remarkable maturation of Jewish medical ethics over the ensuing five decades. First, there has been a veritable explosion

---

47. "Deformed Babies," *Tradition* 5, 2 (1963), 267–268; and "Thalidomide Babies," *Tradition* 5, 2 (1963), 268–270.
48. "Prayers for the Sick," *Tradition* 6, 1 (1963), 88–90.
49. "Abortion," *Tradition* 6, 2 (1964), 114–115.
50. "Circumcision of Proselytes," *Tradition* 6, 2 (1964), 119–120.
51. "Autopsies," *Tradition* 7, 1 (1965), 88–92.
52. "Oral Contraceptives," *Tradition* 7, 2 (1965), 123–126.
53. "Circumcision by Non-observant Mohel," *Tradition* 7, 3 (1965), 66–67.
54. "Accompanying Women in Labor on the Sabbath," *Tradition* 7, 3 (1965), 67–68.
55. "The Blind in Jewish Law," *Tradition* 7, 3 (1965), 319–320.
56. "Artificial Insemination," *Tradition* 8, 2 (1966), 81–83.
57. "Mourning Laws for Babies, *Tradition* 8, 3 (1966), 57–58.
58. "Experiments on Humans," *Tradition* 8, 4 (1966), 105–108.
59. "The Dynamics of Rabbinic Law-making," *Tradition* 4, 1 (1961), 96–97.
60. "Objectivity in the Halakhic Process," *Tradition* 7, 1 (1965), 86–88.

in secondary texts devoted to Jewish medical ethics written in the current vernacular.[61] There has also been an enormous increase in periodical literature. Leading specialty rabbinic[62] and communal[63] journals in this country and abroad almost always include some medically related article in each issue. This growth is reflected in the striking fact that while the original *Jewish Encyclopedia* (1901–1906) had not a single entry devoted to medical ethics, the current *Encyclopedia Judaica* (1972) has over a dozen, many of them contributed by my father.[64] Extensive comprehensive encyclopedias[65] of *halachah* and medicine, in Hebrew, have recently been added as an entirely new genre to the growing library of resources, further attesting to the current vigorous growth in many areas of halachic concern.

---

61. In addition to *Jewish Medical Ethics*, English-language works include: David M. Feldman, *Marital Relations, Birth Control and Abortion in Jewish Law* (New York: Schocken Books, 1968); A.S. Abraham, *Medical Halakhah for Everyone* (Jerusalem: Feldheim Publishing Co., 1980); J.D. Bleich, *Judaism and Healing* (New York: Ktav Publishing House, 1981); J.D. Bleich, *Contemporary Halakhic Problems* (New York: Ktav Publishing House, 1977); F. Rosner, *Modern Medicine and Jewish Law* (New York: Yeshiva University Press, 1972); F. Rosner and J. D. Bleich, eds., Jewish Bioethics (New York: Hebrew Publishing Co., 1979); F. Rosner, *Modern Medicine and Jewish Ethics*, 2nd rev. ed., (New York: Ktav and Yeshiva University Press, 1991); F. Rosner, *Medicine and Jewish Law* I and II (Northvale N.J.: Jason Aronson Inc., 1990 and 1993).

62. For example, *Tradition* and *The Journal of Contemporary Halakha* in English, and *HaPardes* and *Ohr HaMizrah* in Hebrew.

63. *L'Eylah* (now *Le'ela*), *Jewish Action*, and *Jewish Observer*, among others.

64. *Encyclopedia Judaica* articles: "Artificial Insemination," Vol. 3, cols. 660–661; "Birth Control," Vol. 4, cols 1053–1054; "Castration," Vol. 5, cols. 242–243; "Celibacy," Vol. 5, cols. 268–269; "Euthanasia," Vol. 6, cols. 978–979; "Sex," Vol. 14, cols. 1206–1207 (Jerusalem: *Encyclopedia Judaica*, 1971).

65. Examples include the multiauthored *Halakha V'Refuah*, Rabbi Moshe Hirschler, ed. (from 1980); *Nishmat Avraham* organized as a commentary on the *Shulkhan Arukh*, Dr. Abraham Sofer-Abraham (from 1983); and *Encyclopedia Halakhtit Refuit* arranged alphabetically, Dr. Abraham Steinberg (from 1988).

The plethora of books and journals recently has been crowned by the establishment, mainly in Israel, of independent[66] and university-based[67] centers for the study of Jewish medical ethics. Chief in the last-named category are the Jakobovits Center for the Study of Jewish Medical Ethics at Ben-Gurion Medical Center in Beersheva and the Falk Schlesinger Institute at the Shaare Zedek Hospital in Jerusalem. In addition to confirming the expansion and recognition of the specialty as an academic discipline, these developments point to the broadening acceptance of the guiding role that religiously based ethical analysis can provide for those who would submit to its values and guidelines. Such institutes are also now attached to the Albert Einstein College of Medicine in New York and Jews' College in London.

EUTHANASIA AND DEATH

Momentous scientific and social forces have catapulted many medical-ethics issues into the public arena. The overwhelming number of medical-ethical dilemmas[68] are concentrated at or near either end of life. The marriage of technology and medicine in ways that allow physicians to "really make a difference" even in the care of critically ill individuals scares many people and excites many others. Many of medical ethics' most vexing problems converge at the end of life. With the passage of time, the problems of this difficult period have become more complex and perplexing. The growing application of technologically invasive medical techniques in the care of dying patients has led to a concomitant array of general and Jewishly based medical ethical deliberations. The notion of playing God crosses the minds of many. Coupled with the competing claims of limited resources and limitless care are the

66. E.g., the Jerusalem Institute.

67. E.g., at Ben-Gurion University Medical School, Bar-Ilan.

68. "A Modern Doctor's Dilemma," *The Jewish Chronicle* 5, 108 (1967), 7. The title recalls the famous treatise written by George Bernard Shaw.

competing interests of different religious and cultural values. In fact, it is this area more than any other in medicine to which the whole "resurrection" of medical ethics has been largely, and correctly, attributed. Euthanasia and, in its currently fashionable nomenclature, physician-assisted suicide; artificial prolongation of life; distribution of scarce resources; defining death; and transplant technology are among the high-profile medical issues that have captured the attention of the wider public, driving the burgeoning developments in medical ethics.

One of the more contentious areas that the new medicine forced into consideration was the definition of death. Whereas in days gone by this was mainly of academic interest, the pressing demand for viable donor organs engendered by the advent of successful transplant therapy created an urgent need for a precise, but ever-earlier, definition of death. All cultures and legal systems recognize that the donor must be dead before vital organs can be removed, even for a needy recipient. Nevertheless, as an influential medical committee reasoned,[69] death could be redefined in light of new pressures. The concept of "brain death," in contradistinction to systemic death, was introduced. Artificial ventilatory support allows a brain-dead person, even a brainstem-dead person, to carry on vital metabolic functions, thus assuring the vitality of his organs while still being classified as dead in a legal and moral sense for purposes of removal of vital organs.

My father's attitude to the sharp debate that ensued regarding the halachic attitude to brain-death definitions is characteristic of his personal—and rabbinic—demeanor in general. First, he often stresses the principle that, even regarding his own views, though usually firmly argued and not infrequently at odds with the prevailing wisdom, he would never insist that others *kablu da'ati*[70] (should uncritically accept his view). Therefore, he renounces the oft-stated rigid views that have characterized many opinions in the

69. "A Definition of Irreversible Coma. Report of the Ad Hoc Committee of the Harvard Medical School to Examine the Definition of Brain Death," *Journal of the American Medical Association 205* (1968): 337–340.

70. In accordance with the dictate of R. Yishmael in *Pirkei Avot* 4:10.

brain-death controversy. Opinions expressed with aggressiveness are not likely to sound authentic simply because they are declared stridently. A favored dictum cautions: *divrei chachamim b'nachas nishmaim*[71] (the words of the wise are *heard* [as being said] softly). Notice that it does not say that a wise man speaks softly; that degree of propriety is taken for granted. Rather, the dictum stresses that a wise person's pronouncements are "*heard* softly"—crafted in such a way as to be perceived as emanating from a deliberate and thoughtful mind. Declarations issued in a reflective and considered tone are "heard"; views expressed shrilly, or as if they are "shot from the hip," are not. In passing, one might add that this attitude has often governed my father's political views, too.

Second, my father holds the view that it is necessary to establish beyond a shadow of doubt that the *halachah* accepts a person as dead before canceling his hitherto unchallenged presumption of life, *chezkas chai*. Given that we are dealing here with a *safek issur retzikha* (a possibility of murder), one should have to establish the donor's death with absolute certainty. Since the debate regarding brain death continues unabated, one must err on the side of caution. Though of immense concern, the welfare of the recipient could not enter the equation; depriving the donor of even a few moments of life would never be sanctioned, even in order to offer the possibility of many years of life to the recipient.[72]

Incidentally, my father once suggested a compelling mathematical rationale for the absolute halachic prohibition to shorten life, even for the sake of another (*ein dochin nefhesh mipnei nefhesh*[73]). The underlying halachic principle is that all life is infinite in value. Hence, since infinity is indivisible, every fraction of life remains equally infinite in value. Conversely, the reverse is also true: infinity cannot be enlarged by multiplication. Hence, the ruling by Maimonides,[74] that hostages must all submit to death rather than to surrender one of their number to the enemy as a martyr. In

71. Kohelet 9:17.

72. "HaRav Lord Jakobovits Introduces Symposium on Brain Death," *Le'ela* (March 1996), 29.

73. *Yad HaHazakah*, Hil. Yesodei HaTorah, 5:7.

74. Ibid., 5:5, based on *Mishnah Terumot*, Chap. 8.

characteristic fashion, and in contrast with secular legal systems, the *halachah* expresses itself in concrete cases, not in general principles. The principles of halachic thought evolve from specific cases—not the reverse.

MEDICAL EXPERIMENTATION

The continuing development of medical *halachah* directly reflects the developments of medicine itself. Key to the enormous growth of medicine—and often its ancillary problems—is the scientifically based research and development to which thousands of physician-scientists the world over devote their energies and their sponsors' funds. The issue of experimental cures has been often discussed, and many Jewish authorities have analyzed the issues at stake. My father takes the view that medical experimentation per se is permissible, provided that the patient himself would be the first to gain from the "experiment" at hand.[75] Therefore, therapy that is provided solely to determine its usefulness for others would be censured; therapy designed for potential usefulness in the patient at hand, notwithstanding the risks, can be sanctioned, if there are no alternatives.

COSMETIC SURGERY

Most of the ethical dilemmas of medicine occur at one of life's ends, either in relation to conception or abortion at the beginning or in relation to the management of terminal illness and post-mortem at the end. In between these poles, there are relatively fewer halachic

75. "Experiments on humans," *Tradition 8*, 4 (1966), 105–108; A. Steinberg, ed., "Medical Experimentation on the Living," *Sefer Assia 1*, 2 (Jerusalem, 1971), 5–7, in Hebrew; and "Halakhic Guidelines for Medical Research and Experimentation," *Hebrew College Brookline . . . the Milender Institute of Jewish Ethics . . . Jewish Ethics in Medicine* (Brookline, Mass.: Hebrew College, 1982), 117–120.

concerns. One such topic concerns cosmetic surgery, regarding which my father contributed an important set of articles[76] to the literature, establishing some guiding principles. Although, in general, the *halachah* opposes any mutilation of the body, even with the consent of the patient, an exception is made when there are overriding medical concerns. Therefore, cosmetic procedures can be sanctioned in cases of deformity where the patient suffers significant social disabilities. An extension of this principle relates to congenital neonatal deformities, which, if left uncorrected, could have socially—as well as medically—deleterious implications.[77] In other words, provided that cosmetic treatment deals with deformities, the *halachah* would sanction medical intervention.

PERSONAL AUTONOMY

A fundamental disagreement between the values of secular ethics and the *halachah* involves the role of personal autonomy. Over the past several decades, the courts in the United States have repeatedly supported the notion that the ultimate arbiter of a person's care is that person himself. This trend is pervasive in modern society. The authority of parents, teachers, and elected officials have all undergone tremendous erosion. Similarly, in medical questions, the patient's autonomy has taken center stage and is judged supreme. Any action taken in defiance of, or without consideration of, the patient's consent constitutes unauthorized assault.

The halachic view stands in sharp contrast.[78] In fact, the patient

---

76. "Jewish Views on Cosmetic Surgery," *The Eye, Ear, Nose and Throat Monthly 41*, 2 (1962), 133–134 and 142, and *41*, 3 (1962), 220–221; and "Questions and Observations Regarding Medical Topics," *Noam 6* (Jerusalem, 1963), 271–275, reprinted under the title "Plastic Surgery for Cosmetic Purposes," A. Steinberg ed., *Sefer Assia* (Jerusalem: Shaare Zedek Hospital, 1976), 222–223, in Hebrew.

77. "Plastic Surgery on Down's Syndrome children," *L'Eylah 2*, 8 (1984), 1–3.

78. "The Doctor's Duty to Heal and the Patient's Consent," *L'Eylah 2*, (1981), 4–6, and "The Doctor's Duty to Heal and the Patient's

has no proprietary ownership rights over his body at all. A delightful essay by the late Rabbi S.Y. Zevin on halachic aspects of Shakespeare's *The Merchant of Venice*[79] traces the Jewish legal rejection of ownership of oneself in an engaging chapter titled "Shylock's Judgment." Had William Shakespeare been better versed in Jewish law, he would not have created a character—Shylock—who asked that Antonio forfeit "a pound of fair flesh to be cut off and taken in what part of your body pleaseth me" as a security for a loan. One's own flesh is not one's property to barter with. A persons' body is merely in his custody and trust; its treatment must be made in accordance with the overriding dictates of *halachah*, an ethic that devolves on oneself in the first place, but otherwise equally on all members of society: the doctors, the hospital, the courts, and the legislatures.

GENETICS

Perhaps the most significant and far-reaching development in medical science during the closing years of the twentieth century is the geometric escalation of genetic medicine. An early forerunner of applied genetics involves Tay-Sachs screening. It took the personal tragedy of a Brooklyn Chassidic family to focus attention on the need to stem the spread of this dreaded Ashkenazi Jewish disorder that results in a slow neurologic deterioration and eventual death within the first few years of life. Galvanized by the personal losses, individuals solicited the support of leading rabbinic figures in order to establish a community-based anonymous screening project. Thousands of young men and women have been tested by Dor Yesharim, one of the most successful community-based screening services in any community. The organization is credited with

---

Consent in the Jewish Tradition," in G.R. Dunstan and M.J. Seller eds., *Consent in Medicine—Convergence and Divergence in Tradition*, (London: King Edward's Hospital Fund for London, 1983), 32–36.

79. S.Y. Zevin, *LeOhr HaHalakha* (Jerusalem, 1946), referring to *The Merchant of Venice*, Act I, Scene III.

having prevented close to a hundred Tay-Sachs recessive-gene matches and the untold anguish that would have accompanied such unions. The program is conducted with two important stipulations: utmost confidentiality, and targeting of young men and women *before* they are likely to get married. Even being only a recessive gene carrier is likely to prompt a negative stigma within the relatively close-knit Jewish community. By adhering strictly to these policies, these difficulties are largely avoided.

Although this program now has wide rabbinic and general support, such was not always the case. There were significant initial concerns that general, community-based blood screening would foster a "communal neurosis" to which the Orthodox Jewish community, in particular, was thought to be especially prone.[80] In fact, the program has developed remarkably well without any of the negative effects that had been feared at first.

In addition to Tay-Sachs, Dor Yesharim now offers screening for cystic fibrosis, Canavan's disease, and Fanconi's anemia. All these disorders can be prevented by detecting recessive-gene-carrying individuals and avoiding unions between them. The mounting ethical dilemmas here are the escalating cost and the fact that although technically a voluntary procedure, many in the community find themselves under ever-increasing pressure to undergo the full panel of tests. Today's options become tomorrow's obligations. With the expectation that we now stand at the threshold of a veritable explosion of genetically feasible screening because of the Human Genome Project, we can expect numerous recessive disorders to accumulate that will "require" screening. Can—or should—there be a line drawn? Tay-Sachs and the other disorders are devastating, but what about "lesser" disorders? Might a future "*shidduch* (marriage) profile" include recessive-gene status for diabetes, heart disease, or hypertension? Some scientists expect that eventually anger, compassion, and intelligence will all have identifiable genetically based predispositions. Shall these, too, be subject to prenuptial scrutiny?

---

80. "Tay-Sachs Disease and the Jewish Community," *L'Eylah* (Autumn 5737; 1976), 17–20, reprinted in *Proceedings of the Association of Orthodox Jewish Scientists* 5 (1979), 11–17.

Although my father has not focused directly on all these issues, he has been involved in some important legislative deliberations in Britain with regard to embryology and genetic engineering.[81] The essence of these articles presents the Jewish view, which promotes procreation, provided that it is within the framework of marriage. So long as the procedures are designed for the health of the individual, there is no ethical distinction between surgery on whole body parts, microscopic elements, or even stem-cell genetic constituents. Even where genetic manipulation may have a beneficial effect on future generations, there would be no automatic halachic objection, provided that strict guidelines were enforced to guard against abuse. Altogether, the fear of abuse ought not, in itself, provoke the termination of technological enquiry completely. Legitimate apprehensions ought, however, to provoke the formulation of appropriate controls.

CRITICISM

My filial relationship and emotional ties restrict any truly impartial appraisal of my father's contributions. The fact is that little scholarly criticism has been published. One notable exception is a well-documented chapter by Marc A. Gellman, of the faculty of the Hebrew Union College, in a recent book surveying the influence of several theologians on medical ethics.[82] Dr. Gellman is the current chairman of the Medical Ethics Committee of the Federation of Jewish Philanthropies of Greater New York and, as such, has acquired—by way of Rabbi Dr. Moshe Tendler as the intervening chairman—my father's mantle.

Under the subtitle *Bringing the Ancient World to the Modern World*, Gellman first presents a biographical sketch "in tribute to

81. "Genetic Engineering," *L'Eylah 2*, 2 (1981), 3–4; "In Vitro Fertilization and Genetic Engineering," *L'Eylah 2*, 6 (1983), 1–5; and, most notably, *Human Fertilization and Embryology—a Jewish view: Submissions to the Warnock Committee of Inquiry and the Department of Health and Social Security* (London: Office of the Chief Rabbi, 1984).

82. See note 28.

the unique scope and vigor of his life and work" and of his "prescience" in launching the field of Jewish medical ethics a decade before the subject would attract the attention of other philosophers, lawyers, physicians, and theologians. Perhaps Gellman discloses his own bias by suggesting that Jewish medical ethics tests the "flexibility and vitality of Jewish law" and the "intellectual credibility of Jewish moral reasoning in the realm of modern normative ethical thinking." At the same time, he recognizes my father's fidelity to two thousand years of rabbinic moral reasoning and that, though my father "is ready to move the focus of Jewish law into the new realm of medical ethics, . . . he is not willing to alter the Jewish legal process, which has confronted novelty before without surrendering the ancient way." Actually, Gellman's is the correct analysis. Indeed, this is the fundamental approach of every authentic Jewish thinker: *haphoch bo, va'haphoch bo, d'chulah bo*[83]—the Torah encompasses all the guidelines, provided that its depths are plumbed with commitment and consistency.

What Gellman takes to be a point of criticism is, in fact, central to my father's aim in his whole approach to Jewish medical ethics, and, indeed, in his rabbinic leadership and halachic writings in general. An oft-heard complaint by non-Orthodox thinkers is that their Orthodox counterparts are not willing to be "creative" and are bound to the standards of yesteryear. Gellman feels that this has "reduced creative thinkers like Jakobovits . . . to the status of quoting responsa. . . ." Gellman argues that "the layering of interpretation of Jewish sources has thrown [many] off the track and [has] reduced [many] to the Jakobovitsian move of simply citing responsa while withholding personal judgement." Orthodox rabbis, of course, by definition always anchor themselves to the classic sources of our faith and eschew personal opinion. As they exercise their mandate, they examine the authentic Jewish viewpoints and teachings whose basic elements are enshrined in our literature stretching over thousands of years. By conscientious and sincere investigation, rabbis in each generation have unearthed teachings founded on well-defined halachic rules and guidelines. Halachic directives derived by these techniques are applicable and

83. *Pirkei Avot* 5:26.

relevant to the whole gamut of questions raised by the human condition.

THE RABBI'S ROLE

The rabbi's role, then, is decidedly not inventive. It is, above all, interpretive. In this capacity, my father has been eminently successful and renowned. His ability to marshal the sources, as evidenced in *Jewish Medical Ethics* and in the innumerable subsequent publications, is matched by the conviction and consistency, eloquence and dignity of his arguments. He uses every occasion and pronouncement to imbue the *halachah* with the spirituality that has ensured that its message endures beyond the shifting standards and mercurial mores of society and locality. It is this quality that was cited by Viscount Tonypandy, a former Speaker of the House of Commons, when he nominated my father for the 1991 Templeton Foundation's award for progress in religion.[84]

> He conveys Judaism to regulate human life whatever challenges, discoveries and changes confront society. He has continuously sought to provide authoritative Jewish answers to major questions of the day. The Chief Rabbi's contribution to medical ethics is unique and remains pre-eminent. Among his extensive writings are classic expositions of Jewish law of unsurpassed knowledge and enlightened humanity. He has been the pathfinder for a great and growing literature dealing with the most controversial social and ethical problems of our age. . . . Jakobovits' natural authority is based on his knowledge, wisdom and humanity but reflected in his genuine humility, warmth and approachability and has made him the ultimate leader of his people. His unswerving devotion to his principles have at times led him to castigate the self-imposed isolation of spiritual

84. Awarded annually since 1973, this prize endeavors to grant outstanding religious and spiritual contributions status comparable with the recognition of the Nobel Prizes for other prominent contributions to civilization. My father was the first Jewish recipient. Other awardees include Mother Teresa (1973) and Alexander Solzhenitsyn (1983).

leaders indifferent to faiths, cultures and social needs outside their own, whilst he at all times seeks to influence the society around him.

SELECTED CORRESPONDENCE

A particularly engaging presentation of my father's views and reasoning can be found by reading some of the enormous correspondence he has kept with people all over the world, from all sorts of backgrounds, touching upon all sorts of issues. A selection of these letters, written between 1980 and 1990, have been edited and arranged in book form.[85] Thirty selections of medical interest were chosen covering a wide range of topics. Typical of these are my father's responses to:

A Jewish medical-school faculty member from California who inquired as to how he should relate to non-Jewish patients when their religious beliefs governing medical choices are at odds with Jewish teachings.

> In strictly halachic terms, I have little doubt that Jewish physicians should carry out life-saving procedures even against the wishes or religious convictions of the patient concerned, whether Jewish or non-Jewish. . . . However, other considerations may also have to be taken into consideration, possibly modifying this norm. In particular we are required to avoid a *hillul haShem* [desecration of God's name] by causing "enmity" between Jews and non-Jews. . . . A Jewish physician should make every effort to secure the safety of life without consulting patients likely to object, if this can possibly be avoided, i.e., by not fully informing them of the emergency procedure to be adopted.

In explaining the Jewish attitude to the management of Down's syndrome children in *The Times* of London, my father

85. Jeffrey M. Cohen, *Dear Chief Rabbi; From the Correspondence of Chief Rabbi Immanuel Jakobovits on Matters of Jewish Law, Ethics, and Contemporary Issues, 1980–1990* Hoboken, NJ: (Ktav, 1995).

had stressed the "silver lining on the cloud" by pointing out that "the tragedy of a defective child may open up otherwise inaccessible resources of selfless love and spiritual values. The supreme objective value of a cruelly-afflicted being may well lie in the refining influence such a life exercises on those charged tenderly to protect it." Among the many responses—some supportive, but many critical—was that of an irate physician who questioned a rabbi's right to "tell doctors what their function and duties should be when caring for patients." He received this reply:

> . . . [s]urely religion has a right and a duty to speak up. . . . This clearly is a moral rather than purely medical issue, and religious leaders would betray their faith—especially a pioneer of the moral law as acutely concerned with the sanctity of life as Judaism—if they abdicated their responsibility to proclaim and explain their teachings.

An unusual *sheilah* (inquiry) was forwarded from Australia: may *oralot* (foreskins) removed by circumcision be used for medical research, or do they require burial?

> There is basically no objection to the use of *Oralot* for medical experimentation designed to serve therapeutic ends. However, in accordance with established practice, some earth should be symbolically strewn over them to be immediately washed off, and such tissue as is left more or less intact following the experiments should eventually be disposed of by interment, though of course without any ceremony. Particularly in view of the current scandals on the sale of human organs, it should also be stipulated that no payment is to be made for the *Oralot*.

Jewish law, while keeping the death penalty in the codes to indicate the gravity of a capital offense, in practice abolished it two thousand years ago by making its execution subject to effectively impossible conditions. Similarly, my father has argued that homosexuality, even if not punishable, should be kept on the books as a violation of acceptable standards. To one of many respondents, my father wrote:

> I think you should appreciate the distinction I am bound to make between condemning homosexual practice as morally objection-

> able, and encouraging any form of prejudice or discrimination against those who, while recognizing moral norms as valid standards for society at large, nevertheless are themselves unable to resist powerful natural urges which predispose them to depart from the norm. Such encouragement I would oppose as you do, provided the public stance is not compromised. As for condemnation of the practice as immoral, I am frankly not a free agent. As heir to my biblical heritage, I accept by tradition as well as by conviction the injunctions on sexual morality as proclaimed in the Book of Leviticus and elsewhere. Surely anyone raised in the Judaeo-Christian tradition will respect this and not force me—or like-minded Christians—to abandon religious as well as moral principles in which we believe. . . . I feel that society must have some formal expression of approval or disapproval in certain areas of fundamental moral concern. . . . I want to avoid the spread of undesirable practices by official expressions of neutrality or indifference, especially when—as is now evident [due to the AIDS epidemic]—this may have life-and-death consequences. The public disapprobation of these practices should help to reduce those affected and at risk.

My uncle, Mr. Max Munk of New York, sought the opinions of Rabbi David Cohen of Brooklyn and Rabbi Dr. Moses Tendler of Monsey regarding "living wills" and the treatment of the dying. He also solicited my opinion. Subsequently my uncle submitted the three responses to my father, who wrote, flatteringly, as follows:

> On the whole, I go along with the conclusions reached, particularly as formulated by Yoel. . . . I believe the whole notion of a "Living Will" is alien to Jewish thought and law. As Yoel observes, the Jewish imperatives on saving life (or allowing it to expire under certain circumstances) are incumbent equally on patient, doctor, rabbi and friends. Of these, the patient is obviously the least objective, being the most interested party. Moreover, these decisions are made in good health under conditions which may be vastly different when the relevant circumstances arise. The next-of-kin should by all means consult rabbinical and medical opinion when these difficult decisions on maintaining life by "heroic methods" arise. The wishes previously expressed by the patient

have no bearing on this decision, since no one can dispose of his own life any more than of anyone else's. The difficult judgement should be as objective, dispassionate and personally disinterested as possible, and this may exclude even the closest relatives from having a decisive say.

Moreover, I fear that "Living Wills" may often be an excuse for taking liberties in the premature suspension of treatment where the doctor may otherwise feel inclined to continue his medical efforts. I would not therefore encourage the execution of "Living Wills" under any circumstances.

HOMOSEXUAL BEHAVIOR

In exercising rabbinic leadership, my father never shied away from controversial issues and has occasionally championed unpopular views. The most controversial medical issue relates to Jewish attitudes to homosexual behavior. My father has often earned the wrath of the gay community for expressing these views. With characteristic forthrightness he wrote in an op–ed commentary in *The Times* of London[86]:

> There is little maneuverability between the moral absolutes to which I am committed and the popular latitude cherished by many. . . . The Jewish view is plain and uncompromising. All authentic sources of Judaism condemn homosexual relations as a heinous offence. No verbal acrobatics . . . can modify this verdict, harsh as it may be. Anyone who pretends otherwise deceives himself and those he addresses. . . . Moreover, the prohibition is deemed to be binding on all humans, as shown by the term sodomy—the depravity of a heathen city.
>
> We do not share the view, still widely held and advocated in other quarters, identifying the current tribulations of homosexuals as Divine vengeance. AIDS may well be an inescapable consequence of licentious conduct. . . . Such practices are evil even if they do not lead to suffering, just as conversely there are afflictions, such as

86. *The Times*, November 9, 1987.

cancer and multiple sclerosis, which cause fearful suffering although they are unrelated to human conduct.

. . . Jewish sources mention three factors as reasons for the moral abhorrence of homosexuality. The practice is execrated as an unnatural perversion, debasing the dignity of man; as a frustration of the procreative purpose of sex . . . ; and as severely damaging family life.

The "gay" lobby demands public sanction for "alternative lifestyles" principally on the grounds that homosexuality is a natural predisposition in many men and women, just as attraction to the opposite sex is in others. It is precisely a moral order based on resisting nature which the advocates of "gay rights" denounce as oppressive and discriminatory.

In the Jewish view, this argument is the most objectionable of all. What distinguishes man from the animal is above all his capacity to control and sublimate nature, to master his natural instincts and drives. . . . The price to society for tolerating or encouraging such erosion of timeless values will be heavy indeed, not only in normal terms, but in the social and economic cost of impaired family life, not to mention the terrifying burden now added by AIDS. Neither the moral nor natural law can for long be violated with impunity.

My father's elevation to the House of Lords provided yet another avenue for him to express Judaism's eternal truths as they apply to current public issues and debates. The following extract is recorded in *The Hansard*,[87] the official publication of the oral Parliamentary debates:

Quite recently, when I publicly advocated some biblical laws on morality, a demonstration was organized against me in the name of freedom of sexual preference. Presumably such freedom to choose alternative lifestyles now means that adultery or incest between consenting parties should also no longer be denounced as morally wrong. Today it is a sin to speak about moral wrongs. By noisy protests, a minority seeks to impose its views on the morally-sensitive majority under pain of intimidation and defamation. . . . I am sure I speak for many in applauding the Education Secretary for remov-

---

87. *The Hansard* (London: Her Majesty's Printing Office, December 8, 1993), cols. 968–970, in a debate titled "Obligations of Citizenship."

> ing sex education in schools from morally-neutral science and insisting on relating it to moral responsibilities and family values. I recall when the AIDS (educational) campaign was first launched under the slogan, "Don't Die of Ignorance," I told the Education Secretary that this was misleading. Ignorance is not a fatal disease; no one dies of it. People die as a consequence of undisciplined behavior. Indeed, more important than clean needles are clean conduct and clean thoughts.

My father then responded with typical confidence and directness to those liberal opinions that rail against "indoctrinating" children, pleading rather that they should be allowed to decide for themselves when they grow up.

> . . . Imagine we were to adopt the same attitude towards the sciences and the arts. Imagine that we did not teach our children the discoveries of Pythagoras, Archimedes, or Newton and left them to find those insights for themselves. Imagine not introducing them to the artistic creations, the literature or history of past masters, leaving our children to explore those human attainments and discover them on their own. . . . Do we really expect our young people to have the genius of an Abraham or a Moses in discovering monotheism and social justice or the originality of our greatest thinkers and scholars? Do we expect that our youth will arrive unaided and unguided at conclusions which it took mankind's finest brains and most inspired minds to reach in thousands of years of accumulated wisdom? What a strange and pernicious doctrine that in matters of faith and morals we may not communicate the intellectual and spiritual heritage of earlier giants lest our children be subject to indoctrination.

CONCLUSION

In conclusion, I have tried to present a personal yet accurate sketch of my father's contributions to Jewish medical ethics. I have emphasized the courageous way in which he presents Jewish moral teachings, true to authentic sources, on the one hand, and in contemporary terms on the other. Without exaggeration, in addition to being my biologic father, he is the undisputed father of Jewish medical ethics. May he be granted many years in good health to continue to energize this field, along with the many other fields of Jewish concern that have been enriched by his leadership and teachings.

Rabbi Eliezer Yehudah Waldenberg (1920–)

AVRAHAM STEINBERG, M.D.

BIOGRAPHIC NOTES

For many years, Rabbi Waldenberg served as a rabbinic judge (*dayan*) in rabbinic courts in Tel Aviv and in Jerusalem. He was for many years the head of the District Rabbinic Court in Jerusalem, and he subsequently became one of the most distinguished halachic authorities in the Supreme Rabbinical Court of Israel, in Jerusalem.

Rabbi Waldenberg has dealt with all issues of medicine and *halachah* in a most prolific manner. In this field, Rabbi Waldenberg has published more responsa and articles than any other halachic authority. Many of the questions were posed to Rabbi Waldenberg by physicians at the Shaare Zedek Medical Center in Jerusalem, in whose synagogue he prayed regularly and where he gave regular classes in medicine and *halachah* to physicians of Jerusalem. Rabbi Waldenberg did not rule on halachic issues in the haste of the moment; rather, he preferred to receive a written question and learn all the relevant facts and details, including the scientific aspects. Only after a careful and detailed survey of all halachic sources did he arrive at a clear and unambiguous decision.

Rabbi Waldenberg has distinguished himself through the publication of many important halachic texts, including his magnum opus, the multivolume (22 volumes to date) and renowned *Responsa Tzitz Eliezer*. He has earned great respect and has received many important awards, chief among them the Israel Prize and the Shaare Zedek Prize for Medicine and Halachah.

In chronological order, his published books include:

D'var Eliezer, Vol. 1, 1935—novellae on the Talmud and Maimonides' *Mishneh Torah*.

Hilchot Medina, Vol. 1, 1952—concerning judges, courts, and legal punishment in our days.

Hilchot Medina, Vol. 2, 1953—concerning laws of war and the army in Israel.

Hilchot Medina, Vol. 3, 1955—concerning governmental policies and elections.

Shevitat Ha'Yam, 1955—concerning laws of shipping and sea travel on the Sabbath.

Kuntres Hasiru Michshol Miderech Ami, 1956—concerning the Karaites and the translocation of burial sites from around the grave of Maimonides in Tiberias.

Even Yaakov, 1962—novellae on *Shulchan Aruch*, *Yore Deah*, and *Hilchot Semachot*, concerning laws of mourning.

Chief among Rabbi Waldenberg's halachic works and publications are his 22 volumes of *Responsa Tzitz Eliezer*, 1943–1996. Issues from all spheres of Jewish life are discussed and ruled upon in over 1,350 sections. Medicohalachic issues are dealt with in 300 sections, forming 22 percent of the book's sections. Many of these sections are lengthy monographs, including many chapters and paragraphs devoted mainly to Sabbath laws and medicine, medicohalachic problems related to modern fertility technology, triage decisions, and problems related to organ transplantation.

Hilchot Rofi'im U'Refuah, a book that includes all medicohalachic issues discussed in the first 13 volumes of *Responsa Tzitz Eliezer*, was published by Avraham Steinberg (Jerusalem: Mosad Harav Kook Publishing, 1978). This is a compilation, distillation, and arrangement of that material. This book was translated into English as *Jewish Medical Law* by David B. Simon (Jerusalem/California: Gefen Publishing, 1980).

The following discussion is a concise summary of some of Rabbi Waldenberg's halachic contributions to medicine. For a full appreciation of Rabbi Waldenberg's important writings on medicine and *halachah*, the reader is encouraged to search the Hebrew and English versions of *Hilchot Rof'im U'Refuah* and *Jewish Medical Law*, and particularly the 22 volumes of *Responsa Tzitz Eliezer.*

THE PHYSICIAN AND THE PATIENT

A physician is considered to be God's emissary on Earth to heal the sick. The physician is permitted and even required to treat patients according to currently acceptable medical standards and need not fear that he will err. The physician fulfills two positive biblical commandments in the performance of his duties: first, the commandment of returning a lost object (i.e, the patient's health) to its rightful owner; and second, the commandment of loving one's neighbor. A physician who refrains from healing to the detriment of the patient is considered a murderer. However, a court of law cannot punish such a physician, and the patient or his heirs cannot claim compensation in a court of law. The physician must regard his profession with the utmost seriousness and must be extremely meticulous in his medical practice. In case of doubt, he should consult with more knowledgeable physicians and ignore those who may ridicule him for this. It is permitted for a less experienced physician to treat patients even if a more knowledgeable physician is available, provided that the more knowledgeable physician cannot treat all the patients, or if the better physician charges a higher fee than the patient can afford, or where it is difficult to get an appointment with the expert. If a physician is called to treat a seriously ill patient while he (the physician) is in the midst of prayer, he should immediately attend to the patient, even if the proper time of prayer will, in the meantime, pass.

Just as the physician is obligated to heal, the patient is commanded to seek medical attention and is not allowed to refuse standard medical treatment. When a person becomes ill, he is not permitted to rely upon miracles for his cure but is required to consult a physician. He who disregards this norm is not only foolish but self-destructive. Both physician and patient are required to place their trust in God.

References

Responsa Tzitz Eliezer, Part 4, 13:2, Part 8, 15:7:21; Part 9, 17:7:6–7; Part 10, 25:19:2, 25:21:4–7; Part 11, 17:2:2, 41–42; Part 17, 2; Part 19, 63.

MEDICINE ON THE SABBATH

General Considerations

Every rabbi is required to teach his community the laws pertaining to the saving of lives on the Sabbath before the practical necessity arises. The desecration of the Sabbath for a life-threatening illness should be done by any person available at the moment. One should not search for a non-Jew or a minor; it is a greater *mitzvah* to perform the action oneself than to delegate it to another. One should not be self-righteous and say that someone else should desecrate the Sabbath, for it is a great privilege to save a Jewish life. Medical and nursing care preferably should be given by a religious Jewish physician or nurse, even if a non-Jewish healthcare provider is immediately available.

Any action, even if normally prohibited by biblical law, may be performed in the usual manner on behalf of a dangerously ill patient. One is not allowed to be stringent or pious with respect to the desecration of the Sabbath. If a Jewish physician treating a patient would rather have a non-Jew perform the forbidden act—as is customary in certain places—and a non-Jew is readily available, he must inform all present that a Jew also could have performed the same action. Similarly, if an act is performed with a *shinuy* (change from its usual performance), an announcement should be made informing all present that, in life-threatening situations, the act could have been done in the usual manner had it not been just as easy to do it in an unusual manner.

When dealing with danger to life, one must desecrate the Sabbath even for the suspicion of a minority doubt of danger to life.

This is true, however, only on two conditions: (1) The factor giving rise to the suspicion of minority doubt is present now in tangible form, and (2) the seriously ill patient for whom the Sabbath will be desecrated is currently present. In the event of two divergent medical opinions, one should follow the more lenient opinion and desecrate the Sabbath. If one is already desecrating the Sabbath by doing part of what is necessary for the patient, one is permitted to perform the rest, even that which could be postponed until after the Sabbath.

It is permitted not only to initiate therapy for the dangerously ill, but also to continue it after the patient is no longer in life-threatening danger, for we fear that if treatment is stopped, he may suffer a relapse.

It is appropriate to prepare, within a hospital, all necessary medical supplies prior to the onset of the Sabbath. Such supplies include, for example, sterile syringes, sterile bandages of various sizes, paper numbers for recording vital signs, and physician's orders for frequently prescribed medications.

Neighbors who can provide needed supplies or food for a dangerously ill patient before the Sabbath are not legally required to do so, for one is permitted to violate Sabbath laws in order to provide the patient with his demands. However, it is considered an act of kindness and a sanctification of God's name for them to volunteer to supply the patient's needs, thereby obviating the violation of Sabbath or dietary laws.

References

Responsa Tzitz Eliezer, Part 8, 15:1–2, 7; Part 9, 15:7:14, 15:9:7–8, 17:2:6, 17:10:2; Part 11, 17:2:25.

Types of Patients

All the principles of Sabbath desecration for a dangerously ill patient obviously apply to an adult Jew. However, they also apply to the following people: a dangerously ill patient who has no long-term possibility to survive, even if it is doubtful that medical intervention would prolong the patient's life for even a short period; a *tereifah* (nonviable person); a minor; a deaf–mute; a mentally ill person; a fetus; a non-observant Jew; a suicidal patient, or any other patient who has intentionally placed himself in a dangerous situation; and a gentile.

A pregnant woman in labor may be brought to the hospital by car on the Sabbath. If she requests that a companion accompany her because she is afraid to go alone, she may be so accompanied. Even if she does not request a companion, she should still be accompanied by someone, such as her husband, to avoid transgressing the prohibition of seclusion (*yichud*).

References

Responsa Tzitz Eliezer, Part 6, 40:1:8–9; Part 7, 44; Part 8, 15:3:1–15, 15:6, 15:9, 15:89; Part 9, 17:1, 17:2:8–10, 14, 17:6, 17:8, 25:11, 28:11, Part 10, 25:17:3, 25:19:1, 25:27; Part 12, 33.

Types of Diseases

Diseases explicitly stated by the talmudic Sages to be life-threatening retain that status regardless of modern medical opinion. Thus, one should approach these diseases as possibly life-threatening and desecrate the Sabbath for them, although modern physicians consider them as non-life-threatening. One may desecrate the Sabbath for a patient suffering from high fever associated with a toxic appearance or accompanied by chills. However, high fever that is due to a cold is not considered life-threatening. When dealing with a child, however, it is permitted to desecrate the Sabbath for any temperature above 37°C (98.6°F).

Since, according to modern medical conceptualization, isolated danger to a single organ rarely exists, it is permitted to desecrate the Sabbath in order to treat that organ as long as there is a possibility that extension of the local disease to systemic proportion may occur.

For the following medical conditions, it is permissible to desecrate the Sabbath to treat them appropriately:

Dislocated joints and fractures requiring reduction.

Disease of one or both eyes manifested by purulent discharge, pain and tearing, or bloody discharge, provided that the disease is not yet in its terminal stage. This applies to any situation that might cause blindness. However, if the eye is in the process of healing, one may not desecrate the Sabbath during its treatment.

Existing danger of bilateral blindness, even if no systemic danger is present.

Mental illness; this applies, however, only to medical or psychiatric therapy, not to remedies that have no exact scientific basis.

Epilepsy.

Patients whose treatment in the hospital was finished on the Sabbath cannot be transferred home by car on the Sabbath, even if there is a remote possibility of contracting a nosocomial infection in the hospital.

References

Responsa Tzitz Eliezer, Part 8, 15:10:1–14; Part 13, 35:1; Part 18, 13; Part 19, 29.

Types of Treatment

It is forbidden to place a bandage with ointment on a wound on the Sabbath. However, if one prepared bandages with ointment before the Sabbath with the intention of using them on the Sabbath, it is permitted to use them. It is also forbidden to smear any ointment, whether thick or thin, on one's body on the Sabbath. It is permitted, however, to apply ointment to a wound provided that the ointment is only dabbed on.

If a wound is deep—and certainly if it is bleeding profusely—it is permitted for the physician to apply medication and bandages as needed. It is always more desirable to apply a bandage with adhesive tape than to tie a double knot, even if one intends to remove the bandage on the next day. It is preferable to apply tape to the bandage rather than to the patient's skin. One should make all efforts to prepare bandages of various types and sizes before the Sabbath.

It is permissible to apply sutures to a bleeding wound and to tie them if they are to be removed after several days.

It is permitted to reduce a dislocated joint or a fractured bone on the Sabbath.

It is forbidden to use an enema on the Sabbath as a treatment for constipation. However, if the patient complains of abdominal pain, it is permitted.

It is permitted to give an intramuscular or subcutaneous injection to a non-dangerously ill patient on the Sabbath. It is forbidden to inject intravenous substances into a non-dangerously ill patient on the Sabbath. This, however, is forbidden only by rabbinic law. It is forbidden by biblical law to sterilize needles and syringes on the Sabbath. However, on behalf of a dangerously ill patient, such sterilization is permitted. Therefore, a hospital that treats dangerously ill patients may sterilize these instruments on the Sabbath. It is permissible to connect a needle to a syringe on the Sabbath, even for the treatment of a non-dangerously ill patient.

It is permissible to inject a wounded person with antitetanus toxin on the Sabbath whenever there is any doubt as to whether the person has been properly immunized against tetanus.

If a dangerously ill patient requests that his family come to visit him on the Sabbath, it is permissible to violate rabbinic laws to fulfill his wishes. If medical opinion is such that failure to fulfill the patient's wishes may endanger him, it is permitted to violate even biblical laws.

If a critically ill patient is conscious and alert, it is permissible to turn on a light if it will bring tranquility and prevent mental anguish to the patient.

It is forbidden to violate even rabbinically prohibited laws in order to arrange for a special prayer by a *tzaddik* (righteous person) for the patient.

It is forbidden to turn a hearing aid on or off on the Sabbath. It is permitted for the hearing-impaired to carry or wear a hearing aid on the Sabbath as long as it was turned on before the Sabbath started. Even when the hearing aid is turned on before the Sabbath, it is easy to turn off the hearing aid out of habit; therefore, the patient should make a sign to remind himself that it is the Sabbath. If the hearing aid was not turned on before the Sabbath, it is permitted for a gentile to turn it on. It is preferable to use an automatic hearing aid that does not require frequent battery changes. A hearing aid inserted in the sides of eyeglasses may be worn on the Sabbath. However, the patient should take care to put on and take off the eyeglasses in silence and not while being spoken to. It is permitted to speak with a person who is wearing a hearing aid.

It is forbidden to take pills to remain awake on the Sabbath. It is forbidden to take sedatives, tranquilizers, or sleeping pills on the Sabbath. A woman who is taking oral contraceptive pills (with halachic sanction) may take them on the Sabbath. If a patient began taking medication before the Sabbath, and stopping it would cause him pain or a delay in his recovery, he may continue to take it on the Sabbath. People who take vitamins on a regular basis are allowed to take them on the Sabbath. It is permitted to take antipyretics on the Sabbath. It is permitted to treat a cold with nose drops on the Sabbath. A patient with hemorrhoids is permitted to use mineral oil on the Sabbath.

Cardiac patients who take sublingual nitroglycerin, or diabetic patients who take sugar with the onset of hypoglycemic symptoms, are not permitted to carry their medication on the Sabbath in public areas (*reshut harabim*) without an *eruv*. This applies even if they will, as a result, be unable to attend synagogue services or fulfill other *mitzvot* (commandments).

References

Responsa Tzitz Eliezer, Part 4, 4:10, 17; Part 6, 6:1; Part 7, 11, 30:2; Part 8, 14:1–5, 15–18, 15:8:7, 15:9:1–6, 15:14:6–13, 15:15:8–21; Part 9, 17:2:36–37, 40–41, 17:3:1–3, 17:8:2–3, 28:10; Part 10, 25:1:1–5; Part 11, 37, 61:4; Part 12, 41, 45:3–7; Part 13, 34, 45:1–3, 46; Part 14, 50–51; Part 17, 15; Part 20, 18:1–6.

Diagnostic Investigations

It is permissible to take one's temperature with a thermometer on the *Sabbath*. A woman who takes her temperature daily in order to determine her date of ovulation may do so on the Sabbath. It is permitted to shake down the mercury column in the thermometer so that it can be used on the Sabbath. It is permitted to use a thermometer that is applied to the forehead and lights up, whether or not the letters or numbers are already visible; however, it is preferable to use a regular thermometer on the Sabbath.

It is permissible to analyze the urine of a non-dangerously ill patient with a dipstick or a tablet on the Sabbath.

If an X-ray is required but may be postponed, it should be done after the Sabbath.

Drawing blood from a vein or an artery is prohibited on the Sabbath, unless it is required for a dangerously ill patient. In this case, it is permitted to draw only the amount needed for the immediate diagnosis of the dangerous situation. If, however, repeated blood drawings are difficult and dangerous, one may draw sufficient blood even for later testings.

A pregnant woman who suffers from diabetes mellitus is permitted to check the glucose level in her blood on the Sabbath.

References

Responsa Tzitz Eliezer, Part 3, 10; Part 8, 15:15:21; Part 10, 25:1; Part 11, 38; Part 12, 44:5; Part 14, 27:3, 30–31; Part 15, 20; Part 17, 14.

The Physician

It is preferable, whenever possible, to consult an observant physician on the Sabbath, although, according to the letter of the law, one is permitted to consult a non-observant physician. If the patient and his attendants have more confidence in a non-observant physician and are thereby inclined to consult him, they need not refrain from doing so. It is permitted to summon a non-observant physician on the Sabbath on behalf of a dangerously ill patient although it is certain that, because of this consultation, he will unnecessarily desecrate the Sabbath.

The physician may use any type of soap to clean his hands before and after treating a patient on the Sabbath.

A physician whose patients are mostly observant Jews, or who lives in an observant neighborhood, is permitted to answer the telephone on the Sabbath. A physician should preferably have a special number reserved for calls from patients who may be dangerously ill.

A physician who goes to treat a dangerously ill patient on the

Sabbath is forbidden to violate biblical laws in order to return home; he may, however, return home in a car driven by a gentile. Similarly, an ambulance driver who has transported a dangerously ill patient is forbidden to return to his base station on the Sabbath, unless the statistical probability of his being called to transfer another dangerously ill patient is greater than once daily.

If a dangerously ill patient requests a specific physician on the Sabbath, even if other physicians are readily available and the desired one will have to desecrate the Sabbath in order to visit the patient, the requested physician is obligated to go to the patient.

The physician is permitted to accept a fee for his Sabbath visit and may even demand it in a court of law, irrespective of whether he was summoned for only the Sabbath visit or was already involved in the patient's care before the Sabbath and thus includes Sabbath visits in his general fee. However, it is forbidden for a Jewish physician to benefit from a Sabbath fee collected from a gentile patient; he should give it to charity.

The study of medicine does not suspend Sabbath prohibitions, even if the physician is exceptionally studious on weekdays.

References

Responsa Tzitz Eliezer, Part 8, 15:7:10–12, 15:11:6; 15:13:1–14, 15:14:4, 55:2, 56:4–8; Part 9, 17:2:13, 17:2:30, 17:4:1; Part 10, 25:18:3; Part 13, 28:4, 55:1, 56:8; Part 21, 59.

MEDICINE ON FESTIVALS AND FAST DAYS

Festivals (Yomim Tovim)

It is permitted to take medications on festivals as a remedy for normal aches and pains.

In general, elective surgery should not be performed on the eve of any festival, during the weeks between Passover and Pentecost (the *omer* period), or during the three weeks between the seventeenth of Tamuz and the Ninth of Av. If, however, the surgeon or the health insurance group pressures the patient to undergo surgery during the aforementioned periods, the patient may comply if he is of Sephardic background. If the patient may lose his surgical spot because of his refusal, even an Ashkenazic Jew may undergo surgery on the aforementioned dates.

Patients who suffer from celiac disease and therefore are not permitted to eat grain products that contain gluten should not eat *matzah* on Passover. If, however, they wish to fulfill the commandment of eating an olive's weight of *matzah* on the seder evening, they may do so and recite the appropriate blessing, since this small amount is not considered dangerous.

The Day of Atonement (Yom Kippur) and Other Fast Days

A dangerously ill patient is not permitted to fast on the Day of Atonement. If he does, it is not considered an act of righteousness. In fact, he should be fed by the greatest and most prestigious Jews in the area.

A pregnant woman who has a history of repeated miscarriages during fasting should not fast on Yom Kippur, but she should eat less than a critical measure (*shiur*). However, a pregnant woman who has no risk factor for miscarriage should fast regularly. A pregnant woman should not fast on the Day of Atonement if fasting might endanger the fetus, even if it is within the first forty days since conception.

Nonoral routes of alimentation for dangerously ill patients, such as enema, nasogastric tube, and intravenous infusion, are more acceptable on Yom Kippur than eating. Nonetheless, as long as it is halachically permissible for the patient to eat, either normally or less than a *shiur*, he may eat normally and is not required to utilize unnatural routes.

A patient who is permitted to eat on Yom Kippur using the method of less-than-a-critical-measure is required to recite an initial blessing but need not repeat the blessing prior to every act of eating. This rule applies in cases where the patient did not interrupt his thoughts from eating, as by sleeping. Going back and forth between his room and the synagogue is not considered an interruption in thought.

A patient who is required to eat a meal with bread on Yom Kippur should wash his hands before the meal, as usual.

On all fasts except the Day of Atonement, one should not use the method of less-than-a-critical-measure. Thus, a patient who is permitted to eat on Tisha B'Av or any other fast day should eat properly.

References

Responsa Tzitz Eliezer, Part 7, 24–25; Part 8, 15:3, 15:16; Part 9, 17:2:42; Part 10, 25:14:1–7, 25:15, 25:21:1–3; Part 11, 43; Part 12, 1, 46; Part 17, 14:2, 20:4; Part 18, 17:6; Part 19, 22.

GYNECOLOGY AND OBSTETRICS

Contraception

A woman is forbidden to use contraceptive measures without the consent of her husband. If the husband has not yet fulfilled the precept of procreation and his wife may not become pregnant because of danger to her health, he should divorce his wife rather than permit her to use contraceptive measures. Even if the wife is prepared to accept the dangers of pregnancy and delivery, the husband is not required to give his consent, and he may divorce her. If the husband has already fulfilled the precept of procreation, he may permit his wife to use a method of contraception, provided that pregnancy would involve possible danger to her life. If, however, she used contraceptive measures without his permission, she is required to accept a divorce and forfeit the benefits of her marriage contract (*ketubah*).

Under ideal circumstances, a man is not permitted to marry a woman who, before their wedding, has informed him that she will need to use contraceptive measures, even if only temporarily, because of a medical contraindication to pregnancy. They should postpone their marriage until she is medically permitted to become pregnant.

A couple should not get divorced or abstain from sexual relations if the wife has a temporary medical indication for contraception; the wife is then permitted to take the necessary precautions against contraception. Even if there is only a doubtful danger in pregnancy or delivery, the wife may use contraceptive measures. The necessity of contraceptive use must be thoroughly established and medically indicated and not be founded on only an assumption. Therefore, two independent, expert physicians should establish this necessity. However, one should not be stringent and base one's decision on the exceptional case of a woman who became pregnant against medical advice and nevertheless escaped unharmed. In general, the rabbi must deliberate carefully before permitting contraceptive use.

It is permitted to use a contraceptive method for temporary situations, i.e., if the woman is weak, or if it is soon after a recent delivery.

The general principle concerning the selection of a contraceptive measure is to choose the method that is most halachically acceptable, provided that medical effectiveness and safety are not sacrificed. In principle, it is preferable to use those methods that do not involve destruction of sperm but only prevent the mixing of sperm and egg. Similarly, it is preferable to use methods that result in only temporary infertility by means of an indirect mechanism (i.e., hormonal). Therefore, the most halachically acceptable contraceptive method involves the use of oral contraceptives (the pill). The next most acceptable method is the use of an intrauterine device (IUD). If it is not possible to use either the pill or the IUD, it is permitted to use postcoital absorbants or douches. Next in line is the diaphragm, and after this method is spermicides.

If none of these measures can be used, it is permissible to sterilize the woman—preferably in a reversible way, and preferably by a non-Jewish physician. If all these methods are impossible, the husband may use a condom for a temporary period.

In cases where pregnancy does not pose a danger to health but would result in great pain and suffering for the woman, halachically acceptable methods of contraception are limited to the following methods: the pill, the IUD, the diaphragm, and spermicides. In instances where the woman is not physically endangered by another pregnancy but desires contraception because of her inability to cope with an additional child at the present time, she is temporarily permitted to use oral contraceptives or an IUD. These methods also may be used if all the woman's offspring have grown up as delinquent children, causing her to fear bringing additional children into the world. Financial status is not a consideration when deciding whether to permit contraception.

If a woman has significant pain during intercourse and requires temporary contraceptive measures, and the only beneficial method is the use of a condom, the husband is permitted to use it.

References

Responsa Tzitz Eliezer, Part 6, 42:4:1–2; Part 7, 48:5:17; Part 9, 51:2; Part 10, 25:10–13; Part 11, 63; Part 14, 96; Part 15, 43:3; Part 16, 41:1; Part 20, 50.

Abortion

Abortion is forbidden when there is no valid medical reason to allow it. The prohibition against abortion, however, is only rabbinic. Abortion is certainly not considered to be murder.

The following situations are indications that permit therapeutic abortion:

- A clear, life-threatening danger is posed to the mother by the continuation of the pregnancy.
- The pregnancy is detrimental to the mother's health, although not life-threatening.
- A nursing mother becomes pregnant.
- A married woman conceives willfully by a man other than her husband.
- A substantial risk exists that the fetus will be born with a deformity that would cause it to suffer.
- It has been conclusively proven (i.e., by amniocentesis) that the fetus has Tay-Sachs disease.
- It has been conclusively proven (i.e., by amniocentesis) that the fetus has Down's syndrome or other disorders causing severe mental deficiency.

In circumstances where termination of pregnancy has been permitted, it should be done prior to forty days postconception, or within the first three months of pregnancy. Only unusual circumstances permit the abortion to be performed after the first trimester. It is preferable to consult an observant Jewish physician about the indication for abortion. The abortion procedure itself preferably should be performed by a female physician; and, in any case, a Jewish physician is preferable to a gentile one. In all instances where abortion has been permitted, one should also procure the husband's consent.

It is permitted to perform an amniocentesis examination to detect severe abnormalities in the fetus.

In the case of multiple fetuses (i.e, four or more) it is permissible to reduce the number of fetuses in order to save the others.

References

Responsa Tzitz Eliezer, Part 7, 48:1:8; Part 8, 36; Part 9, 51:3; Part 13, 102; Part 14, 27:7, 100–101; Part 15, 13, 43:4; Part 17, 49:12; Part 20, 2, 56; Part 21, 29:1–4.

Artificial Insemination

The practice of artificial insemination using donor semen (AID) in either a married or an unmarried woman is a desecration of the holy concept of marriage, and it violates many strict biblical and rabbinic laws. This is true whether the donor of the semen is a Jew or a gentile. Physicians should refrain from participating in this form of infertility therapy.

If a woman underwent AID without her husband's knowledge and consent, she must accept a divorce and forfeit any rights to financial support, including her *ketubah* and alimony.

A child conceived through AID is considered by many halachic authorities to have the status of a bastard (*mamzer*). In any case, there will always be a suspicion of illegitimacy affecting the child's halachic identity. If the semen donor is a priest (*kohen*) and the child is a boy, he is forbidden to marry a divorcée. If the semen donor is a gentile, the child is a *pagum* (literally, blemished). If the child is a girl, she is forbidden to marry a *kohen*.

Artificial insemination using the husband's sperm (AIH) is

permitted if ten years have passed since the couple married, or if the infertility workup by expert, reliable physicians has established that AIH is the only procedure that may achieve a pregnancy. It is forbidden to augment the husband's semen by mixing it with donor semen. A physician who knows that such mixing occurred is obligated to reveal this to the husband.

A woman pregnant through artificial insemination is forbidden to get married during the period of pregnancy and nursing, similar to any other woman in these circumstances.

References

Responsa Tzitz Eliezer, Part 3, 27; Part 9, 51:4; Part 13, 97; Part 19, 57.

In Vitro Fertilization

It is prohibited to perform in vitro fertilization even if it is done using the husband's sperm and the wife's egg. If, however, such a procedure was performed using an egg-donor woman and a surrogate woman, the child is halachically related to the nurturing, surrogate mother in all aspects, i.e., if one of the two women is gentile or is the daughter of a *kohen*, etc.

References

Responsa Tzitz Eliezer, Part 15, 45; Part 19, 41; Part 20, 49:2.

The Infertility Workup

When evaluating an infertile couple, one should first evaluate the female reproductive tract. If no pathology is found, one may then investigate the male reproductive tract. The husband is not permitted to refuse to participate in such investigations.

Acquisition and examination of the semen is not included in the prohibition against spilling one's semen for naught. However, one should try to procure the semen specimen in the most halachically acceptable manner. The following order of priority is suggested:

- Collection of the ejaculate from the vagina after normal sexual intercourse.
- Collection of the ejaculate following coitus interruptus.
- Collection of the ejaculate from a condom worn during intercourse.
- Collection of the ejaculate from a receptacle placed in the wife's vagina.
- Collection of the ejaculate induced by masturbation.

Testicular biopsy is permitted, if medically indicated.

It is permitted to treat female infertility, whether of natural or induced etiology.

References

Responsa Tzitz Eliezer, Part 7, 48:1:7; Part 9, 51:1; Part 11, 42:8; Part 16, 41:2; Part 20, 48; Part 21, 36.

The Menstruating Woman (Niddah) *and Ritual Immersion*

A woman who undergoes a gynecological examination does not become ritually impure (*niddah*), regardless of whether she was examined bimanually or with a speculum.

If a woman most undergo surgical incision of the hymenal ring, she must count seven "clean" days after the procedure. However, if there is a possibility that the hymen will reanastomose if sexual relations is not permitted on the same day, one may be lenient on the condition that the physician certifies that the blood is of hymenal, not uterine, origin.

One may not rely on scientific tests in order to determine whether vaginal discharge or spotting contains blood in establishing the *niddah* state of a woman. Similarly, one should not rely on a color comparison chart to distinguish among colors of vaginal discharge or spotting.

A woman with a plaster cast on her finger may go to the *mikvah* with the cast in place, if removal of the cast would result in severe pain and danger to her finger.

A woman who, for medical reasons, may not allow water to enter her ears is permitted to occlude her ear canals prior to, and specifically for, ritual immersion. The occlusion should be accomplished with a substance inserted into the ear canal in such a way that it does not extend outside the canal. Therefore, it is preferable to use cotton rather than earplugs.

If a woman who underwent an operation needs to cover the operative site with a bandage so that it will not get wet, she is permitted to immerse in the *mikvah* in that way.

An intrauterine device (IUD) does not interfere with the counting of the seven clean days or with the process of immersion. In addition, the string attached to the IUD, which protrudes through the cervix into the vagina, does not invalidate the immersion.

References

Responsa Tzitz Eliezer, Part 4, 67:6; Part 5, 31; Part 6, 41:6; Part 10, 25:10:3, 25:11–12; Part 11, 63; Part 12, 67:6; Part 13, 81:3; Part 20, 32:2.

SURGERY

Therapeutic surgery involving a significant risk of death may be performed if the patient will otherwise die from his disease in the near future. If the patient's death from the disease is uncertain, but he periodically experiences exacerbations that are life-threatening or that result in severe pain, he is permitted to accept the risks of surgery. This rule applies even if there is a risk that surgery will hasten his death, as long as the chances for cure or palliation are greater with the surgery than without it. These principles apply also in cases where the therapy is very complicated and sophisticated, or where dangerous experimental drugs are used.

An amputated limb does not require burial according to *halachah*, although it should be buried, either according to custom or in order to prevent the ritual defilement of priests (*kohanim*), who are proscribed from coming into contact with it. Under special circumstances, this limb may be concealed in a special room and used by physicians for educational purposes. It is permitted to derive benefit (i.e., study) from a limb or organ that was amputated or removed from a living patient. One is not permitted to treat it disrespectfully but must bury it after the use.

It is permitted for a man to undergo a prostatectomy operation, even though he may be castrated by the procedure. After such an operation, a man may continue to live intimately with his wife.

A patient who has undergone a unilateral orchiectomy is permitted to marry.

Open-heart surgery is permitted when medically indicated, and the patient is not considered halachically dead at any stage of the operation.

A child whose primary sexual characteristics appear female but who, upon genetic investigation, has a male karyotype may undergo bilateral orchiectomy. A hermaphrodite may undergo surgery in order to establish one sexual identity. If possible, the male organs should be preserved and reconstructed; however, if circumstances are such that it would be more advisable to transform the child into a phenotypic female, the surgeon may do so.

Transsexual surgery is forbidden. If one spouse of a couple undergoes sex-change surgery, the marriage is annulled, and no divorce is necessary.

Cosmetic surgery is forbidden unless it is performed for medical purposes, not merely for vanity.

It is permitted to surgically reattach an amputated limb to the body of a *kohen*, even though he thereby becomes ritually defiled.

A baby who was born with meningomyelocele should be operated upon and should receive all necessary medical or surgical therapy, regardless of future difficulties associated with this serious congenital malformation.

References

Responsa Tzitz Eliezer, Part 4, 13; Part 9, 49; Part 10, 25:8, 25:17:1–5, 25:24, 25:26:6; Part 11, 41:8–9, 78; Part 13, 88, 90; Part 14, 78, 95; Part 15, 3:6, 13:3; Part 16, 24, 64.

ORGAN TRANSPLANTATION

Living Donors

A person is not permitted to donate an organ for transplantation if its removal exposes him to a life-threatening danger, whether by the surgical procedure itself or by the lack of that organ. In this circumstance, the surgeon is forbidden to perform such an operation; if he did so and a fatality occurs, he bears responsibility for the death. If, however, there is no risk to the donor, a transplant is permitted. There is, however, no religious obligation to donate an organ in order to save the life of another person.

Kidney donation usually involves a risk to the donor and, therefore, may be performed only if a group of experts decides that the procedure does not pose even a doubtful danger to the donor.

Dying and Dead Donors

It is forbidden to remove an organ from a moribund patient. To obtain an organ from a *tereifah* (nonviable person) is forbidden. It is forbidden to artificially prolong a dying patient's life with the intention of preserving his organs for transplantation. Harvesting an organ from a brain-dead person is considered murder.

There is no religious obligation to donate organs for posthumous use. This applies to any organ, regardless of size (i.e, kidney or cornea), and it applies even in cases where there is a recipient waiting for the organ. Unless the deceased consented to the use of his organs prior to his death, their removal for transplantation purposes is absolutely forbidden.

It is absolutely prohibited to remove an organ from a donor unless he is definitely dead. Brain death is not a halachically acceptable definition of death; hence, no organ should be removed as long as the donor's heart is still beating.

It is forbidden to remove corneas from a Jewish cadaver. If, however, a cornea was harvested from a Jewish cadaver, it is permissible to transplant it in a blind person. If the source of the cornea that is obtained from a cornea bank is unknown, a Jewish physician may transplant it in a blind patient. If a cornea is removed from a Jewish cadaver, the rest of the eye should be buried.

Relatives of a deceased person are permitted to be compensated for their consent to donate an organ of their dead relative (provided that the donation is sanctioned by halachic criteria).

References

Responsa Tzitz Eliezer, Part 9, 17:6, 10, 44; Part 10, 25:5–6, 25:7, 25:28; Part 13, 91:7; Part 14, 84:1–3; Part 15, 13:2; Part 16, 34; Part 17, 66; Part 19, 53:5.

PSYCHIATRY

Mental illness that may result in a patient harming himself or others is considered a life-threatening disease. Therefore, it is permitted to desecrate the Sabbath for such a patient.

It is permitted to perform psychosurgery when medically indicated, even if, as a result, the patient's personality may be changed. If the patient is in the custody of relatives, one should discuss the case with them and procure their consent for the procedure. If the patient is in the custody of the State or has no relatives, the State is permitted to make a decision on the patient's behalf.

A man suffering from schizophrenia should be forced to divorce his wife if she so desires. A woman suffering from catatonic schizophrenia or other severe mental illness diagnosed prior to her marriage may be divorced by her husband if he was not aware of her condition prior to marriage, and she loses all rights to her marriage contract. In such a case, if the husband is, for any reason, unable to divorce her, he is permitted to marry another woman without adhering to the requirements of one hundred consenting rabbis and of handing over her divorce papers and marriage contract payments to a rabbinic court. If a woman becomes mentally ill following her marriage, her husband may force her to accept a divorce, but he is required to pay her marriage contract.

References

Responsa Tzitz Eliezer, Part 4, 13:3; Part 6, 42:1–2; Part 8, 16:12:5; Part 13, 35:1.

MEDICATIONS

A patient should not take medication unless a physician establishes the necessity of the therapy. Pharmacists are forbidden to dispense drugs based on their superficial knowledge of medicine; however, it is permitted for a pharmacist to dispense over-the-counter medication without a physician's prescription. It is forbidden to inflate the price of medications; therefore, even if the patient consents to an inflated price, he is not obligated to pay it. One should not utilize medications and metaphysical remedies recommended in the Talmud, for they are not efficacious in modern times.

It is permitted for even a non-dangerously ill patient to swallow medication whose capsules are made of gelatin. It is not necessary to open the capsule and swallow only the medication in powder form.

A patient who must adhere to a salt-restricted diet may eat meat that has been salted for only eighteen minutes during the process of *kashering*, instead of the usual hour.

References

Responsa Tzitz Eliezer, Part 5, *Ramat Rachel* 22:7–8, 25; Part 9, 17:3:7; Part 10, 25:19:4, 25:20:4; Part 12, 52:6; Part 13, 35:2; Part 20, 33.

BLESSINGS AND PRAYERS

A patient receiving food through a nasogastric tube or a gastrostomy tube is not required to recite a blessing before and after being fed. However, if possible, he should listen to a blessing recited by an individual who is required to recite the blessings over food and thereby fulfill his own religious obligation.

A person who drinks spring water for medicinal purposes is not required to recite the blessing.

A patient is required to recite the thanksgiving blessing *hagomel* in the following situations:

- Following recovery from surgery performed on internal body structures. This includes operations such as herniorrhaphy, hemorrhoidectomy, and eye surgery.
- Following recovery from each episode of an illness, even if one is certain that the disease will recur. Thus, this blessing should be recited following recovery from a heart attack, renal disease, a gallbladder attack, and so on.
- Following recovery from each episode of a mental illness.
- Following recovery from childbirth.
- Recovery from an illness by a patient who is not expected to live for another year, provided that the patient is unaware of his poor prognosis.
- Following recovery from circumcision (in an adult).

A patient should not recite the *hagomel* blessing in the following situations:

Following recovery from organ donation, since he invited the danger upon himself, albeit with altruistic intentions.
Following recovery from an attempted suicide.
The patient is a minor less than thirteen years of age.

This blessing should be recited only upon completion of all dangers; therefore, if a patient is flown overseas for an operation, he should recite *hagomel* only after the operation.

A patient who, under the influence of a cathartic medication, moves his bowels frequently should recite the blessing *asher yatzar* after each bowel movement. However, if he has severe, persistent diarrhea, he should recite the blessing only once daily.

A patient who urinates through a urinary catheter is required to recite *asher yatzar* after voiding, even if the urine is bloody. If it is constantly draining urine, he should recite the blessing at a time when there is a pause in the urinary dripping and no urine is in the catheter. If, however, he is unable to determine a period of time with no dripping, he should recite the blessing only once upon awakening from sleep in the morning. The same laws also apply for patients who have a suprapubic cystostomy. An incontinent patient is required to recite this blessing, as well.

A patient who has an indwelling urinary catheter is permitted to pray, to study Torah, and to wear phylacteries even when urine is draining through the catheter, provided that the catheter and the collecting bag are covered. If a bad odor is present, an air freshener or perfume should be used to dispel the odor. If a bedpan containing feces or urine is present in the room, the patient may fulfill his religious obligation under the following conditions:

- If the bed is 10 *tefachim* (about 40 inches) high, the patient should turn away from the bedpan or cover his body with a sheet.
- If the bed is less than 10 *tefachim* high, the feces or urine should be removed a distance of 4 *amot* (about 2.5 feet) from the patient, and he should turn away from the bedpan or cover his body with a sheet.
- If he is unable to distance himself 4 *amot* from the bedpan, he should place a cover over it.
- If the room has a bad odor because of the feces, air freshener or perfume should be used to dispel it.

A patient with a colostomy or ileostomy may engage in religious activities after giving an enema, cleaning the area around the orifice, and covering it.

References

Responsa Tzitz Eliezer, Part 8, 1:23–26; Part 9, 6; Part 10, 25:27:3, 23; Part 12, 1:12, 2, 12, 18:1–8; Part 13, 35:2; Part 14, 20; Part 15, 32:5; Part 17, 8:1; Part 18, 22:1–5, 78:7; Part 19, 53:1–3, Part 21, 64:7.

THE DYING PATIENT

One is required to do everything possible to save the life of a dying patient, even if the patient will live for only a short time. This applies even if the dying patient is suffering greatly, no matter whether it is an adult or a child. This also applies to a patient in a persistent vegetative state (PVS), even if his continued existence prevents his wife from remarrying. However, if the family requests to withhold further treatment from a terminally ill patient, this request has to be obeyed; otherwise, by secular law, the physician is liable to a malpractice suit. In such a case, the physician is not obligated to resuscitate such a patient.

Any action that results in hastening the death of a dying patient is forbidden. Anyone performing such an action (i.e., discontinuing a respirator) is considered a murderer. Even if the patient is beyond medical help, is suffering greatly, and requests that his death be hastened, one may not do so. The physician is forbidden to hasten a patient's death or to advise him concerning such an act.

If a dying patient is resuscitated and placed on a respirator, the machine may be connected to a timer that will automatically turn the machine off for a short period of time. The patient can then be reevaluated with respect to the presence or absence of spontaneous respiration and cardiac activity. If no spontaneous respirations and no cardiac activity are present, the respirator should not be reconnected; if spontaneous respirations or cardiac activity are present, the respirator must be reconnected.

A dying patient may be given strong analgesics such as morphine, even if they may hasten his death. The medication, however, may be prescribed for purposes of pain relief only and not in order to hasten the patient's death.

Relatives of dying patients are forbidden to pray for the death of a patient even if he is in great pain and requests such prayers on his behalf. However, others may so pray under the following conditions:

- The intentions should be pure, with no ulterior motives.
- The prayer should be offered after an attempt to help the patient accept his suffering is rejected.
- All medical alternatives, as well as offering prayer and charity for the patient's recovery, have been exhausted.

The patient is permitted to pray for his own death.

A prematurely born baby must be treated aggressively with all available measures to sustain his life, even if the treatment may cause harm (i.e., high oxygen that may cause blindness due to retinopathy of prematurity, or a high-pressure ventilator that may cause hemorrhage in the brain). However, if he was born prematurely, there is no obligation to resuscitate him, and one should not desecrate the Sabbath on his behalf.

References

Responsa Tzitz Eliezer, Part 5, *Ramat Rachel* 5, 28:5, 29; Part 7, 49:3:1; Part 9, 47; Part 10, 25:6; Part 13, 87, 89; Part 14, 80–82; Part 17, 72:13; Part 18, 19, 40, 62; Part 19, 10.

ESTABLISHING THE MOMENT OF DEATH

Death is defined as the cessation of both respiration and cardiac activity. One must establish, with the help of all available instruments, that cessation of respiration and cardiac activity have indeed occurred. Brain death in the presence of continuous cardiac activity is not an acceptable criterion for pronouncing a patient dead.

References

Responsa Tzitz Eliezer, Part 9, 46; Part 10, 25:4; Part 13, 89:12–13; Part 17, 66; Part 21, 28.

AUTOPSY

Autopsies performed for forensic reasons, i.e., in order to ascertain whether a suspect is guilty of murder, are permissible.

It is permitted to perform an autopsy on a patient who died of an unknown disease if the results of the autopsy may help in the diagnosis or therapy of other patients physically present with a similar obscure disease. If no other patients are present with a similar condition, it is still permitted to perform an autopsy if such a patient had consented to it before he died or had sold his body for such purposes. If no similar patients are physically present and the patient had not expressed his desires prior to his demise, a special assembly of rabbis must be convened before an autopsy may be permitted. Such permission can be granted only if the deceased has no relatives; otherwise, an autopsy may not be performed without their consent.

If an autopsy is performed, all of the deceased's parts must be returned for interment after the necessary examinations have been performed.

Jewish bodies may not be dissected for the study of medicine, even if the deceased had consented or had sold his body for such purposes. It is forbidden for a person to donate his body to a medical school for the purpose of posthumous anatomical dissection, and it is forbidden for others to attempt to persuade a Jewish person to do so.

Relatives have no right to consent to an autopsy on the body of the deceased if it is not halachically sanctioned.

It is forbidden to perform an autopsy on an unclaimed Jewish body.

Hospital administrators are permitted to remove a cardiac pacemaker from a deceased person under the following conditions:

- The pacemaker will be reused for other patients.
- Preferably, the patient had given written consent, at the time of insertion of the pacemaker, that it be removed after his death.
- Preferably, a relative has been invited to participate at the removal of the pacemaker.

If a pregnant woman dies, there is an obligation to save the fetus if it is at a viable stage of gestation, even if there are doubts as to whether or not it will be normal.

References

Responsa Tzitz Eliezer, Part 4, 14; Part 11, 74:7; Part 14, 83; Part 18, 31.

TRIAGE DECISIONS

A patient who has a prognosis for cure takes precedence in the distribution of limited medical resources over a patient whose prognosis is for only temporary control of his disease. In general, priority for treatment should be decided according to the medical indications, not according to social worth. This applies only when the patient with the poorer prognosis is passively neglected in favor of the patient with a better prognosis. However, active intervention in the less fortunate patient—i.e., terminating his therapy so that the patient with the better prognosis may utilize those resources—is forbidden.

If two dangerously ill patients are present but there is only enough medication for one of them, they should divide the medication equally, thereby providing each with a temporary extension of life. If enough medication is available for only one of two patients, one dangerously ill and the other possibly dangerously ill, the following applies: The medication must be given to the dangerously ill patient unless it belongs to the possibly dangerously ill patient, in which case he is not obligated to give it to the other patient.

If there is a scarcity of life-saving machines, they should be allocated to patients who have the chance to recover and survive and should not be applied to terminally ill patients for the sole purpose of prolonging their short-term survival.

References

Responsa Tzitz Eliezer, Part 9, 17:10:5, 18:3; Part 17, 10, 72; Part 18, 1.

MEDICAL EXPERIMENTATION

A person is permitted to volunteer for medical experimentation, provided that it poses no threat to his own health and the results may benefit others. Although a person is not required to, and should not be forced to, volunteer for such experimentation, he is fulfilling a *mitzvah* if he does so. Should the experiment pose a threat to the volunteer's health, he is not permitted to volunteer; nor may the experimentation be performed.

It is permitted to experiment on animals in order to benefit human beings, but an effort should be made to reduce pain and suffering for the animal being experimented on.

References

Responsa Tzitz Eliezer, Part 13, 101; Part 14, 68.

DIETARY LAWS (KASHRUT)

The halachic rule that when a patient is permitted to consume nonkosher food he should try to use the least prohibited food applies both to a situation in which others feed him and a situation in which he feeds himself.

It is prohibited to hospitalize a mentally retarded person in an institution where nonkosher food is served. However, if such a person is hospitalized in an institution where kosher food is served and subsequently the institution becomes nonkosher, it is the obligation of the community, not the family, to find an alternative institution.

A patient who is nourished by a gastrostomy tube can be fed with meat and dairy products at the same time, and there is no need to wait between such feedings.

References

Responsa Tzitz Eliezer, Part 14, 69–70; Part 19, 53:4.

CIRCUMCISION

One may not use a *Magen* clamp or a Gomco clamp to perform a circumcision. If the circumcision was done this way, it is invalid. A *mohel* (ritual circumciser) who uses these clamps is misleading his clients; if he used them on the Sabbath, he is guilty of Sabbath desecration.

It is forbidden to use local anesthesia for circumcision, except in highly unusual circumstances.

A child with jaundice of any etiology or degree should not be circumcised as long as the jaundice is present, even if the physician has established that it is in the process of resolution. However, when the jaundice has disappeared and the physician feels that circumcision is safe, it may be performed. If the jaundice was physiologic in etiology and has disappeared, circumcision may be performed immediately, without waiting for a period of seven days to pass. If, however, the jaundice was the result of disease, the circumcision should be postponed until seven days have elapsed since the baby's recovery. If the baby underwent an exchange transfusion, the circumcision should be postponed until seven days have elapsed since the transfusion, even if the physician feels that it can be done earlier.

A baby receiving antibiotic therapy for any type of infection should not be circumcised until seven days have elapsed after the antibiotics are discontinued. If, however, the physician certifies that the baby recovered prior to the discontinuation of antibiotics, one may begin counting the seven days from the time of recovery.

A baby placed in an incubator because of prematurity should not undergo circumcision until seven days have elapsed from the time he leaves the incubator, even if the physician feels that he was healthy before leaving the incubator.

A baby who has a fever as low as 37.5°C (99.5°F) is considered to be ill and should not be circumcised until seven days have elapsed after the fever has disappeared. If the fever's etiology is non-pathologic in origin—such as being due to a hot environment or to mild dehydration—the baby is not considered to be ill.

Normal neonatal weight loss is not considered to be an illness.

A baby with an ocular discharge found to be sterile after appropriate laboratory examination may be circumcised only after the discharge clears up. However, one need not wait an additional seven days.

A baby who has a cephalohematoma secondary to forceps delivery or suction extraction, or who has a temporary neurological deficit secondary to traction on his arm or leg during delivery (i.e., brachial palsy), may be circumcised on the eighth day under the following conditions:

- A physician certifies that the baby is not sick.
- The baby has no pain from these temporary disorders.
- The circumcision will not adversely affect these temporary conditions.

References

Responsa Tzitz Eliezer, Part 8, 29; Part 9, 28:8; Part 10, 38; Part 13, 1:1, 82, 83:1–6; Part 19, 68; Part 20, 52:2, 73; Part 21, 64:1–6.

THE PHYSICIAN

Licensing

A physician may practice medicine only if he has mastered the prerequisite knowledge. In modern times, the physician need not obtain permission to practice medicine from a Jewish court. A medical degree and a governmental license serve as a substitute for the permission formerly dispensed by a Jewish court.

References

Responsa Tzitz Eliezer, Part 5, *Ramat Rachel* 22.

Malpractice

A physician who is appropriately licensed is not liable for an error. There is no difference between surgical or medical error, provided that the physician renders care according to acceptable medical standards. If, however, the physician errs and administers the wrong medication to the patient, the physician is liable for harm. Similarly, if an injection was given in an incorrect anatomic location, the physician is liable. (The same is true if a nurse administers an incorrect dosage of medication, or injects it incorrectly; the nurse is liable even if the physician gave the orders.) If the physician admits that the diagnosis was arrived at without the requisite investigations and deliberation and that the patient sustained harm because medication was casually prescribed, the physician is liable. If the physician errs in something that all other physicians would regard as an error, he is liable.

A physician who abuses his medical responsibility and endangers the lives of his patients should have his medical license revoked.

References

Responsa Tzitz Eliezer, Part 4, 13; Part 5, *Ramat Rachel* 23; Part 14, 85.

Physician Reimbursement

A physician may charge a fee for examining a patient, whether the examination was done in the physician's office or at home. Similarly, a physician may charge a fee for teaching medicine to others. If the physician demands a high fee for his expertise, the patient is nonetheless required to pay him; it is a corrupt and immoral practice, however, for physicians to demand a fee that will result in financial difficulties and have deleterious psychosocial effects upon the patient and his family.

A physician is forbidden to charge a consultation fee if he does not examine the patient. A physician also is not allowed to charge a fee for writing a prescription if he does not examine the patient.

A physician is forbidden to charge a fee that a poor person cannot afford to pay. Indeed, according to the letter of the law, the courts may compel a physician to provide such services for free. This, however, applies when there is only one physician in the city; where many physicians are present, one cannot compel any one physician to provide free services. In such a case, the community should pay a fixed salary to a physician so that he can treat the indigent for free.

If a physician was called to see a patient without the patient's prior knowledge, the patient need not repay the third party for medical expenses incurred if the consultation did not benefit him.

References

Responsa Tzitz Eliezer, Part 5, *Ramat Rachel* 24–25; Part 10, 25:29; Part 14, 27:2.

Medical Confidentiality

A physician who swore or explicitly promised a patient that he would not testify against him in court or that he would not reveal medical information that would be detrimental to the patient has sworn or promised to abrogate a positive biblical commandment; thus, his words are not legally binding. As a result he is not only permitted, but is obligated, to testify in court.

The oath or affirmation that all physicians take upon their graduation from medical school, which includes the obligation to uphold the principle of medical confidentiality, is not meant to prevent him from testifying in court or from revealing pertinent medical information to the proper authorities when he has a *mitzvah* to do so. However, if the physician feels bound by his oath not to testify, he may be released from this oath by stating in front of three rabbinical judges that he regrets taking the vow.

The prohibition against revealing confidential medical information does not apply to medical information shared with medical students while at the patient's bedside. If, however, disclosure of such information would embarrass the patient, the physician should first obtain the patient's consent. Should the patient object, the physician should refrain from bringing students to the patient's bedside.

A physician is required to provide medical information to the proper authorities concerning an epileptic patient who may endanger himself or others if the patient is permitted to drive a car. If, however, others are not endangered by the withholding of medical information, the disclosure of such confidential material to others is definitely prohibited.

A physician who diagnoses a disease or a defect in a patient that may harm others (i.e., severe myopia and driving license, or severe defects in the sexual organs) has an obligation to notify the appropriate authorities or the third party (i.e., potential spouse) that might be harmed, in order to avoid significant harm to innocent third parties. It is preferable to explain to the patient his obligation to notify the third party or the appropriate authorities about his disease or defect. However, even if the patient insists that his secret not be revealed, the physician is obligated to notify the appropriate party.

References

Responsa Tzitz Eliezer, Part 13, 81:2, 104:1; Part 15, 13:1; Part 16, 4.

Refusal of Treatment

If a patient refuses a well-established treatment without which he may die or be seriously damaged, the physician should force the patient to receive the treatment.

References

Responsa Tzitz Eliezer, Part 17, 2:1.

Treatment that Exposes the Physician to Danger

In principle, a person may not place himself in possible life-threatening danger in order to save his friend's life. However, in regard to physicians, this law is somewhat modified. It is permitted for a physician to assume the risk of treating patients with any type of contagious disease. Indeed, he is credited with the fulfillment of an important religious duty. When preparing to treat a patient with a contagious disease, the physician should pray to God for special guidance and protection since he is endangering his own life.

A military physician is permitted to render medical care to a wounded soldier in a combat zone, although he is endangering his own life. This applies even if it is not known whether the wounded soldier will live, die, or be killed. Similarly, another soldier is allowed to place his own life in danger in order to rescue a wounded comrade from the combat zone.

References

Responsa Tzitz Eliezer, Part 8, 16:10:13; Part 9, 17:5; Part 12, 57; Part 13, 100; part 18, 1:9–11.

Laws of Seclusion (Yichud)

A male physician may examine a woman, even internally, when they are alone in an unlocked room, under the following conditions:

- Three people are in the waiting room.
- A husband and wife are in the waiting room.
- The woman's husband is in the same city.
- The physician's wife is in the same city, has a key to the room, and may enter it at any time.
- Another person besides the physician has a key to the room and may enter it at any time.
- The examining room is in the apartment inhabited by the physician and his family.

A female physician may examine a male patient, even in a locked room, on the condition that her husband is present in the same city.

The laws of *yichud* apply even when dealing with a sick or moribund patient or an elderly man.

References

Responsa Tzitz Eliezer, Part 6, 40:12:7–12; Part 8, 27:5; Part 13, 67:25.

SMOKING

There is a biblical prohibition against smoking, since smoking is an established life-threatening behavior. In public areas, everyone is entitled to protest against smoking and to require people who smoke to stop smoking in their presence.

In general, the prohibition against smoking also includes the manufacturers and the sellers.

References

Responsa Tzitz Eliezer, Part 15, 39; Part 17, 21–22; Part 21, 14.

THE BATTERED-CHILD SYNDROME

It is permitted to inform the authorities about a significant battered-child situation in order to remove the child from his battering parents. This rule applies in situations of physical battering as well as sexual abuse.

References

Responsa Tzitz Eliezer, Part 19, 52.

CONCLUSION

Medicohalachic problems include issues of general ethical concern (i.e., abortion, transplantation, triage, etc.) as well as issues of special and "pure" halachic interest (i.e., Sabbath, *niddah*, *kashrut*, etc.). Rabbi Waldenberg may be considered as the most prolific writer on all issues of medicine and *halachah*. There is no topic or subject of interest within the sphere of medicine and *halachah* that Rabbi Waldenberg did not discuss and rule clearly upon. His contributions to modern life and *halachah* in general, and to modern medicine and *halachah* in particular, are enormous and long-lasting.

Contemporary Specialists in Jewish Medical Ethics

DR. NISSON E. SHULMAN

INTRODUCTION

Recognized, authoritative *poskim*, or rabbinic decisors, in the area of medicine and *halachah* include the late Rabbis Moshe Feinstein and Shlomo Zalman Auerbach. One of the living authorities in medical *halachah* is Rabbi Eliezer Yehudah Waldenberg.

Other great men—both rabbis and physicians—who do not concentrate in the area of *psak*, or rabbinic decision making, by virtue of their well-rounded personality and the scope of their activity are highly regarded in this area, as well. That is the common denominator with which we group together, in alphabetical order, Abraham S. Abraham, M.D.; Rabbi Dr. J. David Bleich; Rabbi Dr. David M. Feldman; Rabbi Mordechai Halperin, M.D.; Fred Rosner, M.D.; Rabbi Avraham Steinberg, M.D.; and Rabbi Dr. Moshe David Tendler. These seven men and their important contributions to medical *halachah* will be highlighted in this chapter.

Other rabbis and physicians in the United States and in Israel lecture or write on Jewish medical ethics and contribute their scientific, legal, talmudic, and halachic expertise to elucidate important aspects of this many-faceted field. This chapter, however, focuses on only the seven aforementioned contemporary specialists in Jewish medical ethics.

BIOGRAPHIES

ABRAHAM S. ABRAHAM was born in Jerusalem, studied medicine at the Universities of Leeds and Birmingham, England, and is presently Professor of Medicine at the Hebrew University–Hadassah Medical School and Director of the Department of Medicine B of the Shaare Zedek Medical Center in Jerusalem. In 1975, he received the Faculty Prize of the Hebrew University–Hadassah Medical School for outstanding clinical research.

Dr. Abraham has published many articles in the general medical literature. His books, however, are all devoted to medical *halachah*. They include: *Lev Abraham* (2 vols., 1977), translated into English as *Medical Halakhah for Everyone* (1980); *Nishmat Avraham* (5 vols., 1984, 1986, 1988, 1992, 1995, covering all parts of the *Shulchan Aruch* (Code of Jewish Law); *Halachot for the Physician on the Sabbath and Festivals*, a pocket-sized book of practical *halachah* (1995), translated into English under the same title (1995); *Halachot of the Patient and Attendant on the Sabbath, Festivals and Yom-Kippur; A Pocket Book of Practical Halakhah* (1995); and *Comprehensive Guide to Medical Halakhah* (1990).

His magnum opus is his five-volume *Nishmat Avraham*, which pertains to halachic rulings in all areas of modern medicine and is already a classic work that established Dr. Abraham as a giant in the field of Jewish medical ethics. He is a prolific writer and a sought-after lecturer in this field.

DAVID J. BLEICH is presently Rosh Yeshiva (Professor of Talmud) and Rosh Kollel LeHora'ah (Head of the Postgraduate Institute for Jurisprudence and Family Law) of the Rabbi Isaac Elchanan Theological Seminary of Yeshiva University; Professor of Law, Benjamin N. Cardozo School of Law; Tenzer Professor of Jewish Law and Ethics, Yeshiva University; and Rabbi of the Yorkville Synagogue in New York City. He has taught at several universities. He was a Woodrow Wilson Fellow, Post-Doctoral Fellow at the Hastings Institute for Ethics, and Visiting Scholar at the Oxford Center for Post-Graduate Hebrew Studies. He is the Editor of the contemporary *halachah* department of the prestigious periodical *Tradition*; Contributing Editor to *Sh'ma*; Associate

Editor of *Cancer Investigation*; past Chairman of the Committee on Medical Ethics of the Federation of Jewish Philanthropies of New York; Founding Chairman of the Section in Jewish Law of the Association of American Law Schools; Contributor to the *Encyclopedia of Bioethics*; New York State past Chairman of the Committee on Law of the Rabbinical Alliance of America; Member of the Governor's Task Force on Life and the Law; and Member of numerous medical ethics committees and advisory boards.

Rabbi Bleich is the author of *Contemporary Halakhic Problems* (4 vols.); *Providence in the Philosophy of Gersonides*; *Judaism and Healing*; *Time of Death in Jewish Law*; and *Birchat HaHammah*. In addition to numerous published original articles on topics of Jewish law and ethics, he edited *With Perfect Faith: Readings in the Foundations of Jewish Belief* and, with Fred Rosner, *Jewish Bioethics*. His four-volume *Contemporary Halakhic Problems* is recognized as a masterful elucidation of Jewish law in many areas of modern medicine and biomedical technology.

Rabbi Bleich's background in law, as well as his concentration on teaching practical *halachah*, makes medical and legal ethics an ideal partnership with talmudic law. This synthesis of modern bioethics and Jewish law is apparent in his meticulous and scholarly methods and approach to sources. His scope is broad, and he cites legal systems and sources from other faiths with skill and profound Torah learning. The scope of his knowledge and the expertise with which he articulates and writes about the topics are truly remarkable.

DAVID M. FELDMAN is the author of a now-classic book titled *Birth Control in Jewish Law: Marital Relations, Contraception, and Abortion, as Set Forth in the Classic Texts of Jewish Law*, published by New York University Press. The book then appeared in several paperback editions and has now been republished in augmented form, dubbed "Third Edition—With Epilogue 1995." He is also author of *The Jewish Family Relationship* and *Health and Medicine in the Jewish Tradition*. He is Coeditor of the *Compendium on Medical Ethics*, and he has written several articles for the *Encyclopedia Judaica* and the *Encyclopedia of Bioethics*.

Rabbi Feldman pursued graduate studies at Columbia University and at the University of Illinois, and he holds degrees from Yeshiva University and the Jewish Theological Seminary. Having served as Chaplain in the U.S. Air Force and then, for many years, as Rabbi of the Bay Ridge Jewish Center in Brooklyn, he is now Rabbi of the Jewish Center of Teaneck, New Jersey. He recently was awarded the "Rabbi of the Year" Award from the New York Board of Rabbis.

Rabbi Feldman served as Chairman of the Committee on Medical Ethics of UJA-Federation and as Chairman of its Committee on Marriage and Divorce, as well as Vice-Chairman of the Interfaith Commission of Marriage and the Family. A long-standing member of the Law Committee of the Rabbinical Assembly, he served on the Faculty of the School for Chaplains of the New York Board of Rabbis, and as Visiting Associate Professor at the Jewish Theological Seminary. He is a Founding Fellow of the Hastings Institute of Society, Ethics and the Life Sciences, and a member of the Editorial Advisory Board of the *Encyclopedia of Bioethics*, sponsored by the Kennedy Institute.

Dr. Feldman has lectured widely before synagogue, university, and medical groups. He has given testimony in Albany and Washington on abortion and population issues. He was invited to Rome to address a Vatican-sponsored conference on the subject of his first book, and he delivered a series of lectures on Jewish law at the Law School of the Hebrew University in Jerusalem.

MORDECHAI HALPERIN received rabbinic ordination "Yoreh Yoreh, Yadin Yadin" from Yeshivat Ponevez in Bnei Brak, Israel. His medical degrees (M.D. and M.B.Sc.) are from the Hebrew University–Hadassah Medical School in Jerusalem. He is, thus, an example of the scientist–rabbi combination.

He specializes in gynecology and obstetrics, with emphasis on impotence and infertility. He is the Director of the Jerusalem Medical Center for Impotence and Infertility, and Director of the Falk Schlesinger Institute for Medical Halakhic Research at the Shaare Zedek Medical Center in Jerusalem. He is the editor of *Assia*, a renowned Hebrew quarterly journal on *halachah* and medicine.

Dr. Halperin has served on many governmental committees investigating sexual abuse of psychiatric patients, the status of pregnancy termination, and surrogate motherhood and in vitro fertilization in Israel. He is a founding member of the Israeli Society for Medical Ethics and a member of the Israel Academy of Sciences and Humanities. He has lectured widely, at scholarly conferences in Israel and abroad. He has edited or coedited eleven journals and periodicals, has over 100 publications (books and articles) to his credit, and has received several prizes and awards.

FRED ROSNER is Director of the Department of Medicine of the Queens Hospital Center in Jamaica, New York, a major teaching campus of New York's Mount Sinai School of Medicine, where he serves as Professor of Medicine. He is a diplomate of the American Board of Internal Medicine and a Fellow of the American College of Physicians. He is also Visiting Professor of Medicine at his alma mater, the Albert Einstein College of Medicine of Yeshiva University.

Dr. Rosner is the recipient of the Maimonides Award from the Michael Reese Medical Center and Chicago College of Jewish Studies for "Notable Contributions to the Field of Medicine and Judaica"; the Bernard Revel Memorial Award from the Yeshiva College Alumni Association for "Distinguished Achievement in the Arts and Sciences"; the Maimonides Award of Wisconsin for "Distinguished and Extraordinary Service to Learning and Science"; a medal from the Ben Gurion University in Beersheba, Israel; and the Lawrence D. Redway Award for "Excellence in Medical Writing" from the Medical Society of the State of New York.

Dr. Rosner is listed in *Who's Who in America*, *Who's Who in World Jewry*, the *Dictionary of International Biography* (London), *American Men and Women of Science*, and the *National Social Directory* (New York). He is a contributor to the *Encyclopedia Judaica*, and the *Encyclopedia of Bioethics*, a member of the Advisory Board of the Israel Institute for the History of Medicine, and Consultant to the Medical Research Council of Canada. He is also a member of numerous professional and scientific organizations.

Dr. Rosner is an internationally known authority on medical ethics. He has lectured widely on Jewish medical ethics and is in great demand as a speaker on this and related topics. He has served as Visiting Professor or Lecturer in Australia; Canada; Denmark; England; France; Germany; Holland; Israel; Mexico; New Zealand; South Africa; Sweden; and the United States. He is a member of the Professional Advisory Board of the prestigious Kennedy Institute for Ethics of Georgetown University. He is also Chairman of the Medical Ethics Committee of the Medical Society of the State of

New York and former Cochairman of the Medical Ethics Committee of the Federation of Jewish Philanthropies of New York and Coeditor of its popular *Compendium on Medical Ethics.*

Dr. Rosner is a manuscript reviewer for sixteen professional medical journals and serves on the editorial boards of three of them. He has published 36 books and has written by invitation chapters in several dozen books. His bibliography contains over 800 items. He is the author of six widely acclaimed books on Jewish medical ethics, including *Modern Medicine and Jewish Ethics* (2nd enlarged ed., Ktav, 1991) and *Medicine and Jewish Law I* and *II* (Jason Aronson, 1990 and 1993). These books are up-to-date examinations of the Jewish view on many important bioethical issues in medical practice.

Dr. Rosner has also published extensively on Jewish medical history, including an English translation of Julius Preuss' classic reference work titled *Biblical and Talmudic Medicine* (reprinted in 1993). Dr. Rosner is also the translator, editor, or author of many books on Moses Maimonides and is recognized as an authority on this medieval giant of Judaism.

In addition to being a prolific writer, Dr. Rosner is also a superb organizer of views from the classic Jewish sources and modern rabbinic responsa. Although he claims not to issue *psak halachah*, or rabbinic decisions, his writings clearly indicate where the preponderance of halachic opinion lies. He collects the views of many and arranges them so that the subject is clear to the reader because the literature is succinctly summarized.

AVRAHAM STEINBERG received rabbinic ordination following study at Yeshivat Merkaz Harav Kook in Jerusalem. His medical degree was obtained at the Hebrew University–Hadassah Medical School in Jerusalem. Following service in the Israeli Air Force, he obtained postdoctoral training in adult and pediatric neurology at the Albert Einstein College of Medicine of Yeshiva University in New York. He presently practices his specialty at the Shaare Zedek Medical Center in Jerusalem, where he formerly directed the Falk Schlesinger Institute for Medical–halachic research.

Dr. Steinberg is Director of the Center for Clincal Ethics at the Hebrew University–Hadassah Medical School. He is a member of the editorial boards of the *Israel Journal of Medical Sciences, Assia*, and *Jewish Medical Ethics.* He is a member of numerous professional societies and is listed in several international biographies and directories. He is the recipient of numerous awards and prizes, including the Rabbi Kook Prize from the municipality of Tel Aviv–Jaffa, the Katz Prize, the Gerta Schwartz Prize, and the Abramowitz–Zetlin Prize.

Dr. Steinberg has written or edited 15 books, another 15 chapters in books, and over 180 articles, nearly all dealing with Jewish medical ethics. His most important work is a six-volume Hebrew *Encyclopedia of Jewish Medical Ethics and Law* (1988–1997), which has established itself as the classic reference work on this subject. It is a masterful and scholarly work that reviews all the important topics in medial ethics, giving linguistic and scientific backgrounds on each topic followed by exhaustive discussions of all halachic sources from classic Hebrew writings such as the Bible and Talmud to the modern rabbinic Responsa literature. This massive work is currently being translated into English by Dr. Fred Rosner.

Dr. Steinberg is also an internationally renowned lecturer on Jewish medical ethics and is invited frequently to major conferences in Israel and abroad to lecture on these subjects.

MOSHE DAVID TENDLER is a combination of rabbi, biochemist, scientist, and Professor of Talmud, thus representing an ideal of the Jewish people found more often in early times than today. He has published many scientific articles in leading medical journals. His contribution to Jewish medical ethics, however, lies more in his oral lectures and rabbinic decisions on crucial ethical dilemmas than in formal publications.

Rabbi Tendler has headed cancer-research laboratories in New York and for the Unites States government. At present, he is a medical-ethics consultant for the American College of Chest Physicians, the Society of Critical Care Medicine, and the National Association of the Bioethics of Embryo Research, the research arm of the American College of Obstetrics and Gynecology. He is also Consultant in fermentation chemistry to several pharmaceutical firms, such as Hoffmann-LaRoche.

Rabbi Tendler is University Professor of Medical Ethics at Yeshiva University and its Albert Einstein College of Medicine and was Chairman of the Medical Ethics Commission of the Federation of Jewish Philanthropies of New York. He is also Professor of Talmudic Law. His father was one of the leading rabbis of America of the last generation and one of the early leaders of the Rabbinical Association (*Agudat Harabanim*) of the United States and Canada. Rabbi Tendler is the son-in-law of the late Rabbi Moshe Feinstein, who was, until his death in 1986, the leading world authority in Jewish law as it relates to practical issues. For thirty-six years, in addition to his many scientific and pedagogic interests, Rabbi Tendler served as Rabbi Feinstein's right hand and was consulted on many of the responsa that that great man issued.

Rabbi Tendler is a teacher par excellence and was among the first to teach medical ethics as a halachic discipline. He was the first to introduce courses on this subject in any university, with his pioneering classes at Yeshiva University and later at the Albert Einstein College of Medicine. His teaching style flows into his decision making so that his halachic discussions are laced with the philosophy and rationale of the *halachah* in question. He often finds fascinating and even startling biological or chemical evidence that corresponds to a halachic principle.

Rabbi Tendler's contribution is, therefore, threefold: his responses to the many questions he is asked in the field of medical *halachah*; his frequent lectures and his many courses on the subject; and his published writings, both articles and books.

DISCUSSION OF ISSUES

The following are a few examples of the way some of these contemporary specialists in Jewish medical ethics approach specific issues in medicine and *halachah*. Medical ethics can be divided into categories in many ways: from birth until death of the human being; from the point of view of the physician, the patient, and society; by comparing universally agreed-upon issues and those under controversy; and from many other such vantages. For the purposes of this chapter, I have selected certain issues that underscore the approach some of these modern pioneers of medical ethics use in dealing with the sources, highlighting areas of agreement and disagreement, and incidentally noting how their citations often complement each other, though with different emphasis and style.

THE PHYSICIAN AND THE PATIENT

Rabbi Bleich contrasts the legal system of our country with that of Judaism. In the Unites States, the relationship between a physician and his patient is contractual, so that a doctor has the absolute legal right to refuse to treat a patient who is not yet under his care.[1] A physician in fact may not, except in an emergency, treat patients without their consent.[2] In Jewish law, we have a responsibility to heal the patient beyond that of a legal contract.[3]

Rabbi Tendler, Dr. Rosner, Rabbi Bleich, and others agree that there are three primary sources indicating that Judaism encourages the practice of medicine. None are based on the assumption of a legal contract. Rabbi Tendler indicates that each of these sources adds a more inclusive dimension to the authorization. "Heal, ye shall heal" authorizes the doctor to practice his art. "Return lost property" requires all individuals, skilled as physicians or not, to do what they can for the patient, to the limits of their skill and ability.[4] "Thou shalt not stand idly by while the blood of your neighbor is being shed" requires involvement, even if it costs money and extra effort.[5]

Rabbi Bleich cites later Sages who add additional sources to the requirement to heal. Thus, Nachmanides states that the obligation to heal is inherent in the commandment *And you shall love your*

---

1. J.D. Bleich, *Judaism and Healing* (Ktav Publishers, New York 1981) p. 11.
2. Ibid., pp. 18–20.
3. See H.A. Broide, "*Hovat Harofe Lachole . . .* "*Assia 51–52*, Vol. 13, Iyar 5752, for a discussion of whether a doctor must force healing on a patient in the event that there is a difference of opinion between them.
4. If you must return his lost donkey, you must certainly return his lost health.
5. See Maimonides, *Mishnah Commentary*, Tractate *Nedarim* 4:4. See also *Shulchan Aruch, Yoreh Deah* 336:4, and *Sifsei Cohen*; see also *Chafetz Chaim, Hilchot Issurey Rechilut*, 9, and *Beer Mayim Chayim*, ibid., for a discussion including monetary and physical damage under the commandment not to stand idly by while your neighbor's blood is shed.

neighbor as yourself (Leviticus 19:18).[6] In his Bible commentary (Leviticus 25:36), he adds the source *And your brother shall live with you* as constituting a general obligation to preserve the life of one's fellow. The Talmud (*Yoma* 85b) interprets this passage to mean *And he shall live through* [the commandments] *but he shall not die by any means of them*, and accordingly Nachmanides interprets this verse as establishing the principle that Torah commandments are suspended in the face of life-threatening dangers.[7]

Characteristically, Dr. Rosner gives a general review of major sources, adding Ibn Ezra's opinion that only external wounds are to be healed by mortals, but internal ailments should be left to God. However, he indicates that this restriction is almost universally rejected.[8] He adds a discussion about whether a patient is required to seek healing. Among the sources he quotes is Maimonides' statement that a person should care for his health, since one cannot properly comprehend God's wisdom when hungry, or ailing, or if one of the limbs is aching.[9]

In discussing the physician's obligation to heal, Dr. Rosner also summarizes modern ethical questions facing physicians from the moment they enter medical school throughout their time of practice, including issues from sexuality and procreation through death and dying.[10]

PHYSICIANS' FEES

May a physician charge a fee? After all, if he is obligated to heal, perhaps that healing should be available to all free of charge. While it is acceptable to charge a fee, Rabbi Bleich cites sources indicating

---

6. J.D. Bleich, *Contemporary Halakhic Problems*, Vol. II (Ktav Publishing Co. and Yeshiva University Press, New York, 1983), p. 54ff.

7. Ibid., p. 55.

8. F. Rosner, *Modern Medicine and Jewish Ethics* (Ktav Publishing and Yeshiva University Press, Hoboken, NJ and New York, NY 1986), p. 10.

9. Ibid., pp. 15–21.

10. Ibid., pp. 23–58.

that the physician must make his services available to rich and poor alike. The Rabbinical Court (*Beit Din*) has coercive power to ensure this, for the *Beit Din* is the executive and administrative arm of society.[11]

Rabbi Tendler and Dr. Rosner deal with the question of whether a physician may charge a fee for caring for a patient on the Sabbath or a Festival. They conclude that, ordinarily, the physician may not charge for medical care on the Sabbath, for the fee would constitute payment for work performed on the Sabbath. However, if the absence of a fee would prevent the availability of medical care, then such a fee may be charged.[12]

PRIVACY

Refusal of Treatment

Rabbi Tendler stresses that Judaism denies the "right to refuse treatment." Giving such a right is tantamount to affording someone the right to commit suicide, which is forbidden in *halachah*. He explains that to refuse treatment that can "keep life going" is an act of suicide. He objects to the New Jersey Supreme Court decisions made on the basis of the so-called "right of privacy," which give patients the legal right to refuse treatment even if they are not critically ill and have no shortened lifespan owing to a disease.

---

11. Bleich, *Judaism and Healing*, p. 16f, citing R. Eliezer Fleckles, *Teshuvot me-Ahavah, III, Yoreh De'ah*, No. 336; R. Shalom Schachneh, *Mishmeret Shalom*, II, 99; and R. David Katz, *Bet David, II, Yoreh De'ah*, No. 306. See also Rabbi Yitzchok Zilberstein and Dr. Pinchas Nemeth, "*Schar Harophe BeHalakah*," *Assia*, Vol. 10, No. 3, Tevet 5745, p. 26–31, for a discussion on payment for medical services. There, Rabbi Goren discusses whether physicians may go on strike (32–45).

12. F. Rosner and M.D. Tendler, *Practical Medical Halakhah*, 3rd rev. ed. (Association of Orthodox Jewish Scientists and Ktav Publishing, Hoboken, NJ 1990), p. 151, citing *Shulchan Aruch, Orach Chaim* 245; 246; 330:9; 407:3.

Rabbi Tendler declares that, from a religious point of view, such patients are committing suicide.[13]

Right to Know

Rabbi Tendler also objects to the way the law is interpreted in regard to the "right to know." He indicates that the *halachah* differs greatly from the broad interpretation the courts have given to the concept of the "right of privacy," which, in effect, gives the right to know everything. He cites the Code of Jewish Law,[14] which states: "It is forbidden to tell a patient if he is seriously ill or that someone else has died, *shelo yishbor es libo, shelo titrof es daato*," which literally means: "lest you break his heart or upset his mind." Properly interpreted, "not to break his heart" means not to cause depression, and "not to upset his mind" means not to cause him to give up the will to live.

Dr. Abraham S. Abraham agrees, and, in his commentary to the Code of Jewish Law, states that:

1. Deathbed confession applies only to a patient whose death is imminent.[15]
2. One does not reveal the extent of illness to a timid soul who would lose courage and become depressed.[16]
3. A doctor may not declare a patient to have no hope whatsoever, nor may he issue an opinion about how much time a patient has yet to live.
4. Nowadays, since a patient's help, consent, and cooperation are necessary for treatment, and types of treatment such as chemotherapy indicate, in themselves, the extent and often the type of illness, it is frequently necessary to share information with the patient in order to bolster his courage and give him hope.[17]

---

13. *Tendler Lectures, First Sidney Conference on Jewish Bioethics* (Nisson Shulman, ed., Sydney, Australia, August 1987), p. 33.

14. *Hilchot Bikur Cholim*, No. 383.

15. *Yoreh Deah*, No. 338; la. He cites differing opinions as well.

16. Ibid., 338:3; lc. He also cites Rabbi M. Feinstein, who holds this opinion.

17. *Assia*, Vol. 11, No. 2–3, a letter added to the discussion, 24ff.

Dr. Rosner agrees with the necessity to withhold information if the disclosure may discourage the patient, while acknowledging that modern treatments often reveal the extent of illness. In discussing this issue in their work *Practical Medical Halakhah*, Rabbi Tendler and Dr. Rosner conclude that, in the Jewish view, patients suffering from a fatal illness should not be so informed if there is the slightest chance that such knowledge may further impair the physical or mental well-being of the patient. Jewish ethics permit, and even require, that the facts concerning the true severity of the illness be withheld from the patient. The patient should be made aware that he is seriously ill so that he may be forewarned to "set his house in order," but this should be done without giving that patient a wholly negative outlook. Rather, the positive side of the illness—including the chances for cure, however remote—should be emphasized. Only in exceptional circumstances should the truth be divulged to the patient. Even then, it should be emphasized that medical prognostications may be grossly inaccurate, lest they further reduce the morale and defense capabilities of the patient and his family. Mention of death should be avoided if possible, lest the will to live be undermined.[18] In summarizing the opinions relating to informing the patient, Dr. Rosner stresses that the act of telling is an art that requires experience, knowledge, and understanding.[19]

Privileged Communication

Rabbi Bleich discusses the problem of privileged communication. He cites the source *You shall not go as a bearer of tales among your people* (Leviticus 19:16) as forbidding the divulgence of personal information concerning another. "Such activity is forbidden even when not accompanied by malicious intent and even if the information is not derogatory in nature."[20]

Judaism acknowledges that in certain circumstances even professional confidences must be revealed. Disclosure of medical infor-

18. Rosner and Tendler, *Practical Medical Halakhah* (1990), p. 53.
19. Rosner, *Modern Medicine and Jewish Ethics*, p. 62.
20. Maimonides, *Mishneh Torah, Hilchot Deot*, 7:2.

mation, in particular, is discussed in detail in a work titled *Chafetz Chaim*, where the author discusses a person seeking disclosure of medical information concerning a prospective marriage partner. While the author permits disclosure, he makes the following four conditions:

1. The presence of a disease or a physical defect may be disclosed. However, a vague, general weakness or deficiency that does not directly compromise health may not be disclosed.
2. The nature or extent of a disease or injury must not be exaggerated in any way.
3. The sole motivation prompting disclosure must be the benefit of the person to whom the information is supplied. No disclosure may be made when prompted, even in part, by personal animosity.
4. Disclosure is permissible only when reasonable grounds exist for assuming that the information divulged will be the determining factor in terms of the contemplated marriage.[21]

In general, Rabbi Bleich stresses the "need to know" principle as the determining factor in disclosing such information. He also indicates that "the respect for privacy and the inviolability of the professional relationship certainly do take precedence over protection of the lives and safety of others."[22]

THE ALLOCATION OF SCARCE RESOURCES, AND INDIVIDUAL VERSUS SOCIETAL ETHICS

The allocation of scarce medical resources is one of the most vexing problems of our time.

Brian Glenville, a London heart surgeon, gives an excellent

21. Bleich, op. cit., p. 34ff. He cites *Chafetz Chaim, Hilkhot Issurei Rekhilut*, Klal 9.

22. Ibid.

insight into some of the problems facing physicians on a daily basis. He states:

> Planning for intensive care is . . . a problem. We have a fixed number of beds and if I do not plan my week in a fairly crude and harsh manner, I will not be able to practice. If I operate on an eighty-three year old who needs a double valve replacement, she will occupy an intensive care bed for five days. If I select that patient for a Monday, her bed will not be available to me until Saturday. If I perform that operation on a Friday, there is a good chance that I might be able to get her to a High Dependency Unit on the following Monday. If so, I will be able to carry on with the list. If I operate on a Monday, I am stopping four CABG (bypass) patients, who would have zipped through on Tuesday, Wednesday, Thursday, and Friday.[23]

Dr. Rosner gives an overview of the issues and some of the leading opinions in *halachah*.[24] He stresses the difference between societal and individual decisions in this area. Rabbi Bleich, too, discusses the difference between individual ethics and societal ethics and concludes that an individual physician could sidestep his responsibilities by removing himself from situations in which his aid might be sought. While such conduct does not merit approbation, the physician who acts in this manner does not incur the guilt of a technical *halachah* infraction. Society, however, has wider responsibilities that are accompanied by broad-ranging authority. Within autonomous Jewish communities, society's responsibility for the promotion of communal well-being is discharged through the *Beit Din* (Rabbinical Court). Thus, the *Beit Din* is empowered to compel the physician to make himself available and to function in his professional capacity.[25]

Rabbi Tendler discusses the question of triage in connection with the allocation of scarce medical resources and develops the discus-

---

23. Brian Glenville, *Yearbook of the Centre for Medical Ethics* (Nisson Shulman, ed., Jews' College, London, Vol. 1, 1993), p. 113.

24. Rosner, *Modern Medicine and Jewish Ethics*, pp. 339–352.

25. Bleich, The Role of the Physician, in *Judaism and Healing*, Ch. 1, p. 13.

sion as follows: Triage at the societal level is a series of conflicts of one good against another, rather than good versus bad. Everyone seeks to heal, but everyone has his own priority in achieving this goal. In this series of conflicts of good versus good, the individual must react differently than society may, for there is more to society than the individuals in it. Rabbi Tendler marshals two talmudic texts to support his thesis.

Triage decisions are made between two communities—one has water, the other does not (*Nedarim* 80b). They are made between two departments—who gets the allocation of funds? But triage decisions between our generation and those yet unborn must also be made. With all our modern technology, we have great difficulty in disposing of radioactive waste. Can we seal it in cement canisters and sink it into the sea? We have enough technology now to hide waste for five hundred years. But what happens after that? What about the yet-unborn generations? After five hundred years, how many people will develop leukemia and how many will have malformed children? Whose concern is this? Do triage concerns extend to other generations? Of course they do.[26]

VISITING THE SICK

Rabbi Bleich cites the actions of Rabbi Akiva Eger, who, despite his extreme reluctance to spend precious moments in other activities, made it a constant practice to personally visit the sick. Frequently he would spend the entire night at the bedside of a critically ill patient.[27] Rabbi Tendler cites the Talmud,[28] which discusses reasons for visiting the sick and tells of a disciple of Rabbi Akiva's who took sick, but where friends did not visit him. So Rabbi Akiva himself came to visit his disciple. The honor that the student felt, and the care Rabbi Akiva gave him, prompted him to say: "My

26. Moshe D. Tendler, "Rabbinic Comment: Triage of Resources"; *The Mount Sinai Journal of Medicine*, Vol. 51, No. 1, (Jan.–Feb. 1984), 106–109.

27. Bleich, op. cit., p. 44 and n. 1.

28. *Nedarim* 39a.

teacher, you have enlivened me." Rabbi Akiva then went into the study hall and taught: "If you do not visit the sick, you are a [moral] murderer." In other words, if it is within your ability to enliven someone, failure to do so is passive euthanasia.

When Rabbi Dimi heard Rabbi Akiva's disclosure, he added to it and said, "Whoever visits the sick causes him to live. Whoever does not visit him causes him to die." The Talmud explains how the visit impinges upon the physiology of the patient in such a way as to cause life or death:

> What is the reason for this? Is it because I pray he should live, does that mean that if I do not visit him I pray he should die? No! By failing to visit him I do not learn of his status, and I do not know what to do! Should I pray for life or for death?[29]

Rashi explains that if the patient wants to die, one must provide him at least with helpful solace. Maimonides rules that if one visits the sick at a time when he is suffering and close to death, one may pray that he should die. Based on this discussion, Rabbi Tendler makes the following comment:

> A person cannot delegate his obligation of visiting the sick to another person, since the latter is also obliged to fulfill the commandment of *bikur cholim*. Nor should one delegate the recitation of prayers for the patient to others because all are so obligated and the more people that pray, the more likely it is that God will hear them.[30]

Dr. Rosner outlines procedures for visiting the sick, beginning with the statement in the Talmud that there is no limit to such visitation, and the interpretations of the statement.[31] He cites the limitations quoted by the rabbis, all in order to ensure the patient's well-being.

---

29. Ibid.

30. *Practical Medical Halakhah*, p. 165, citing Rabbi Moses Feinstein, *Iggrot Moshe, Yoreh Deah*, responsum 223 (New York, 1959), pp. 450–451.

31. *Nedarim* 39a; See Rosner, *Modern Medicine . . .* , p. 69ff; Rabbi Joseph, that the reward is unlimited; Abaye, that a prominent person must visit a simple person; Rava, that there is no limit to the number of visits.

JEWS AND GENTILES

Restrictions against touching a dead body apply to the corpse of a gentile as well as to that of a Jew.[32] Dr. Rosner and Rabbi Tendler deal with a question about whether a Jewish physician attending a non-Jew on the Sabbath must treat him exactly as if he were attending a Jew so that all exemptions from Sabbath laws that apply to a critically ill Jewish patient apply equally to the non-Jewish patient. They conclude that the Sabbath laws, both rabbinic and biblical, are set aside when a Jewish physician is actively involved in the care of any patient, Jew or non-Jew. (This rule applies, of course, only in a medical situation that Jewish law classifies as *pikuach nefesh*—danger to life.)[33]

PROCREATION: BIRTH CONTROL, ARTIFICIAL INSEMINATION, IN VITRO FERTILIZATION

Dr. Rosner writes that "the most extensive study of the principles of Judaism concerning contraception, based on a wealth of primary sources, is that of David Feldman. In his book[34] Rabbi Feldman examines the relevant precepts of the Talmud, codes, commentaries, and rabbinic Responsa. Feldman's work is so exhaustive that recent articles on the subject add very little to the overall picture."[35]

Rabbi Bleich is very strict about birth control, but he does permit

32. Bleich, op. cit., p. 38, citing *Shulchan Aruch* and *Rema, Yoreh Deah* 372:2.

33. *Practical Medical Halakhah*, p. 149, citing the Chatam Sofer on *Yoreh Deah* 131 (abstract printed in margin of *Shulchan Aruch, Orach Chayim* 329).

34. D. Feldman, *Birth Control in Jewish Law* (New York: New York University Press, 1968).

35. Rosner, *Modern Medicine . . .*, p. 78.

postcoital devices in certain circumstances, although he cites some Sages who are more lenient. Rabbenu Tam's lenient view regarding postcoital devices permits them in some circumstances, but not for precoital control. Rabbi Chaim Ozer Grodzinski of Vilna maintains that in the case of a clear hazard, the Sages would concur in permitting even precoital contraception.[36]

Dr. Abraham cites opinions[37] that forbid artificial insemination even with the husband's semen[38] and those that permit it if the husband's semen is used. Some rabbis permit it only after unsuccessful years of attempting to procreate[39]; other opinions permit the practice when necessary without the limitation of years of effort (Rabbi Shlomo Zalman Auerbach and others).[40] Dr. Abraham adds that since there is often a need to concentrate the semen to attain an adequate sperm count, it is extremely important to be assured that the physician is trustworthy and would not mix in semen from an outside donor.[41] He also cites Rabbi Moses Feinstein's statement that in certain rare instances he had permitted insemination with donor semen provided that the donor was not Jewish, although he limited this ruling to a particular case where the woman was suffering intense emotional stress.[42]

Dr. Mordechai Halperin adds that there is a possible advantage to embryo transfer with a foreign donor (IVFD) to artificial insemination with a foreign donor (AID), since there is no prohibition of

---

36. Bleich, op. cit., p. 58.

37. A.S. Abraham, *Nishmat Avraham* (Jerusalem, 1987), *Even Haezer, Hilkhot Priyah Ureviah*, No. 1.

38. Responsa *Divre Malchiel*, part 4, No. 107; and the Chazon Ish as quoted by *Responsa Tzitz Eliezer*, part 9, No. 51, Section 4:86; and *Responsa Mishpetei Uziel*, part II, No. 19; and *Responsa Yaskil Avdi*, part 5, *Even Haezer*, No. 10.

39. *Responsa Maharsha'm*, part III, No. 268; Har Zvi comment on Tur cited in *Otzar HaPoskim* 23:1:1; *Responsa Minchat Yitzchak*, part I, No. 50, and part III, No. 108; *Responsa Zekan Aharon*, No. 97.

40. *Noam*, Vol. 1 (5718), p. 157; *Responsa Seridey Esh*, Part III, No. 5; *Responsa Yabia Omer*, part II, *Even Haezer*, No. 1.

41. *Nishmat Avraham, Even Haezer*, loc. cit., p. 6ff.

42. A letter cited by *Responsa Helkat Yaakov*, part III, No. 47.

embryo transfer, while scholars forbid donor insemination directly from a Jewish donor, and most from a non-Jewish donor.[43]

Rabbi Bleich mentions the opinion of Catholic theologians who say that interference with barrenness is in violation of natural law but says that this argument is alien to Judaism.[44] He is also doubtful whether fertilized zygotes can be discarded during the protocol of IVF. Thus, the use of one fetal egg and the discarding of many "extra" eggs in IVF procedures is not acceptable to him. He would limit the procedure to the fertilization of a single ovum.[45] Rabbi Tendler agrees with the first point and disagrees with the second. In a series of lectures in Australia[46] he offered the following analysis.

> 1. *Tampering with this world*: Our Jewish view of man's role in nature differs from that of other religions. For the Pope, artificiality by its very nature is immoral, whereas for the Jew it may very well be a *mitzvah*, fulfilling a commandment of the Almighty.
>
> When we add artificiality to the world and peel off veils from nature to reveal the hidden mysteries that lie underneath, we are not tampering with God's world. Rather, we are fulfilling the *mitzvah* of *v'chibshuhah*.[47]
>
> 2. *Endangering or causing pain to a woman for the sake of an IVF protocol*: When Rachel realized she would not become pregnant, she said to Jacob, *Hovoh li bonim ve'im ayin meisah anochi* (Give me children, or else I shall die). The Torah records that language to teach that one is dealing with a deathly ill woman. Rachel said that she was dying, and hence infertility is

---

43. M. Halperin, "Applying the Principles of Halakhah to Modern Medicine: In-Vitro Fertilization, Embryo Transfer and Frozen Embryo," *Proceedings of the Association of Orthodox Jewish Scientists*, Vol. 8–9, Charles S. Naiman, Ph.D, ed. (New York: Sepher Hermon Press, Inc., 1987), pp. 203ff.

44. Bleich, op. cit., p. 88.

45. Ibid., p. 90.

46. *The Tendler Lectures, First Sydney Conference of Jewish Bioethics*, Nisson E. Shulman, ed. (August 11–19, 1987), pp. 7–17.

47. Ibid., p. 8ff.

defined halachically as an illness. Using that definition is the only justification for a woman to subject herself to the rigors of infertility-management protocols. Furthermore, there is a *mitzvah* to return a lost object. Lost fertility, to a woman, is more important than a lost diamond ring. It is a *mitzvah* to return a lost diamond ring; it is a *mitzvah* to return her lost reproductive capacity. Hence, we have the commandment to reach out and help within the boundaries set by Torah, set by *halachah*.[48]

3. *The actual protocol*: Among the issues that arise from the actual protocol is the discarding of fertilized human eggs. Under the physiological stimulus of exogenous hormones, the woman superovulates, and multiple eggs are removed from her ovary and fertilized. Several are inseminated as part of the IVF procedure. What happens to the others? There is, certainly, wastage of these embryos if one decides not to freeze them. Most experts recommend not to freeze the excess embryos. Rabbi Tendler is convinced that the disposal of the excess fertilized eggs involves no violation of any Jewish or moral ethical law.[49]

4. *Who is the mother?* Who is the mother of a child that was conceived from the egg of another woman or carried to term in the womb of another ("incubator") woman? Do we consider gestational motherhood? Do we consider genetic motherhood? The sperm determines paternity. What determines motherhood? Rabbi Tendler cites a decision by Rabbi Moshe Feinstein to the Chief Rabbi of Israel, stating that such a child must be considered as having two mothers, and that consanguinity laws apply to both families. Hence, gestational motherhood cannot be discounted.[50]

While Rabbi Tendler emphasizes the mandate to treat infertility since it is considered an illness, Dr. Mordechai Halperin takes a different approach to come to the same conclusion. He offers the general halachic principle, based on the Mishnah,[51] that emphasizes

48. Ibid., p. 10ff.
49. Ibid., p. 13ff.
50. Ibid., p. 14ff.
51. Mishnah, *Yadayim* 4:3.

that only the *prohibitive* requires juridical substantiation or supportive precedent, but *permissibility* needs no supportive precedent. "The very absence of a prohibitive substantiation is to be equated with halakhic permissibility. The practical implication is that any scientific or technologic innovation is permissible unless there is a halakhic reason for prohibiting it."[52] Of course, one must consult a competent halachic authority before acting on such a principle. Dr. Halperin presents steps to be taken to establish such permissibility, particularly the search for parallel precedents and analogous rulings. He finds these in three basic principles: the commandment to be fruitful and multiply; the *mitzvah* to show lovingkindness; and the importance of family integrity.[53] The second of these principles, lovingkindness, which requires that we alleviate suffering, corresponds to Rabbi Tendler's biblical citation of the suffering of Rachel. Rabbi Tendler goes further, however, and considers the intervention in the category of "healing" the mental anguish of a childless woman.

STUDYING ANATOMY

Rabbi Bleich concentrates on two issues as problems in the study of anatomy: the prohibition of *nivul hamet*, desecrating the dead; and the prohibition of deriving benefit from the dead. The prohibition of deriving benefit from the dead would not allow advance directives by the patient to permit anatomical dissection, since this is a commandment between man and God. The prohibition of desecrating the dead, however, according to some rabbis, can be set aside if a patient donates his body to science in advance. He cites Rabbi Abraham Isaac Hakohen Kook (responsa *Daat Kohen* no. 199), who sanctions the use of non-Jewish cadavers without reservation, though the question of *eivah*, causing hatred of Jews, remains. Rabbi Tendler attests that Rabbi Feinstein was very care-

52. Op. cit., p. 197.
53. Ibid., p. 198.

ful about the latter question. Rabbi Jakobovits quotes Rabbi Soloveitchik,[54] who states that no distinction may be made between Jew and non-Jew. *Thou shalt not allow his corpse to remain hanging because* [his corpse reflects] *a cursing of God* [since he was created in God's image] (Deuteronomy 21:23) applies to Jew and gentile, who are alike created in the image of God.

HOMOSEXUALITY

Halachic authorities make a clear distinction between homosexuality and homosexual conduct. In recent times, it has been suggested that homosexuality may have genetic causes. The argument has therefore been raised that, because of its possible genetic base, the conduct of homosexuality is, in some individuals, unavoidable. Others have voiced the opinion that as a genetic "disorder" it may be curable. Rabbi Bleich writes:

> If homosexuality is an aberration, then, of course, a cure must be attempted. . . . It must be recognized that this tendency may not be acted upon because homosexual contact is forbidden[55]. . . . If he cannot help himself he is considered an *onus*—deprived of the ability to exercise free will[56]. . . . *Tosafot* and *Rosh*, Nedarim 51a, indicate that the homosexual goes astray in the sense that he abandons his family. . . . The Talmud, in enumerating the relatively few meritorious practices of pagan societies of old, praises them because "they do not write a marriage contract for a male."[57]

Society has a definite obligation not to bestow a seal of legitimacy upon homosexual activity. Rabbi Bleich expresses the general view of halachic scholars when he says that "removal of the odium

54. Kovetz, *Torah Shebe'al Peh* (Jerusalem, Mosad Harav Kook, Y.L. Hacohen Maimon, ed.), Vol. I, 5724, p. 64.
55. Bleich, op. cit., p. 71.
56. Ibid., p. 72.
57. Ibid., p. 70.

associated with a transgression is even more serious a matter than the transgression itself."[58]

TRANSPLANT SURGERY

Dr. Mordechai Halperin discusses transplants from live donors where minimal or no risk attends to the donor.[59] He offers examples, such as kidney, skin, blood, and bone marrow. He addresses the following halachic and social questions: Is the risk of the donation permitted? Are there instances where we can compel the donor to offer the donation? Is it possible to permit the sale of "human spare parts"? Is the recipient permitted to accept a donation from someone who was forbidden by *halachah* to offer it? He indicates kidney donation, though associated with some risk, is permitted for the great benefit of saving life. So, too, with skin, marrow, and blood. The risk of these is even less than with kidney donation.

Dr. Halperin leaves the question of compulsion to donate unresolved. For example, if a patient with a rare blood type is bleeding to death and an unwilling donor is available, can the donor be coerced to give? Dr. Halperin indicates that though one may save a life by means of another's possessions, this rule may not apply to torts such as forcibly taking a person's blood.[60] On the other hand, there may be a requirement to force someone to save another's life. Rabbi Tendler clearly disagrees, since he stresses the prohibition of enslaving another, for we are "God's servants and not servants to servants." Both Dr. Halperin and Rabbi Tendler agree that a donor may be paid for his effort and discomfort, although a market for "body spare parts" is abhorrent.

Rabbi Tendler notes that the *halachah* concerning live kidney donation may change in light of recent medical findings of added

---

58. Ibid., p. 72, citing the severity of Sodom's punishment because they legitimized it.

59. M. Halperin, "Transplants from Live Donors," *Assia*, Vol. 12, Nos. 1–2 (January 1989), 34–61.

60. Ibid., 48ff.

risk to the donor of later developing high blood pressure, measured against greater success with cadaver kidney donations where the success rate is approaching that of live matched donors because of new antirejection drugs. According to Rabbi Tendler, while *halachah* once encouraged and commended live donor matches for kidney donation, now *halachah* would prefer use of cadaver kidneys. The heightened risk to the donor and the diminished relative benefit to the recipient would change the view of *halachah* and require the use of cadaver kidneys wherever available.[61]

TIME OF DEATH

The determination of the moment of death is one of the most important issues facing halachic scholars today, and upon this decision rests the ability to perform many of the organ transplants made possible by recent advances in medicine. The following is the summary of the opinions of some major halachic authorities.

Rabbi Aaron Soloveitchik states that death is an ongoing process and is not complete until all organs no longer function, including the heart; he thus precludes heart transplants altogether. He quotes Maimonides, who declares: "If the brain . . . spills like water . . . the animal is a *tereifah*" (unable to survive; literally "torn").[62] Since by definition a *tereifah* is alive, reasons Rabbi Soloveitchik, it follows that an animal or human being is regarded as still alive even though the brain has liquefied.

Rabbi J. David Bleich agrees with Rabbi Soloveitchik and states that mere cessation of blood flow to the brain is not the halachic equivalent of decapitation. He further argues that if respiratory activity is regarded as the sole determining criterion of the presence of life, it would follow that a polio victim who is entirely dependent upon an iron lung machine or a similar device in order to live would be regarded as dead despite the fact that such an individual is fully conscious and is capable of engaging in intellectual activities

61. *Tendler Lectures, First Sydney Conference* . . . , p. 81.
62. *Shulchan Aruch, Hilkhot Shekhitah*, 6:4.

requiring a high degree of cognition. He also argues that in the light of the halachic prohibition against moving even the limb of a *goses* or an imminently dying patient lest the patient's death be hastened thereby, it would be difficult to perform testing procedures upon a moribund patient without violating applicable halachic strictures.

Rabbi Tendler writes about Rabbi Joseph Soloveitchik's view as follows:

> Although a student of Hagaon Horav Yoseph Dov Soloveitchik, of blessed memory, for almost half a century, I cannot recall a clear *pesak* [legal decision] from him on this issue. I can recall numerous conversations in which his only expressed reservation was to the accuracy and reproducibility of the testing protocol. Rabbi Walfish, [past] Executive Vice President of the Rabbinical Council of America and also a student of his, asserts that the "*Rav*" did unequivocally accept brain-stem death as halakhically valid. Rabbi Walfish is a man of great integrity whose respect for *halakhah* and love of the *Rav* is second to none. I would also add that the *Rav* established RCA policy to support all halakhic decisions of the Chief Rabbinate of Israel that are of international, not local import.[63]

Rabbi Tendler's own views can be summarized as follows: Brain-stem death does not mean that the brain died and the body lives. It is not analogous to cardiac failure or liver failure, which is the failure of an *organ*. The Mishnah (*Ohalot* 1:7) instructs that anatomical decapitation (actual removal of the head) results in halachic death

---

63. Rabbi Herschel Schachter, also of Yeshiva University, seeks to indicate that life is defined by heartbeat, not by respiration. Lack of breathing merely indicates the lack of heartbeat. Rabbi Eliezer Waldenberg agrees with this point of view. He wonders why Rabbi Moshe Feinstein, in his responsa, ignores the question of heartbeat. He argues against Rabbi Tendler, saying, "If we accept the view that the death of any one of the vital organs defines the person as dead, it might result in some rather startling conclusions. If a person's liver is removed, or, according to Rav Moshe Feinstein's understanding even if it is gangrenous, although that person can still walk, talk and think, he would be considered halachically dead!" He therefore accepts the idea that a person is not considered dead until all the vital organs are "dead."

of the entire body, even though the heart still beats and the limbs twitch. The Talmud (*Chullin* 21a), in its statement *Zikna Shaani*, concludes that anatomical decapitation is not an absolute requirement. Even if no external wounding occurs, if the connection between the brain and body is interrupted, the entire body is dead, i.e., organismal death. Therefore, a *kohen* (priest) may not enter the room. It is forbidden to transgress the Sabbath for such a "cadaver," and there is a duty to bury the body. The clinical picture is described by Rashi in *Yoma* 85a in referring to a person buried under rubble on the Sabbath: "If he appears clinically dead, and does not move his limbs, how much does one dig to determine the truth?" The Talmud concludes, "until one exposes the nose," so as to determine if he makes any respiratory efforts, "because the source of life is in the breath."

Brainstem death that is determined after careful neurological examination affirms that the following criteria of death are all present: completely unreactive pupils; no spontaneous or elicited eye movements; no motor response to stimulation; no grimacing, blink response, or gag response; and no respiratory movement, cough, sigh, or hiccup, confirmed by an apnea test in which the patient is hyperoxygenated prior to disconnecting the ventilator.[64]

Rabbi Tendler points out that his father-in-law, Rabbi Moshe Feinstein, wrote four responsa concerning the determination of the time of death. In three responsa, he clearly refers to the type of patient now known in medical literature as the Karen Ann Quinlan or Nancy Cruzan cases. He clearly defines such a patient as *yachol linshom* (able to breathe independently). This is not a brainstem-dead patient but one referred to as cerebrally dead, or in a persistent vegetative state, or having a locked-in syndrome. Such a patient is entitled to full medical care. In his fourth responsum on brainstem death, Rabbi Feinstein identifies the patient as follows: "The doctors put him on a ventilator so that he breathes even though he is dead. Such breathing does not qualify to consider him alive."[65]

This position is discussed at greater length by Dr. Rosner and

---

64. T.P. Bleck and M.C. Smith, "Diagnosing Death and Patient Vegetative States," *Journal of Critical Illness*, 1989 4(11); 60–65.

65. *Iggrot Moshe, Yoreh Deah*, Part 3, #132.

Rabbi Tendler.[66] Dr. Mordechai Halperin[67] and Dr. Avraham Steinberg also support Rabbi Tendler's position on brain death.

CONCLUSION

The issues discussed in this chapter are but a few examples of a vast number of areas addressed by modern halachic scholars interested in medical ethics. The issues ranging from theoretical and practical research to the practice of medicine from before conception to postmortem are of deep concern to individuals, community, and society. These issues are not new in the sense that age-old Jewish principles can provide guidance. They are new in the sense that they frequently arise from advances in science and medicine, such as in genetic engineering and in vitro fertilization. They are made more significant by society's concern for the health and welfare of all its members, with the resultant astronomical growth of costs of health care. These costs grow still greater because of the ever-increasing costs of research, medicines, and treatments. New discoveries, ever-more-complicated drugs that are difficult and costly to produce, engender new problems of triage and increase the tensions and pressures upon government, community, and physician to provide treatments often beyond the reach of the patient.

These problems will not go away. They are a small sample of the great issues addressed by the medical ethicist. Almost all are met in halachic thought and illuminated by principles of Jewish law.

---

66. F. Rosner and M.D. Tendler, "Definition of Death in Judaism," *Journal of Halakhah and Contemporary Society*, No. 17, Spring 1989, 14–31.

67. See M. Halperin, "*Al Daato Shel Hagaon Rav Moshe Feinstein zt'l Besugyat Hamavet Hamochi,*" *Assia, 47–48*, Vol. 12, Kislev 5750.

Future Trends and Currents in Jewish Medical Ethics

Dr. Immanuel Jakobovits

Without the gift of prophecy, likely developments in the future can only be extrapolated from an analysis of the past—and then only with a liberal margin of error.

Certain parameters within which developments are possible or probable can be discerned. For instance, the essential building blocks of modern Jewish medical ethics, if they are to be authentically Jewish, are rulings given by leading experts on Jewish law. Such verdicts, when collected and published, are known as "responsa." By definition, they are reactive rather than proactive. They meet a demand for guidance by patients, physicians, or scholars who seek to govern their lives by Jewish teachings.

Jewish medical ethics is, therefore, not usually the product of conclaves of conferences, of formal pronouncements or edicts. The rulings become normative and assume the force of law by virtue of the (often worldwide) recognition accorded to their authors.

These conditions show every sign of remaining a permanent feature of Jewish medical ethics. The constituency seeking, and respecting, rabbinic rulings is at present experiencing a record growth—in fact, it is the only element of the Jewish people, which far from shrinking dramatically, as the rest does, proliferates at an unprecedented rate. This predisposes to a high degree of consistency in anticipated trends.

Obviously, the second crucial factor determining the future

course of medical ethics will be the development of medicine itself. Most important from a Jewish point of view will be where to draw the line between the blind march to mechanical perfection and the capacity to control the forces science and technology can now generate at our bidding for the exploitation of nature's infinite energies.

The conflict between religion and science no longer lies in a competitive search for the truth—especially on the origin of the universe and its destiny. The clash is now mainly between excesses and controls—the capacity to create, and the knowledge of where and how to stop. Jewish thought will be particularly concerned to preserve man's spirituality and humanity against the encroachments of mechanization in which human love will be replaced by syringes and test tubes in the generation of life, and the designs of Providence by the arbitrary manipulation of genes and lethal agents in the determination of life and death, or in which human beings will be constructed to specified orders.

Behavioral patterns, too, may be subject to forms induced by medicinal, chemical, or psychiatric agents—possibly denying us the freedom of choice and thus the full responsibility for our actions. Artificially operated humans are morally little different than mechanical robots. Jewish medical ethics will urge the utmost caution against the surrender to mindless powers and moral unaccountability.

In some areas, halachic issues raised in modern medicine are still unresolved and subject to heated controversy. Two such moot questions are particularly glaring examples—one at the beginning of life and the other at its end—both thrown up by the spectacular advance of modern medicine.

Certain grave genetic abnormalities in an unborn child can now be identified by amniocentesis during pregnancy, with a view to aborting the affected fetus. Particularly regarding Tay-Sachs, opinions on terminating such a pregnancy and, therefore, on carrying out such tests, are still sharply divided. Some leading halachists strongly and unreservedly object. Others give permissive rulings even up to the seventh month of gestation. Arguments in favor of the latter conclusion include the doubtful viability of a Tay-Sachs child, who is not expected to live longer than about four years.

Equally controversial, at the opposite end of life, is the definition of death with enough precision to warrant the excision of vital organs for transplant purposes. Particularly for heart transplants, the donated organs to be successfully grafted must still be functioning. Once the heart stops contracting and thus circulating the blood, it is useless as a transplant.

When I discussed this problem with Christian Barnaard within a year of his pioneering heart-transplant operation while I was on a visit to his hospital in Cape Town, it was clear to me that his definition of death differed widely from the commonly accepted halachic norm. As has been argued, one certainly would not bury a patient whose heart was still beating!

To treat the increasingly acute shortage of organs—fresh hearts in particular, especially after car seat-belt regulations considerably reduced the supply of healthy organs—the new concept of brain death or brainstem death, soon to be legalized by legislatures in many countries, was introduced by the medical fraternity. The artificial respiration of the lungs keeps the heart sufficiently oxygenated to keep the heart beating and the blood circulating; the cessation of brainstem functions, ascertained twice within forty-eight hours by a very simple test of responses to external stimuli, is deemed to constitute death.

Again, how far the new criteria of death can be reliably accepted remains the subject of fierce, often bitter, arguments among leading authorities.

Within the next few years, as medical as well as halachic research progresses, both disputes are likely to be resolved—if only by the preponderance of halachic verdicts one way or the other. The final decision depends on facts, and facts are bound to emerge convincingly in the end.

The history of halachic rulings on the very subject of heart transplants illustrates this. Among the first verdicts was a severe condemnation of the practice by the foremost halachist, Rabbi Moshe Feinstein. He called the operation "double murder"—killing the patient as well as the donor. At the time, this view was endorsed by virtually all other authorities.

But then the circumstances changed, as the problem of organ rejection was largely overcome, leading to a very high success rate—up to 95 percent survived at least for a year, and 80 percent for five years. Correspondingly, permissive rulings increased, and will no doubt continue to predominate.

A large new area that is still rather fallow and which is bound to engage ever-increasing attention is the distribution of scarce resources and the allocation of limited funds. Among the limited resources is the Jewish source material. This need, too, will eventually be met by intensified search for precedents in earlier statements of principles and decisions.

Professional ethics will also feature even more prominently. Professional secrecy, for example, does not enjoy a high priority in Jewish sources, especially when it may conflict with the public interest. Having regard to the supreme value of human life, Jewish opinion may well support greater care in controlling the spread of AIDS, such as by favoring its registration just as is required for much lesser forms of contagion.

Finally, the significant growth of Jewish medical ethics, both for practical guidance and as an academic discipline of ever-greater sophistication, will call for the more intensive training of experts proficient in Jewish law and medicine alike. Such professional specialists are beginning to emerge, although we presently lack an institution specifically dedicated to filling this need.

Contributors

Shimon Glick, M.D. Head, Medical Faculty and Center for Medical Education, and former Dean, Faculty of Health Sciences, Ben Gurion University of the Negev, Beersheva, Israel; Head, Internal Medicine Department C, Soroka University Hospital, Beersheva, Israel

Lord Immanuel Jakobovits, Chief Rabbi (Retired), British Commonwealth of Nations

Yoel Jakobovits, M.D. Attending physician, Divisions of Medicine and Gastroenterology, Sinai Hospital of Baltimore; Assistant Professor, Department of Medicine, Johns Hopkins Hospital and University School of Medicine, Baltimore, Maryland

Samuel S. Kottek, M.D. Harry Friedenwald Chair of the History of Medicine, Hebrew University–Hadassah Medical School, Jerusalem, Israel

Edward Reichman, M.D. Attending physician, Montefiore Medical Center, Bronx, New York; Assistant Professor, Department of Epidemiology and Social Medicine, Albert Einstein College of Medicine of Yeshiva University, Bronx, New York

Fred Rosner, M.D. Director, Department of Medicine, Mount Sinai Services at Queens Hospital Center, Jamaica, New York; Professor of Medicine, Mount Sinai School of Medicine, New York, New York

Nisson E. Shulman, M.D. Director, Department of Rabbinic Services, Rabbi Isaac Elchanan Theological Seminary of Yeshiva University, New York, New York

Avraham Steinberg, M.D. Director, Pediatric Neurology, Shaare Zedek Medical Center, Jerusalem; Director, Center for Clinical Ethics, Hebrew University, Hadassah Medical School, Jerusalem, Israel

Rabbi Moshe D. Tendler Chairman, Department of Biology, Yeshiva College; Rosh Yeshiva, Rabbi Isaac Elchanan Theological Seminary, Yeshiva University; Rabbi Isaac and Bella Tendler Chair in Jewish Medical Ethics, Yeshiva University, New York; Rabbi, Community Synagogue of Monsey, New York

Index

About the Editor

Dr. Fred Rosner is Director of the Department of Medicine of the Mount Sinai Services at the Queens Hospital Center and Professor of Medicine at New York's Mount Sinai School of Medicine. Dr. Rosner is an internationally known authority on medical ethics, has lectured widely on Jewish medical ethics, and is in great demand as a speaker on this and other related topics. He is the author of five widely acclaimed books on Jewish medical ethics, including *Modern Medicine and Jewish Ethics* and *Medicine and Jewish Law*. These books are up-to-date examinations of the Jewish view on many important bioethical issues in medical practice. Dr. Rosner is also a noted Maimonidean scholar and has translated and published in English most of Maimonides' medical writings.